Addicted to Crime?

The Wiley Series
in
Offender Rehabilitation

Edited by

Clive R. Hollin

*Rampton Hospital, Nottinghamshire
& University of Leicester, UK*

and

Mary McMurran

*East Midlands Centre for Forensic Mental Health, Leicester,
& University of Leicester, UK*

Young Offenders and Alcohol-Related Crime
Mary McMurran and Clive R. Hollin

What Works: Reducing Reoffending
Guidelines from Research and Practice
Edited by James McGuire

Therapeutic Communities for Offenders
Eric Cullen, Lawrence Jones and Roland Woodward

Addicted to Crime?

Edited by

John E. Hodge
Rampton Hospital, Nottinghamshire, UK

Mary McMurran
East Midlands Centre for Forensic Mental Health, Leicester
& University of Leicester, UK

Clive R. Hollin
Rampton Hospital, Nottinghamshire
& University of Leicester, UK

Other Wiley Editorial Offices

John Wiley & Sons, Inc., 605 Third Avenue,
New York, NY 10158-0012, USA

VCH Verlagsgesellschaft, Pappelallee 3,
0-69469 Weinheim, Germany

Jacaranda Wiley Ltd, 33 Park Road, Milton,
Queensland 4064, Australia

John Wiley & Sons (Asia) Pte Ltd, 2 Clementi Loop #02-01,
Jin Xing Distripark, Singapore 129809

John Wiley & Sons (Canada) Ltd, 22 Worcester Road,
Rexdale, Ontario M9W 1L1, Canada

Library of Congress Cataloging-in-Publication Data

Addicted to crime?/edited by John E. Hodge, Mary McMurran, Clive R.
Hollin.
    p.   cm. — (The Wiley series in offender rehabilitation)
    Includes bibliographical references and index.
    ISBN 0-471-95079-3. — ISBN 0-471-95777-1 (pbk.)
    1. Criminals—Rehabilitation. 2. Recidivism. 3. Criminal
psychology. I. Hodge, John E. (John Edward), 1948–
II. McMurran, Mary. III. Hollin, Clive R. IV. Series.
HV9275.A424   1997
364.3—dc21   96-39235
                                                            CIP

British Library Cataloguing in Publication Data

A catalogue record for this book is available from the British Library
ISBN 0-471-95079-3 (cased)
ISBN 0-471-95777-1 (paper)

Typeset in 10/12pt Times by Mathematical Composition Setters Ltd, Salisbury, Wilts.
Printed and bound in Great Britain by Biddles Ltd, Guildford
This book is printed on acid-free paper responsibly manufactured from sustainable
forestation, for which at least two trees are planted for each one used for paper
production.

Contents

About the Editors

John E. Hodge Psychology Department, Rampton Hospital, Retford, Notts DN22 OPD, UK.

John Hodge is Head of Psychology Practice at Rampton Hospital. As a chartered clinical psychologist and chartered forensic psychologist, he has had a long-term interest in the application of research on addiction to criminal behaviour and has published in this area. He has worked with people with addiction problems as well as with offenders. At present he has a particular interest in developing psychological knowledge and understanding about personality disorder.

Mary McMurran East Midlands Centre for Forensic Mental Health, Arnold Lodge, Cordelia Close, Leicester LE5 OLE, and Department of Psychology, University of Leicester, Leicester LE1 7RH, UK.

Mary McMurran is Head of Psychology Services at the East Midlands Centre for Forensic Mental Health and Honorary Reader in Psychology at the University of Leicester. A chartered psychologist, both clinical and forensic, she has worked with offenders in prisons, in secure psychiatric hospitals, and in the community. Her major academic interest is in alcohol and crime, and she has published widely in this area. She is a Fellow of the British Psychological Society, co-editor of the Society journal *Legal and Criminological Psychology*, and Chair of the Society's Division of Criminological and Legal Psychology.

Clive R. Hollin Psychology Department, Rampton Hospital, Retford, Notts DN22 OPD, and Department of Psychology, University of Leicester, Leicester LE1 7RH, UK.

Clive Hollin is currently Consultant Forensic Psychologist at Rampton Hospital and Reader in Psychology in the Centre for

Applied Psychology at the University of Leicester. His professional background is both as a forensic practitioner working in secure settings and as an academic psychologist. He has worked as a prison psychologist and as a forensic psychologist at the Glenthorne Centre in Birmingham for disturbed adolescents; and has held academic appointments at the University of Birmingham and the University of Leicester. He has written and edited 14 books, published more than 100 academic papers and book chapters, and is co-editor of the journal *Psychology, Crime, and Law*. He is a Fellow of The British Psychological Society and a Chartered Forensic Psychologist.

Contributors

Iain Brown Department of Psychology, University of Glasgow, Adam Smith Building, Glasgow G12 8RT, Scotland.

David M. Gresswell Lincoln District Healthcare NHS Trust, Francis Willis Unit, The County Hospital, Greetwell Road, Lincoln LN2 5QY, and Psychology Department, Rampton Hospital, Retford, Notts DN22 0PD, England.

Kevin Howells Psychology Department, Edith Cowan University, Joondalup Campus, Joondalup, WA 6027, Australia.

Rosemary Kilpatrick School of Education, Queen's University of Belfast, 69 University Street, Belfast BT7 1HL, Northern Ireland.

James McGuire Department of Clinical Psychology, The Whelan Building, The Quadrangle, University of Liverpool, Liverpool L69 3GB, England.

Gail McGregor Newcastle City Health NHS Trust, Department of Forensic Psychology, St Nicholas' Hospital, Jubilee Road, Gosforth, Newcastle upon Tyne NE3 3XT, England.

Derek Roger Department of Psychology, University of York, Heslington, York YO1 5DD, England.

Jessica Whitman Formerly: HMYOC Glen Parva, Tigers Road, Wigston, Leicester LE8 2TN, England.

Series Preface

Twenty years ago it is doubtful that any serious consideration would have been given to publishing a series of books on the topic of offender rehabilitation. While the notion of rehabilitation for offenders was widely accepted 30 years ago, the 1970s saw the collapse of what we might call the treatment ideal. As many other commentators have noted, the turning point can be pinpointed to the publication of an article titled 'What Works—Questions and Answers about Prison Reform', written by Robert Martinson and published in 1974. The essential message taken from this article was that, when it comes to the rehabilitation of offenders, what works is 'nothing works'. It would be stretching the case to say that Martinson single-handedly overturned the rehabilitative philosophy, but his message was obviously welcomed by a receptive audience. As writers such as Don Andrews have suggested, there are many reasons why both the academic community and politicians and policy-makers were more than willing to subscribe to the 'nothing works' philosophy although the evidence suggests that the public at large did not buy completely the need to abandon rehabilitation). Thus the 1970s and 1980s saw a return to hard sentencing, the predominance of punishment, and the handing out of just deserts to those who transgressed the law of the land. Throughout this period of rehabilitative nihilism a small group of academics and practitioners kept faith with the rehabilitative ideal, led perhaps by Paul Gendreau and Robert Ross, and slowly began to look for new ways to argue the case for rehabilitation. The turnabout, when it came, was dramatic. Through the development of a methodology for statistically reviewing large bodies of research, called 'meta-analysis', unequivocal evidence was produced that rehabilitative programmes did work. The view that 'nothing works' is simply wrong: rehabilitation programmes do have a positive effect in reducing recidivism. The effect is not always large, although sometimes it is; nor is it always present, although on average it is. However, it is there and that cannot be ignored. Since 1990, armed with these findings, there has been a remarkable resurgence of the rehabilitative ideal: practitioners have eagerly attended conferences, seminars, and training courses; researchers are working not to make the case for rehabilitation, but to improve and refine techniques for working with offenders.

While it is critically important to build upon existing knowledge and to evaluate rehabilitative work with offenders, it is equally important that time and space are given to the exploration of new ideas. It would, in our opinion, be most unwise to settle for evermore within an exclusive and restricted style of thinking and a one-track approach to working with offenders. As psychological and criminological theory and research grows, which it continues to do at an exponential rate, so new possibilities arise for the synthesis of different fields of enquiry. Of course, as ideas meld so they give rise to practical advances in the development of new ways of working with offenders.

This book looks at a way of thinking about criminal behaviour as yet hardly explored in the current literature—the application of models of addictive behaviour to the understanding and treatment of criminal behaviour. This approach seeks to make sense of some criminal behaviour, mainly repetitive or serial offending, by drawing on models of addictive behaviour. This line of thought has, arguably, been prompted by the apparent relevance and effective application of addiction treatment approaches to criminal behaviours, for example the use of relapse prevention in the treatment of sex offenders. For interventions to develop rationally, some level of conceptual under-pinning is essential. This book is a first step in drawing together theory and practice, addictions and crime.

We think that the contributors to this book have shown considerable insight in developing and applying new ideas. We are grateful to John Hodge for his editorial lead in this particular project; to all the contributors for the excellence of their work; and to our publishers for having the foresight to encourage this particular book in the Series.

Mary McMurran
Clive Hollin
March 1997

Preface

As all practitioners will know, many offenders present with a range of problems that sit alongside their criminal acts. As well as a focus on offending, practitioners are accustomed to working with mental health problems, family problems, sexual and relationship difficulties, disadvantages in education and employment, and problems with gambling, drug abuse and drinking. When seen in this light, the task facing practitioners who work with offenders is daunting in the extreme. As well as keeping pace with the burgeoning 'what works' developments in offender rehabilitation [see J. McGuire (Ed.), *What Works: Reducing Reoffending*. Wiley, 1995], practitioners need to be aware of effective interventions in all those areas noted above. Similarly, researchers in the field of offender rehabilitation need to keep abreast of advances in these other areas of concern. For practitioner and researcher alike, this can be seen as either an intimidating task or a professional challenge!

Following the above, one of the effects of the demands of working with offenders is that very often practitioners and researchers develop expertise in two areas. For example, practitioners and researchers concerned with sexual offending will not only be aware of issues centrally related to sex offences, but will also be highly knowledgeable about human sexuality generally. It was this need for duality of knowledge that sparked the idea for this book.

Substantial numbers of offenders present with drug and alcohol problems; sometimes these problems are an inherent part of their offending, sometimes not. Nonetheless, we need both to understand the parameters of such problems and to work with them for the benefit of the community generally and the offender specifically. Thus, a previous book in this Series considered the overlap between juvenile offending and drinking [M. McMurran & C. R. Hollin, *Young Offenders and Alcohol-Related Crime: A Practitioner's Guidebook.* Wiley, 1993], while elsewhere the work of one of us has branched into the mainstream of theories of addiction [M. McMurran, *The Psychol-*

ogy of Addiction. Taylor & Francis, 1994]. At some point in this process, the possibilities of a theoretical link between addiction and offending began to emerge from the haze. Some criminal behaviour is highly repetitive, as are addictive behaviours; some criminal behaviour appears to bring about 'internal rewards' for the offenders, as do addictive behaviours; understanding of criminal behaviour often invokes concepts such as motivation and emotion, excitement, control, and reward, as similarly found in the addiction literature. Could there be more than coincidence to this overlap?

In setting out to develop this idea, we contacted several researchers and practitioners and offered them the germ of the concept. Several caught the bug, indeed some were already infected, and they set to work to expound on the theme. Within the broad remit of the text, contributors were given total freedom to speculate as they saw best. Drawing on as many sources as they wished—including previous research, theoretical speculation, their own empirical work, and casework—contributors were at liberty to wander where they felt the ground was fertile. When the chapters appeared, it was evident that three took a primarily theoretical orientation, the remainder leaned towards practice.

The first part of the book contains the three theoretical chapters. The first of these, by Iain Brown, best known from his contribution to research in gambling addiction, presents an overview of current thinking in behavioural addictions. This chapter very clearly sets the agenda for what follows in that it takes current knowledge of addictions and applies this knowledge to offending. Naturally, there are strengths and weaknesses in such an exercise: to consider the possibilities is the challenge. The second chapter, by Derek Roger, considers the issue of emotional control and its development into operational use. It is clear that the concept of emotional control spills into theorising about both addiction and offending. This chapter considers the possibilities and begins to define an empirical approach to taking the next steps in testing the ideas. The third chapter, by John Hodge, offers some theoretical insights into the possibilities when seemingly unconnected strands of the literature—in this case models of addiction and knowledge of post-traumatic stress disorder—are applied to develop our understanding of violent behaviour. One of the tantalising strengths of this particular chapter is to be found in the hypotheses it begins to define for further research to explore.

In the second part of the book the contributors have applied the concept of 'addicted to crime' to a particular type of offence, sketching ideas for both theory and practice.

The offences covered in these chapters are all offences that are typically repetitive in nature. Gail McGregor and Kevin Howells show how an addiction model can be applied to sexual offending; David Gresswell and Clive Hollin do the same for multiple murder. In both chapters the authors show how the concept of addiction can be usefully applied, although clearly the application is not without difficulties and raises many further questions. The offence of car theft is one that greatly troubles contemporary society, but remains much under-researched by psychologists. The two chapters here, one by Rosemary Kilpatrick, the other by Mary McMurran and Jessica Whitman, show how psychological ideas and research, sympathetic to an addictions model, can be applied to car theft. It is commendable that both chapters display theoretical sensitivity alongside practical innovation. Rather like car theft, shoplifting is of much concern without perhaps attracting the degree of attention from psychologists that it merits. The chapter here by James McGuire provides an outstanding example of how psychological ideas and concepts, here from the standpoint of addiction, can be used both to enhance our understanding of this particular criminal behaviour and to develop practice with some shoplifters.

Finally, we hope that this book will be seen as a valuable addition to the Wiley Series in Offender Rehabilitation. Unlike other books in the Series that aim to consolidate current knowledge, this book is primarily and unashamedly speculative in nature. While most books will cover an existing field of knowledge, we believe that there must always be room for speculation. Without surmise, theorising, and hypothesising, we run the grave risk of intellectual stagnation. It is heartening to think that there are publishers who are prepared to give room to conjecture, and that there are academics and practitioners who can offer the level of insight exhibited here. We are grateful to our publisher and contributors alike for their work on this project which, at the very least, has reduced any danger of our own intellectual stagnation.

John Hodge
Mary McMurran
Clive Hollin
March 1997

Introduction: Current Issues in the Treatment of Addictions and Crime

Mary McMurran

East Midlands Centre for Forensic Mental Health, & University of Leicester

John E. Hodge

Rampton Hospital

and

Clive R. Hollin

Rampton Hospital, & University of Leicester

What is happening to the construct of addiction? In the recent past, the term 'addict' has been reserved for those who overindulged in certain behaviours, with apparent associated loss of control, and in whom a biological abnormality was suspected. This construct of addiction could most readily be applied to substance use, where craving and loss of control might logically be understood in terms of a substance ingested, inhaled or injected into the body causing changes in cell metabolism or neural activity in the brain, particularly in those with a biological vulnerability to the effects of substances. With the rise of social-psychological models of addiction, however, the emphasis on the biological element has been reduced; that is, whilst a person's biology undoubtedly affects his or her behaviour, cultural,

Addicted to Crime? Edited by J.E. Hodge, M. McMurran and C.R. Hollin.
© 1997 John Wiley & Sons Ltd.

social and psychological factors have an important role to play. If we accept that addiction is a product of the person–environment interaction, with biology playing only a part, then we may look at addiction as a behaviour explicable in terms of the same psychological principles as other behaviours. This view allows for the inclusion of non-substance-based behaviours as addictions. Gambling and sex have already received attention in the academic literature (Orford, 1985), and more recently the notion of some types of crime as addictions has been proposed (Hodge, 1991). Non-academics have suggested an even wider array of addictions amongst which feature work, exercise, love, and using computers. (See McMurran (1994) for a review of addiction.)

Substance-based addictions have been the subject of a considerable amount of scientific enquiry over the years, and one positive aspect of widening the usage of the term addiction is that we can draw upon developments in the understanding and treatment of substance use to inform thinking and practice relating to non-substance-based addictions. Current issues in the study and treatment of addiction may inform the study and treatment of criminal behaviours, and, indeed, there may also be scope for fruitful exchange in the opposite direction. Furthermore, substance use and crime commonly occur together, in that the same people are heavily involved in both types of behaviour, and explanation of this phenomenon might help in the prevention and treatment of a variety of problem behaviours.

COMMON ANTECEDENTS

Criminal behaviour and substance use share many common antecedents along their developmental pathways (see review by McMurran, 1996). These include hyperactivity in childhood (Klinteberg et al., 1993), poor family management practices and low family bonding (Hawkins et al., 1992), conduct problems in childhood (Maughan, 1993; Wilens & Biederman, 1993), low commitment to school (LeBlanc, 1994), and association with delinquent peers (Elliott et al., 1985). Indeed, problem behaviours frequently appear in a cluster in adolescents, these behaviours including both delinquency and substance use (Jessor & Jessor, 1977). The person–environment interactions that lead to the development of these problem behaviours suggest that the difficult child may elicit poor family management practices by parents or carers, with the child consequently developing conduct problems. This disadvantages the child in the school setting in that he or (less commonly) she becomes unpopular with peers and teachers, fails to attend to lessons, does not achieve academic success, and eventually avoids the unpleasant experience by truanting. Truancy presents the opportunity for association with like-minded peers who as a group engage in a range of antisocial activities. As time passes, the individual's *curriculum vitae* progressively precludes acceptance by conventional society and a criminal lifestyle becomes entrenched. Beliefs and attitudes simultaneously take shape in ways that justify or rationalise behaviour (Walters, 1995).

These observations bear many implications for the prevention of both delinquency and substance use through interventions such as family support, family management training, preschool enrichment programmes, and classroom management strategies (Farrington, 1994). One may also conclude that crime and substance use, for some people at least, serve similar functions. This may provide a rationale for interventions aimed at reducing individuals' involvement in both substance use and crime, including help with emotion control, interpersonal skills, and problem solving. Once an antisocial lifestyle has developed, then efforts may be needed to alter this. Walters (1994) suggests that the entire lifestyle should be addressed, with interventions encompassing relationships, leisure activities, education, and work.

PERSISTENCE AND ESCALATION

Most people grow out of both crime and problematic substance use in early adulthood, yet some persist and escalate. There appears to be a core group which displays a continuity of antisocial behaviour throughout life, and, interestingly, heavy drinking at age 18 years predicts the continuity of crime into adulthood (Farrington & Hawkins, 1991; Loeber, 1990). Persistence of crime, particularly violent crime, is associated with high levels of psychopathy (Hare, 1996), and psychopathy is also associated with alcohol and drug problems in offenders (Smith & Newman, 1990). Treatment programmes for these people may need to address substance use and crime separately, yet perhaps there are common underlying features that need to be addressed to change both types of behaviour. Serin and Kuriychuk (1994) suggest the need to address impulsivity, thinking styles, and hostile attributions.

There is scope for investigating new pathways to violence and addiction. Solursh (1989) noted that some American veterans returning from Vietnam showed symptoms of post-traumatic stress disorder. They also showed an increased likelihood of becoming involved in both violent crime and substance abuse, even though they had not engaged in these behaviours before their war experiences.

Hodge (1992) explores the relationships between childhood experiences of abuse, post-traumatic stress disorder, violence and
addiction, hypothesising connections amongst them.

The role of fantasy in the persistence of behaviours to addiction
levels requires further exploration. Pithers (1990) suggests that the
use of fantasy by sex offenders may mediate the development of an
addictive style of offending. Cognitive rehearsal of ever more risky
behaviours may contribute to maintenance and escalation. The role of
fantasy in substance use is only just beginning to receive attention
(Long et al., 1997).

MATCHING

In the mid-1970s, Martinson (1974) reviewed the effectiveness of
treatments for offending, and Emrick (1974, 1975) reviewed treatments for 'alcoholism'. Both came to similar conclusions in that there
was no single superior treatment for either of these problem
behaviours, and that treatment was not very effective at all. At that
time, in the criminological field this was taken to mean that 'nothing
works' and the rehabilitation ideal was gradually replaced by the
justice model in dealing with offenders. Although therapeutic nihilism
was not unknown in the field of alcohol treatment, over the years the
direction taken has been to refine the basic question of 'What works?'
into 'What works with which clients under what circumstances?' This
latter question raises the issue of matching clients with interventions
appropriate to them. These days, treatments for substance-use
problems include a wide variety of goals—abstinence, moderation,
harm minimisation—and a range of treatment approaches—advice,
self-help, and psychological interventions; individual therapy, group
therapy, and family therapy. It is only recently that programmes for
offenders have been subject to analysis to identify effective components
(e.g. Andrews et al., 1990). Effective programmes are those which
match the intervention with the needs, circumstances, and learning
styles of individuals (Andrews, 1995). Studies of the processes of
change in addictive behaviours have provided a rationale for matching
clients with appropriate interventions.

THE PROCESS OF CHANGE

In the addictions field, it has been observed that, whilst interventions have only modest success rates, large numbers of people

successfully control their behaviour without recourse to formal intervention. A similar picture presents itself in the criminological field; whilst interventions addressing criminal behaviours have limited success, many people 'spontaneously' grow out of crime.

The phenomenon of 'spontaneous remission' has been a focus of attention in addictions. The use of the term 'spontaneous' may be seen to reflect a lack of knowledge about the factors involved in behaviour change and identification of these factors may help in the development of effective interventions. Reductions in alcohol consumption may be a consequence of increasingly negative out-comes, either in the form of a critical event, for example involvement in an accident or commission of a crime, or by the gradual worsening of important aspects of life, for example illness, deterioration of personal relationships, or financial problems; alternatively, positive life events may cause a person to reduce consumption, for example finding a job, getting married, or becoming a parent (McMurran & Whitman, 1990; Tuchfeld, 1981). At this point, the individual makes a resolution to change and a number of action strategies are employed to control drinking.

Stall and Biernacki (1986) suggest a three-stage model of 'spontaneous remission' from problematic use of substances: Stage 1: Motivation to change as a result of negative consequences; Stage 2: Redefinition of economic, emotional and social relationships that are influenced by or predicated upon the problematic use of a substance; and Stage 3: Development of a new lifestyle to avoid problematic substance use. These three stages have clear similarities with the model of stages of change in psychotherapy, now widely used to understand processes of change in the addictions field. Prochaska and DiClemente (1986) describe the stages of change as a predictable motivational route through: (i) Precontemplation, where the person is unaware of or unconcerned by the negative consequences of his or her behaviour; (ii) Contemplation, where the person is considering change; (iii) Action, where change attempts are being made; and (iv) Maintenance, where change is consolidated in the long term. Progress is often impeded by relapse, where people return to their former problematic behaviours.

This process of change is well understood in the treatment of addictions and may have application in the understanding and treatment of crime. One major implication of such a model is that strategies for change may differ depending upon which stage the individual is in. Prior to making a decision to change, there needs to be recognition of a problem. Motivating clients to change has been recognised as a treatment need in the addictions field, and ways of enhancing motivation to change have been developed (Miller & Rollnick, 1991). These techniques are now being tried with offenders (St. Ledger, 1991; Mann & Rollnick, 1996).

The action stage of change requires skill acquisition. Examination of correctional programmes and addictions treatments has identified a remarkable consistency between the two fields in what treatments are most effective. Structured cognitive-behaviourial skills training serves both offenders and substance users best (Andrews et al., 1990; Miller & Hester, 1986). Cognitive-behaviourial programmes show most promise for substance users in the criminal justice system (Husband & Platt, 1993; McMurran, 1995; Peters, 1993). The content of such programmes may address, according to need, emotion control, behaviourial self-control, problem solving, and interpersonal skills.

Maintenance of change is a particular challenge and the problem of relapse has long been recognised in the addictions field. Both rates and temporal patterns of relapse show consistency across a variety of addictive behaviours (Marlatt, 1985a) and relapse to crime may follow a similar pattern. Marlatt (1985b) has identified and classified situations which predict relapse and designed an intervention programme aimed at enhancing maintenance of change by teaching clients how to recognise and cope with high-risk situations (Marlatt, 1985c). This intervention has been used with sex offenders (Laws, 1989; Pithers et al., 1983) and may have applications with other types of offender.

CONCLUSION

Miller (1991) points out that the commonalities among addictive behaviours are substantial and informative, and that further research should focus on these commonalities in the design of assessment procedures, interventions, and evaluation measures. He also suggests a need for the development of organising theories in addictions, and the integration of theory, research, and practice. It might be useful to include crime in this endeavour, further to test the goodness of fit of crime with addictions models, and also to stimulate innovative practice. We hope that this text will promote such a venture.

REFERENCES

Andrews, D. (1995). The psychology of criminal conduct and effective treatment. In J. McGuire (Ed.), *What Works: Reducing Reoffending*. Chichester: Wiley.

Andrews, D. A., Zinger, I., Hoge, R. D., Bonta, J., Gendreau, P. & Cullen, F. T. (1990). Does correctional treatment work? A clinically relevant and psychologically informed meta-analysis. *Criminology*, **28**, 369–404.

Elliott, D. S., Huizinga, D. & Ageton, S. S. (1985). *Explaining Delinquency and Drug Use*. Newbury Park, CA: Sage.

Emrick, C. D. (1974). A review of psychologically oriented treatment of alcoholism. I The interrelationships of outcome criteria and drinking behavior following treatment. *Quarterly Journal of Studies on Alcohol*, **35**, 523–549.

Emrick, C. D. (1975). A review of psychologically oriented treatment of alcoholism. II The relative effectiveness of different treatment approaches and the effectiveness of treatment versus not treatment. *Quarterly Journal of Studies on Alcohol*, **36**, 88–108.

Farrington, D. P. (1994). Early developmental prevention of juvenile delinquency. *Criminal Behaviour and Mental Health*, **4**, 209–227.

Farrington, D. P., & Hawkins, J. D. (1991). Predicting participation, early onset, and later persistence in officially recorded offending. *Criminal Behaviour and Mental Health*, **1**, 1–33.

Hare, R. D. (1996). Psychopathy: A clinical construct whose time has come. *Criminal Justice and Behavior*, **23**, 25–54.

Hawkins, J. D., Catalano, R. F. & Miller, J. Y. (1992). Risk and protective factors for alcohol and other drug problems in adolescence and early adulthood: Implications for substance abuse prevention. *Psychological Bulletin*, **112**, 64–105.

Hodge, J. E. (1991). Addiction to crime. In M. McMurran & C. McDougall (Eds), *Proceedings of the First DCLP Annual Conference*. Issues in Criminological and Legal Psychology, No.17, Vol.2. Leicester: The British Psychological Society.

Hodge, J. E. (1992). Addiction to violence: A new model of psychopathy. *Criminal Behaviour and Mental Health*, **2**, 212–223.

Husband, S. D. & Platt, J. J. (1993). The cognitive skills component in substance abuse treatment in correctional settings: A brief review. *Journal of Drug Issues*, **23**, 31–42.

Jessor, R. & Jessor, S. L. (1977). *Problem Behavior and Psychosocial Development: A Longitudinal Study of Youth*. New York: Academic Press.

Klinteberg, B. A., Andersson, T., Magnusson, D. & Stattin, H. (1993). Hyperactive behavior in childhood as related to subsequent alcohol problems and violent offending: A longitudinal study of male subjects. *Personality and Individual Differences*, **15**, 381–388.

Laws, D. R. (1989). (Ed.), *Relapse Prevention with Sex Offenders*. New York: Guilford Press.

LeBlanc, M. (1994). Family, school, delinquency, and criminality: The predictive power of an elaborated social control theory for males. *Criminal Behaviour and Mental Health*, **4**, 101–117.

Loeber, R. (1990). Development and risk factors of juvenile antisocial behavior and delinquency. *Clinical Psychology Review*, **10**, 1–41.

Long, C. G., Hollin, C. R. & Williams, M. J. (1997). Self-efficacy, outcome expectations, and outcome fantasies as predictors of post-treatment alcohol use in problem drinkers. *Manuscript submitted for publication*.

Mann, R. E. & Rollnick, S. (1996). Motivational interviewing with a sex offender who believed he was innocent. *Behaviourial and Cognitive Psychotherapy*, **24**, 127–134.

Marlatt, G. A. (1985a). Relapse prevention: Theoretical rationale and overview of the model. In G. A. Marlatt & J. R. Gordon (Eds), *Relapse Prevention*. New York: Guilford Press.

Marlatt, G. A. (1985b). Situational determinants of relapse and skill-training interventions. In G. A. Marlatt & J. R. Gordon (Eds), *Relapse Prevention*. New York: Guilford Press.

Marlatt, G. A. (1985c). Cognitive assessment and intervention procedures for relapse prevention. In G. A. Marlatt & J. R. Gordon (Eds), *Relapse Prevention*. New York: Guilford Press.

Martinson, R. (1974). What works? Questions and answers about prison reform. *The Public Interest*, **35**, 22–54.

Maughan, B. (1993). Childhood precursors of aggressive offending in personality disordered adults. In S. Hodgins (Ed.), *Mental Disorder and Crime*. Newbury Park, CA: Sage.

McMurran, M. (1994). *The Psychology of Addiction*. London: Taylor and Francis.

McMurran, M. (1995). Alcohol interventions in prisons: Toward guiding principles for effective intervention. *Psychology, Crime and Law*, **1**, 215–226.

McMurran, M. (1996). Substance use and delinquency. In C. R. Hollin & K. Howells (Eds), *Clinical Approaches to Working with Young Offenders*. Chichester: Wiley.

McMurran, M. & Whitman, J. (1990). Strategies of self-control in young offenders who have controlled their alcohol consumption without formal intervention. *Journal of Adolescence*, **13**, 115–128.

Miller, W. R. (1991). Emergent treatment concepts and techniques. *Annual Review of Addictions Research and Treatment*, **1**, 1–14.

Miller, W. R. & Hester, R. K. (1986). The effectiveness of alcoholism treatment: What research reveals. In W. R. Miller & N. Heather (Eds), *Treating Addictive Behaviours: Processes of Change*. New York: Plenum Press.

Miller, W. R. & Rollnick, S. (1991). *Motivational Interviewing: Preparing People to Change Addictive Behaviors*. New York: Guilford Press.

Orford, J. (1985). *Excessive Appetites: A Psychological View of Addictions*. Chichester: Wiley.

Peters, R. H. (1993). Treatment in jails and detention centres. In J. A. Inciardi (Ed.), *Drug Treatment in Criminal Justice Settings*. Newbury Park, CA: Sage.

Pithers, W. D. (1990). Relapse prevention with sexual aggressors. In W. L. Marshall, D. R. Laws & H. E. Barbaree (Eds), *Handbook of Sexual Assault*. New York: Plenum Press.

Pithers, W. D., Marques, J. K., Gibat, C. C. & Marlatt, G. A. (1983). Relapse prevention with sexual aggressives: A self-control model of maintenance of change. In J. G. Greer & I. R. Stuart (Eds), *The Sexual Aggressor: Current Perspectives on Treatment*. New York: Van Nostrand.

Prochaska, J. O. & DiClemente, C. C. (1986). Toward a comprehensive model of change. In W. R. Miller & N. Heather (Eds), *Treating Addictive Behaviours: Processes of Change*. New York: Plenum Press.

Serin, R. C. & Kuriychuk, M. (1994). Social and cognitive processing deficits in violent offenders: Implications for treatment. *International Journal of Law and Psychiatry*, **17**, 431–441.

Smith, S. S. & Newman, J. P. (1990). Alcohol and drug abuse-dependence disorders in psychopathic and non-psychopathic criminal offenders. *Journal of Abnormal Psychology*, **99**, 430–439.

Solursh, L. (1989). Combat addiction: Overview of implications in symptom maintenance and treatment planning. *Journal of Traumatic Stress*, **2**, 451–462.

St. Ledger, R. J. (1991). Motivational interviewing with special hospital patients. Paper presented at the First Annual DCLP Conference, University of Kent at Canterbury.

Stall, R. & Biernacki, P. (1986). Spontaneous remission from the problematic use of substances: An inductive model derived from a comparative analysis of the alcohol, opiate, tobacco, and food/obesity literature. *International Journal of the Addictions*, **21**, 1023.

Tuchfeld, B. S. (1981). Spontaneous remission in alcoholics: Empirical observations and theoretical implications. *Journal of Studies on Alcohol*, **42**, 626–641.

Walters, G. D. (1994). *Drugs and Crime in Lifestyle Perspective*. Thousand Oaks, CA: Sage.

Walters, G. D. (1995). The psychological inventory of criminal thinking styles. *Criminal Justice and Behavior*, **22**, 307–325.

Wilens, T. E. & Biederman, J. (1993). Psychopathology in preadolescent children at high risk for substance abuse: A review of the literature. *Harvard Review of Psychiatry*, **1**, 207–218.

PART I

Theory

CHAPTER 1

A Theoretical Model of the Behavioural Addictions — Applied to Offending

Iain Brown

University of Glasgow

But pleasures are like poppies spread—
Your seize the flow'r, its bloom is shed;
Or like the snow falls in the river—
A moment white, then melts for ever;
Or like the borealis race,
That flit ere you can point their place;
Or like the rainbow's lovely form
Evanishing amid the storm.

('Tam o' Shanter,' Robert Burns)

The central metaphor of this book draws attention to the likeness of some forms of criminal offending to some addictions. This has many creative possibilities. All metaphors are, of course, imperfect, but this one opens up the possibility that we may be able to use our theoretical understanding of addictions to improve our understanding of criminal offending. Indeed perhaps we may even learn to apply to our management of some offenders some of the intervention strategies

Addicted to Crime? Edited by J.E. Hodge, M. McMurran and C.R. Hollin.
© 1997 John Wiley & Sons Ltd.

developed for addictions—such as motivational interviewing and relapse management and prevention.

It is still controversial in a few quarters to assume that there is a unified field of study of addictions. The medical profession sometimes seems to be making strenuous efforts to render the word 'addiction' obsolete, notably in promoting the concept of 'dependency' based almost exclusively around the phenomena of withdrawal from, and tolerance of, substances. In a more recent break with the past, the latest version of the *Diagnostic and Statistical Manual* (DSM-IV)(American Psychiatric Association, 1994) seems carefully to eschew the concept of addiction, referring only to 'substance abuse' and 'disorders of impulse control'.

Nevertheless most scholars and clinicians point to what are seen as common features in problems humans have with eating, alcohol, gambling, heroin, cocaine, medically prescribed tranquilliser drugs, tobacco and many other substances (Milkman & Sunderworth, 1987). Common features in successful treatment of these problems are also pointed to (Miller & Heather, 1986). More recently the field of addictions has expanded. Gambling is now widely recognised as an addiction and it has no clear physical base. Recent activities which have been identified and written about in the professional literature as potentially addictive include sexual addictions, some forms of religious practice, fast driving, watching television, playing computer games, physical violence, work for the sake of being busy, and exercise (especially jogging) (Witman et al., 1987; Brown, 1993a).

Some cautious recognition has been given, even in the bastions of orthodoxy, to this growing field of relevance in the study of addictions by officially allowing the existence of 'behavioural addictions' (Marks, 1990a,b). Sometimes this expansion has led to comments that the concept of addiction is becoming so overinclusive as to become almost meaningless (Jaffe, 1990). There is almost literally an explosion in the concept of addictions (Milkman & Sunderworth, 1987) and to avoid all of psychological and physical experience becoming classified as potentially addictive it is necessary to rediscover the essential core of the concept and define boundaries between it and other related phenomena, such as obsessions, attachments and compulsions (Brown, 1993a). None of these 'new' addictions fit the simple 'chemical dependency' and substance abuse model.

Most people who have not studied addictions too closely think of good examples of an addiction as to heroin, to alcohol or, less commonly, to tobacco. These addictions are all connected with taking in too much of some substance, and the popular belief is that addictions are diseases which cause addicts to lose all control over the taking of the substance. Or that just taking even one dose of it (in the case of heroin) can produce irreversible physical effects on body tissue so that the addict will need more and more of it for the rest of their life. The most common allied belief is that total abstinence and constant dependence on AA groups, doctors, or Jesus groups is then for ever necessary to avoid being overwhelmed by the craving and by the urges to take the substance again in the same destructive way.

Such a simple model of addiction based on the physical effects of what the Americans call 'chemical dependency' and on 'substance abuse' is just about plausible as long as it is applied *only* to the sucking, swallowing, breathing and injecting of substances. But the treatment deriving from that model is not particularly effective (Armour et al., 1978; Polich et al., 1980; Lindstrom, 1992) and such a narrow conception of addiction is useless in understanding a whole range of psychological and social problems such as gambling or sexual excesses. An illness model centred on the use of substances is still a powerful force among medically educated laymen and journalists, and, of course, is favoured by the medical profession. Illness, however, is mostly a process over which the patient, as victim, has little or no control. This view leads to the widespread belief that people caught in an addictive process, say to heroin, are helpless—an effect which Peele (1985) sees as producing a self-fulfilling prophesy of defeat and Davies (1992) sees as part of the modern 'myth of addiction'.

Nevertheless, the illness analogy has made an important contribution to the understanding of addictions, drawing attention to the role of processes within the individual which reduce control and to the phenomena of increased tolerance to substances and the effects of sudden withdrawal. However, criminal behaviour is clearly *not* about taking in a substance. Therefore, many, especially in the medical profession, but also in popular journalism, may argue that criminal behaviour *cannot* be an addiction. Thus the analogy central to this book is labelled as certainly useless and probably even perniciously misleading because it may lead to the confusion of 'illness' with 'crime', or even 'sin'.

Moral models both of criminal offending and of addiction tend to interpret both behaviours as bad, the product of personal weakness and inadequacy at best and, more usually, of a deliberate choice of wickedness and evil. Moral prescriptions are taught, chosen and have to be conformed to, regardless of the 'temptation' of subjective feelings, beliefs, thoughts or impulses. Punishment, deterrence, evangelical 'conversion' and/or spiritual regeneration are the principal remedies recommended by that most widely held model of explanation.

A social learning model, perhaps predominantly accepted inside psychology, sees addiction as mainly the product of faulty learning from a distorting and problem-generating environment. Addictive patterns of behaviour can be corrected, according to this model, by manipulation of the environment and by educational systems derived from learning theory in the well-established processes of behaviour therapies. Social learning theory has been invaluable in drawing attention to the role of immediate triggers in setting off the addictive activity, and identifying patterns of reward and punishment that sustain and even modify the addictive behaviour. Early behaviourism was also important in calling in question the whole theoretical system that conscious feelings and cognitions were direct causes of actions which Skinner dismissed as 'mentalism', but it made the mistake of neglecting the importance of the subjective perception of the role, in everyday decision making, of emotion, and of expectancies about feeling states. The most sophisticated cognitive social learning models of personality used to explain addiction (Bandura, 1986; Rotter, 1982; Mischel, 1973) have gone far to correct that early neglect. Contemporary learning theories now allow room for expectancies, belief systems, self-control, internally administered rewards and decision making. However, they still tend to undervalue the addict's subjective experience of feeling and mood, the interpretations he or she makes of their feelings, and the beliefs they have about their internal state. There are some outstanding exceptions such as Marlatt and Gordon (1985) who found a central role played in relapses by more internal phenomena such as strong emotions or abrupt changes in mood states, and Beck et al. (1993) who concentrates on the role of repetitive patterns of thought.

To exploit the metaphor 'offending is like addiction' rationally and systematically we need a conception of addictions which has a credible inner content and clear boundaries. We also need a theoretical model of how addictions arise, what they are, and of how they decline. None of these requirements for a model of addictions can be fully met by the major ways of understanding addictions which are dominant today. There is room for a new emphasis in our thinking about addictions which is not necessarily intended to replace any of our favourite models (e.g. psychodynamic, behavioural, moral, medical) but may marginally enhance their aggregated power and may be likely to illumine and direct our work with criminal behaviour.

It is contended here that the factor in all these currently accepted models which has not been given enough importance is the role of the conscious subjective experiences, beliefs and decisions of the addicted person. It is the aim of the *Hedonic Management Model* of addictions presented here to recognise the central role of subjective experience, and of the addict's own interpretation of it, in the development, dominance and decline of addictions. Historically it has been left to humanistic and existential psychologists to reinstate subjective experience (and people's very idiosyncratic interpretations of it) at the centre of the explanation of human conduct. Although this model might be labelled as broadly a 'humanist/existentialist' view of addictions, it owes no allegiance to any particular humanist theorist such as Rogers, Maslow, or Kelly.

The model of addictions presented and applied here, then, is predominantly a psychological one. It classes addictions as clearly motivational phenomena, and it adopts an expectancy-value theory of motivation consonant with cognitive social learning theory rather than the more mechanistic motivational models previously associated with early behaviourist and psychodynamic approaches (Weiner, 1993). It is neither a disease model nor a moral model and is potentially value-free (Brown, 1993a). It identifies the major factors in the development and recovery from addictions as psychological ones—although physical processes are seen as providing strong secondary support. Although it draws on conceptions from widely differing addiction models accepted by different groups on both sides of the Atlantic, it does not conform to any of the current major orthodoxies on either side. It presents addictions as extreme examples of a range of ordinary everyday motivational and self-management phenomena.

It would be ideal if a model of addictions could be presented based on ready-made research findings. Unfortunately the research techniques available to us in the social sciences are, themselves, as yet limited and unsatisfactory. If we were to demand in advance that all parts of a theory must be backed by experimental, correlational or survey-type research we would devalue those elements of human psychology that are currently not open to full empirical investigation, merely out of our arrogant belief in the omnipotence of our struggling research techniques. The theoretical model is, therefore, presented here in a series of propositions, some of which are researchable (or even already researched), but others of which are not yet researched or are even unresearchable with the techniques we currently have available.

MOOD MANAGEMENT IN THE EVERYDAY MAINTENANCE OF GOOD HEDONIC TONE

Most of our actions and experiences have consequences, however slight, in changes in subjective feelings of pleasure and well-being. These feelings and subjective experiences are called here, for convenience, *hedonic tone*, what the founding fathers of the United States Constitution called 'the pursuit of happiness'. This pursuit obviously involves not just the care of the physical self in the maintenance of sleeping, eating, exercise, shelter, etc., but also the taking of whatever steps are open to us for the arrangement of a future schedule of rewarding events and experiences which will keep us 'in a good mood' and 'enjoying life'. No one imagines that all negative feeling states can be banished. If they were, even the positive ones would become meaningless for lack of contrast. We all recognise that our 'pursuit of happiness' has often to be indirect and that it is frequently only very partially successful or even a failure. But we also know that if we do not attempt some planning and management of our immediate and future states of hedonic tone, the consequences can be even more punishing. And so we all do it.

The hedonic management model set out here sees the phenomenon of addiction as a failure in this function of the maintenance of an optimum level of hedonic tone by the normal methods of management and integration of rewards from a wide variety of sources and activities in everyday life. Instead, through bad planning, poor decision making and mismanagement the addicted individual acquires a drive for continuous high hedonic tone. This drive is achieved through a single 'addictive' activity (or a single reward source) which is expected repeatedly to produce an identifiable state as a goal. It follows that so-called 'cure' lies in better strategies and techniques of hedonic management.

The Factor Structure of Emotional Experience

Recent factor analyses of data from empirical studies of emotional experience have repeatedly produced the suggestion that emotional experience is best summarised in terms of two major orthogonal dimensions of (i) arousal and (ii) pleasure/displeasure or hedonic tone (Russell & Mehrabian, 1977; Russell, 1980; Russell & Ridgeway, 1983; Watson & Tellegen, 1985; Thayer, 1989; see Figure 1.1).

Hedonic Tone, Mood, Emotion and Feeling States

Subjective experiences of pleasure and well-being are notoriously difficult to define and even more difficult to quantify, but they are nevertheless factors of crucial importance in the experience, thinking and behaviour of mankind. It has often been a catastrophic mistake to limit psychology to only that which we can quantify, especially when our best techniques of quantification are so primitive and crude. 'Hedonic tone' is used in this chapter to refer to a subjective experience which is a combination of both mood and emotional state. 'Momentary hedonic tone' refers to a combination of phasic emotional experience with a tonic background of mood at any single moment in

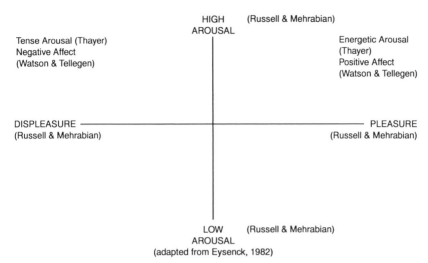

Figure 1.1. The two-dimensional space formed by Russell and Mehrabian's factors of emotional experience and the location of Thayer's self-report arousal factors within it.

time. 'Average hedonic tone' refers to the central tendency of a series of such momentary states over a given period. Such concepts are inevitably difficult to define and measure and perhaps the most easily measurable element in them is the phenomenon of arousal which is a dimension common both to moods and to emotional states.

The Concept of Arousal

Level of arousal is the other major defining characteristic of emotional states and it has been extensively researched and has played a major role in many theories of emotion. There are several conceptions of arousal (reviewed in Brown, 1993b) and it would be manifestly premature to single out any one as the best fit for the explanation of addictions. However, it seems safe to affirm that it is often useful to conceive of arousal as a single unitary dimension and that in general subjective feelings of arousal relate very closely to physiological measures of arousal such as, especially, heart rate (Thayer, 1989). The term arousal will be used in this general sense throughout this paper.

Returning to the everyday management of good hedonic tone described above, everyone uses a wide range of personal techniques every day for lowering and for raising their arousal levels and, through that, managing their hedonic tone. These have been well explored by Apter (1982) (see Figure 1.2).

Some Common Techniques for Reducing Arousal

Production and continuing entertainment of biased underestimates of the likelihood of failure or disaster

Development of short- long-term contingency plans and strategies for coping with failure, if it should occur plans which promise an acceptable level of goal satisfaction by other means

Some Common Techniques for Raising Arousal

Non-conforming or disruptive behaviour such as the flouting of social norms

Deliberate creation of challenges and suspense

Search for novelty and uncertainty through unfamiliar and unexpected stimuli, exploration of the unknown

Risk taking – fast driving, gambling, or, vicariously, by watching dangerous sports

Searching for, or exaggerating the significance of, current actions, e.g. imagining they have lifelong repercussions

Figure 1.2. Some common techniques for reducing and for raising arousal. (Adapted from Apter (1982).)

THE ROLE OF THE MANIPULATION OF AROUSAL IN THE DEVELOPMENT AND MAINTENANCE OF VARIOUS ADDICTIONS

The role of arousal in the development and maintenance of addictions is most clearly seen in gambling and in addictions to illegal drugs. Such manipulations of arousal are an integral part of the process of hedonic management.

Arousal in Gambling Addictions

The best illustration of the importance of the role of arousal is in the development and maintenance of gambling addictions. This is now now well established (Brown, 1993c). In two major studies, one by the Federal *Commission on the Review of National Policy Towards Gambling in America* (1976) and one in the UK (Anderson & Brown, 1984), the most frequent reason given for betting was 'excitement'. It was found (Anderson & Brown, 1984) that the heart rate of normal regular gamblers playing blackjack in the real casino increased by a mean of 24 beats per minute throughout the cycle of blackjack, with some individual increases of up to 54 beats per minute recorded, as great as for fairly considerable physical exercise. They concluded that gambling is very exciting and that some form of arousal or excitement is a major, and possibly the major, reinforcer of gambling behaviour for regular gamblers. This was corroborated twice in Australia (Leary & Dickerson, 1985; Dickerson & Adcock, 1987) and psychobiological underpinnings of a functional disturbance in the noradrenergic system have been traced in the brain chemistry of addicted gamblers (Roy et al., 1988), indicating raised sensation-seeking needs as predicted by Anderson and Brown (1984).

These empirical studies gave rise to new theoretical orientations in the explanation of gambling and gambling addictions. This new view proposed that the central phenomenon of normal gambling is a personal experience and an objectively verifiable state of arousal, not sexual, but probably autonomic and/or cortical. This arousal component of normal gambling was open to explanation by an optimal level of stimulation model or a biological optimum-pessimism model (Brown, 1986), or by a more sophisticated model of the role of arousal in all addictions derived from reversal theory (Brown, 1988). Subsequently Brown (1993a) has reviewed the role of arousal in a wide range of addictions, including alcohol, various legal and illegal drugs, tobacco and eating disorders.

In addition to the classic 'uppers' and 'downers' such as heroin, cocaine and tranquillisers, the regulation of arousal is recognised as playing an important part in drinking, smoking and eating to excess. This points to the function of arousal in all addictive activity in managing emotional and mood states and in attaining and maintaining positive feeling states as goals in their own right.

STATES AS GOALS AND ADDICTIONS AS ACQUIRED DRIVES

For many people certain 'peak experiences' and even some more regularly reproducible feeling states become goals in themselves, to be sought and enjoyed. For example, it may not be the sexual orgasm itself that is sought but the feeling state of calm low arousal that follows it or the prolonged state of arousal and anticipation preceding it.

People regularly sense their levels of arousal and even when they are not clearly aware of them they regularly employ techniques of self-management, often half-consciously or even unconsciously to improve their hedonic tone. Morris and Reilly (1987) review the wide variety of strategies people use to modify mood, including self-reward, alcohol consumption, distraction, expressive behaviour, cognitive transformations (e.g. altering interpretations), problem-directed action, and affiliation (e.g. seeking associations with others). Even within the range of non-addicted behaviour, the use of these strategies frequently becomes sophisticated enough to be accurately described as goal-directed behaviour motivated by a secondary acquired drive (Bejerot, 1972, 1975; Keup, 1982).

As with any other goal-directed behaviour, people make plans for the attainment and maintenance of these desirable feeling states. In colloquial terms 'they arrange a treat for themselves'. Attempts to manipulate hedonic tone over long periods of time can be seen in the normal person in, for example, the formation and execution of career plans or the making of marriages. These attempts might be called strategic manipulations which produce an omnipresent but perhaps less obvious background of good hedonic tone. Alternatively, middle-term planning of the manipulation of hedonic tone, for example through the arranging of a good vacation, and the more immediate short-term 'tactical' manipulations of, for example, hustling a cup of coffee, produce shorter lasting, but often more intense, satisfactions. In adverse conditions or while experiencing negative emotions many people simply 'arrange a treat for themselves'.

The short-term maintenance of happiness or good hedonic tone is a perilous and unpredictable business for normal people. Attempts to intervene and manipulate our moods and feeling states are often ineffective, have undesirable side-effects, or even provoke the exact opposite to what was intended. If we were better at it we would all be able to maintain high positive hedonic tone for extended periods. Even if we were successful in achieving perpetual happiness there would be no unpleasantness to compare and contrast with the unbroken positive feeling state, so that 'happiness' would soon become meaningless in itself. No one manages to maintain good hedonic tone for much of the time. As a consequence we all develop some tolerance for negative emotional states, for poor or low hedonic tone. As Apter (1982) puts it:

> It is hardly to be wondered at that high levels of positive hedonic tone are not typically maintained for extended periods. To put this in everyday terms, it is not surprising that people have difficulty in remaining happy for very long. (p. 330)

This analysis of the tactical manipulations of arousal to maintain short-term hedonic tone in normal day-to-day living provides an essential contrast which makes it possible to define and understand addictions. Simply, addictive activities are chosen to replace and improve upon normal coping strategies. *In contrast to the normal state of poorly managed uncertainty and acquired tolerance for aversive states, the core of the addictive process can easily be seen as the discovery and continuous use by the individual of relatively reliable and effective methods which enable him or her to manipulate arousal and hedonic tone in the directions he or she wants—reliably and immediately.*

The particular personal states sought as goals in this way vary to some extent from addiction to addiction. In gambling addictions they are most obviously identifiable as very high general arousal and sometimes as escape. In other addictions what is sought is sometimes excitement and sometimes oblivion, even by the same person using the same drug at different times (as in the case of alcohol), calm or heightened sharpness (as with tobacco), fullness (as with eating), euphoria or invulnerability (as with opiates) and so on. The subjective experience of arousal reported by gamblers and monitored physiologically happens to be more accessible to systematic study, and it can be seen as only one of a class of states of consciousness, mood states or types of subjective experience sought in other addictions.

This simple general observation that what are sought in addictive activity are the by-products or epiphenomena of the activity itself in 'altered states of consciousness', 'changes of mood' or 'escape from the usual self' has often been made before, particularly among the American AA-derived disease model 'chemical dependency' theorists of the Hazeldean and Johnston Institutes. There has also been interest in altered states of consciousness as goals among the phenomenological and existential theorists of addiction (Greaves, 1974; Weil, 1972; Peele, 1980). In Sweden, Bejerot (1972, 1975) conceived of addictions to specific pleasures as acquired drives (in the Hullian sense) with all the flexibility and purposiveness of drive-related, goal-directed behaviour.

At this point the first of the twelve basic propositions of a hedonic management model of addictions can be outlined below:

1. *Management of Hedonic Tone* **All individuals learn to manipulate their arousal, mood and experiences of subjective well-being to sustain good hedonic tone (states of relative pleasure and euphoria) for as much of the time as possible, in the normal pursuit of happiness. Some regularly reproducible feeling states become secondary goals or drives.**

INDIVIDUAL VULNERABILITY EFFECTS

If it is accepted that all individuals may accidentally discover how to manipulate, or may be induced to manipulate, their moment to moment states of pleasure/displeasure to achieve high hedonic tone in the short term at the expense of the long term, then, it follows that all individuals are, to some extent, vulnerable to addictions. But some individuals are clearly, on this explanation, likely to be more vulnerable than others.

The term 'hedonic gap' is a useful shorthand to refer to the discrepancy between the level of pain, frustration, deprivation and negative feeling states that the individual can tolerate and the level that they experience. Reduced tolerance to negative feeling states may arise because certain individuals have been either constantly overexposed (i.e. the emotionally and economically deprived), or they have been underexposed and so never learned to cope (i.e. the emotionally 'spoiled' or overprotected, or [economically] the bored, satiated and idle rich). An individual's hedonic gap may also be widened by subjective appreciation of the discrepancy between what is being currently experienced and the most intense euphoria that has ever been experienced. Thus a single 'revelational' experience of heroin or a first episode of gambling with a big win can permanently alter the individual's average hedonic gap. The greater the hedonic gap, the greater the personal vulnerability.

Large hedonic gaps (and so major personal vulnerabilities to addictions) may be expected to arise from seven main sources :

1. *Planlessness.* Possibly because the individual's life has become (or has always been) so confusing and unpredictable that long-term, or even middle-term, strategies for securing high sustained hedonic tone are unlikely to pay off; also possibly because the individual's life situation is inherently devoid of the possibility of anything except short-term reward; or possibly because, in contrast, the individual has always had readily available short-term rewards, making for an easy style of life relying almost solely on short-term immediate satisfactions (the myth of the 'idle rich').

2. *Individual differences in lability of arousal and in its perception and interpretation and therefore in hedonic tone.* This applies especially to chronic low hedonic tone, and dysphoric states. Established feedback loops which produce recurrent patterns of states of intense low hedonic tone, and even just the restriction of an individual's experience to a range of very mediocre hedonic tones, may all make an individual equally vulnerable to the discovery of

effective methods of producing noticeable changes in short-term positive hedonic tone.

3. *Poor skills in manipulating hedonic tone.* This skill deficiency may result in frequent periods of dysphoria. It may arise from difficulty in learning caused by the variability and unpredictability of the consequences of attempts to manipulate arousal and hedonic tone. Or it may arise from low tolerance for dysphoric moods, or from poor feedback awareness of somatic sensations (Greaves, 1974), or from the measurable general characteristic known as alexithymia, involving deficits in awareness of feelings and ability to identify and express them, and unimaginative concrete thinking (Nemiah, 1977; Apfel & Sifneos, 1979; Newton & Contrada, 1994; Lumley & Robey, 1995; Pinard et al., 1996).

4. *Low frustration tolerance.* Low frustration tolerance is seen as resting 'on a complex set of beliefs and cognitive distortions' and as 'magnifying the usual sources of frustration and leading to excessive disappointment and anger' (Beck et al., 1993, p. 39).

5. *Previous, probably childhood, emotional deprivation.* Emotional deprivation and insufficient emotional support or security for experimentation may result in a history of poor interpersonal relations. This may lead to severe or chronic patterns of conflict, frustration and deprivation, as seen in many of those with emotional distress amounting to clinical or subclinical neurotic and psychotic states

6. *Individual differences in personality and temperament.* The use of experience-changing substances and activities more usually produces very crude or marked effects on experience compared to the normal 'pursuit of happiness'. It is therefore expected that those low on Zuckerman's (1979) Sensation Seeking Scale (SSS) and those with weak nervous systems in the Pavlovian sense will more often find these substances and activities repugnant. Thus the population of abusers will be predicted to be biased towards high scores on the SSS. Similarly vulnerable may be those who have a habitually manipulative approach to people, problems and situations. Thus the population of abusers may contain more than its share of individuals with hysterical and psychopathic tendencies (Brown, 1988).

7. *Social, economic and cultural influences.* Other vulnerable people may be those who belong to and have absorbed the values of more manipulative cultures. For example those believing in active manipulation of the environment, often ignoring long-term broader ecological consequences, as is characteristic of the application of modern technology (Brown, 1988). Absence of economic opportunity and belonging to a threatened social grouping, such as the North

American Indians, may also have subtle adverse effects on feelings of well-being which make an individual more vulnerable.

The important role of individual vulnerabilities is summarised in the second of the twelve basic propositions of a hedonic management theory below:

2. *Vulnerabilities* **Personal predisposing vulnerabilities to addiction (i) increase the individual's hedonic gap, defined as the difference between the levels of relative dysphoria they can tolerate and those they habitually experience, and (ii) narrow the range of easily accessible rewarding activities.**

INITIATION

For the present purposes it is useful to think of the probabilities that, at any given moment, a specific individual will behave in any one of variety of ways, which has been expressed as the outcome of a behaviour potential equation (Rotter, 1982). The habitual choices made can be ordered in a hierarchy of behaviour preferences which depend (in games theory terms) on the interaction of desirability and ease of access (Rotter et al., 1972). For example, at any given moment the guesses as to what John Doe will do next depend on a balance between what he wants most, say intercourse with Mary McGintie, and what is available to him, say intercourse with Jean Doe, or, if that is not available, a half bottle of whisky, or, if that is difficult to obtain, a cigarette. There is a hierarchy of preferences which tends to be quite stable on average over time.

Initiation to an addictive activity typically upsets this normal hierarchy of behaviour preferences. This first stage of 'Initiation' to the addiction may be quite short in those instances where a longstanding period of dysphoria may be relieved in a sudden 'rush' of euphoria and one-trial-learning takes place. For example, a person with chronic low arousal goes gambling and wins a large sum at the very first attempt. They have an 'Aha' experience (as the Gestalt psychologists would say) and wonder where they have been all their life that they did not know about gambling. In this instance their hierarchy of preferences among the various activities easily accessible to them has been instantly and dramatically changed. However, the period of initiation may be quite extended, as when an individual is drawn into the addictive activity by social pressures and only gradually discovers for him or herself a rewarding pattern of use. After this discovery the activity grows insidiously in importance until some incident makes him or her aware of how much he or she has come to depend on it for the day-to-day management of happiness and feelings of well-being. During this initiation period the addict-to-be becomes increasingly skilled in the use of the activity to maintain the desired hedonic tone. The person gradually develops an acquired drive for the state or states normally produced by the activity.

The phenomena of initiation are summarised in the third of the twelve basic propositions of a hedonic management model below:

3. *Initiation* **An addiction is initiated when there is either the gradual development or the sudden discovery of an activity which provides a relatively powerful and effective means of manipulating hedonic tone to sustain long periods of euphoria or relief from dysphoria and so changes the preference hierarchy of the repertoire of easily accessible activities.**

SPECIALISATION IN ADDICTIVE ACTIVITY OR SUBSTANCE

Choice of addictive substance or activity, apart from accidences of availability, culturally induced prejudice, etc., depends upon how efficiently the individual can learn to use it to manipulate their own individual naturally occurring patterns of arousal and subjective experience in the pursuit of the acquired drive for sustained high positive hedonic tone. Many of the widely used substances and activities, such as smoking and drinking, are 'bi-directional', i.e. can be used as both 'uppers' and 'downers' (Frith, 1971), depending on the skilled titration of the dose to match the circumstances and the desired feeling state (Brown, 1993a). Even gambling, which may appear in some forms to be an exclusively arousing activity, can be used as a soothing, completely absorbing escape in the long monotonous play of the one-arm bandits or bingo, punctuated only occasionally with a flutter of excitement. Other drugs are more specialised. It is difficult to see how cocaine or amphetamines could be used as 'downers', for example.

Apart from the accidences of personal discovery and availability, it takes time to learn the skilled use of most of these instruments of change of subjectively experienced state. Thus unless the user is particularly dissatisfied or adventurous, there is a tendency towards stable use of just one or two major techniques. This means that psychological factors determining choice of substance or activity are complex. Many individuals, having become skilled in the use of one widely available 'bi-directional' technique, never have reason to learn the use of another. Others, perhaps less satisfied with the degree of control of hedonic tone achieved, experiment constantly with new substances, activities and techniques. Such factors may go some way to explain poly-addictions, the ease of formation of cross-addictions, and the frequent parallel and sequential uses of, for example, alcohol and gambling. However, in general it is not the choice of substance or activity which is so important as the ways in which it is used.

Addictive activities all possess, to greater and lesser extents, the property of being able to intervene to effect hedonic tone for the immediate future. Some activities and some substances lend themselves more readily to abuse in the gross manipulation of hedonic tone. For example, activities and substances which have only delayed, mild or very subtle effects on hedonic tone, such as jogging, may take longer to become established as agents of abuse as compared to substances such as cocaine which have immediate, crude, massive, powerful and obvious effects. Gradients of tolerance may also play some role with those substances and activities which rapidly need higher doses to produce the same effects (i.e. they have particularly steep gradients of tolerance) and are also more likely to be chosen as a means of hedonic management.

Some specialisations in a single addictive activity are not stable. For example, if drinking becomes difficult because of a new working life as a taxi driver, gambling may take its place.

This is summarised in the fourth major proposition of a hedonic management model of addiction set out below:

4. *Addictive Activity* **Choice of addictive activity depends on (i) the range of activities available in the environment, (ii) social support for that activity, (iii) inherent properties of that activity to affect the individual's hedonic tone (e.g. through changes in arousal), and (iv) acquired skills in using that activity to manipulate hedonic tone. Activities with stronger reinforcement effects lead to faster development of addictions and a few substances have physical properties which produce steeper tolerance gradients leading to the same effect.**

THE DEVELOPMENT OF AN ACQUIRED DRIVE AND THE 'GOLDEN AGE' OF AN ADDICTION PRODUCE INCREASING SALIENCE

An addiction develops its maximum power and momentum through the prolonged action of several positive feedback loops. These positive feedback loops begin with a series of cognitive failures which lead to the strengthening of an acquired drive for particular feeling states as a goal associated with the performance of the addictive activity. As the acquired drive strengthens, so the single activity becomes more and more salient as almost the sole source of reward.

Entry to the feedback system probably begins with the cognitive failures. There is deficient self-awareness and vigilance. The person fails to retain an overall picture of their own current activities and the spread of the sources of their satisfactions so that they are not aware of the extent to which their rewards and satisfactions have become concentrated on a single activity. Alternatively, if they *are* aware, they do not see its significance, nor are they sufficiently concerned, far less alarmed. This is the point at which education and prevention are most effective. There is a similar narrowing of vision and normal awareness of time-span becomes contracted, so that the middle and more distant future loses significance and all planning becomes focused on the short-term, and all management becomes crisis management.

According to this model, in the development of an addiction the normal functions of planning for intermediate and long-term goals that might bring satisfaction to the addicted person and might reach and maintain tolerable levels of hedonic tone are increasingly disrupted or become progressively deficient. This can be because an individual's life situation is so confusing and unpredictable that the participant loses the conviction that long-term strategies for securing high sustained hedonic tone will ever pay off and therefore fails to invest in them. Alternatively, in another individual, it may be because their life situation is objectively and inherently devoid of the possibility of reward. This situation may be partly contributed to by previously inherited or acquired skills deficiencies before the process of development of the addiction began any progressive further deterioration. In yet another individual, the addictive process may develop because of the ready availability of easy short-term rewards, making for a style of life that gradually brings the individual to rely almost solely on immediate and short-term satisfactions.

When the normal management functions of planning for intermediate and long-term goals are thus made deficient, a 'crisis management' style of conducting day-to-day, hour-to-hour, and even minute-to-minute, manipulations of arousal and subjective perceptions is developed in order to sustain high hedonic tone by lurching from one 'crisis intervention' (more of the addictive activity) to another (yet more of the addictive activity). After some time, the person gradually loses the management skills for any other way of living involving intermediate and long-term goals, and so becomes locked into or enslaved in their particular addictive activity and lifestyle (Brown, 1989)

Poor-quality decision making also contributes to the initiation of the positive feedback loops. Decision making deteriorates to a quality very similar to that which characterises people who chronically engage in criminal activity. As with many criminals, most decisions about addictive activity are made on the basis of the perception of the immediate positive consequences of action (Hare, 1970). There is no attempt or even ability to foresee the negative consequences, but only a concern with what is tangible and with what is felt in the present. Yochelson and Samenow (1976), in their description of criminal thinking, state: 'In most of the criminal's decision making there is no weighing of pros and cons, no careful evaluation of course of action' (p. 402). According to them, the criminal has not learned that there are a number of alternative courses of action. In fact he or she does not need to consider alternatives because he or she trusts his or her initial assumptions above all others. He or she therefore bases his or her decisions on unvalidated assumptions and his or her immediate desires. This could easily be a description of the concept of 'easily accessible rewarding activities' to be introduced below.

Hare (1970) suggests that what he calls 'inability to delay gratification' is perhaps related to the criminal's low expectancies of positive long-term consequences and inability to give equal value to long-term rewards in comparison with the acute awareness of short-term rewards. This view matches the observations of the deterioration of planning operations and their restriction to the short term outlined above which are typical of addictive thinking. As stated by Yochelson and Samenow (1976), in describing criminal thinking: 'There is no realistic long-term planning, no consideration of injury to others, and no putting himself in the place of others' (p. 403). Many writers have emphasised the criminal's apparent lack of empathy (e.g. Cleckley, 1964; Hare, 1970; Yochelson & Samenow, 1976). These characteristics in thinking and feeling shared by significant proportions of the populations of both addicts and criminals are strongly reminiscent of the deficits in awareness of feelings and inability to identify and express them, and the unimaginative concrete thinking characterising the trait of alexithymia (Nemiah, 1977; Apfel & Sifneos, 1979; Newton & Contrada, 1994; Lumley & Robey, 1995; Pinard et al., 1996). It seems that in the addict, the criminal's well-known failure of empathic imagination to forecast the severity of the long-term negative consequences to victims of short-term crisis management is extended into the failure of the addict even to forecast them for him or herself.

A useful concept here may be that of *easily accessible rewarding activities* which may have important explanatory potential within this catalogue of cognitive failures, especially in relation to decision making. Where short-term crisis management is becoming the habitual style of coping, and tolerance for immediate dysphoria has significantly declined, the person with the growing addiction increasingly needs easily accessible rewarding activities. What has often been described in medical model terms as an apparent 'loss of control', can be better conceptualised as a problem of decision making and the immediate balance of utilities. The utility of a behaviour is a dependent function of both desirability and credibility of the antici-pated reward. This is pure games theory as used in mathematics and economics but can be translated into psychological terms. If, in any given situation, each alternative behaviour is subjected to a cost-benefit analysis, some rewards, although seen as great, will be perceived as having too high a preliminary cost in relation to the benefit expected. This will be particularly true when the time-scale of costs and rewards is taken into account. To extend the economic analogy, the individual experiences acute pleasure-flow problems in the same way as others experience cash-flow problems. The concept of easily accessible rewarding activities describes the subjective value of the behaviour in relation to the available alternatives, i.e. the place of that behaviour in the hierarchy of likelihood of responses. This concept is taken direct from normative decision theory (Von Neumann & Morgenstern, 1944) and it has a central function within some cognitive-behavioural theories of personality (e.g. Rotter, 1982). Most analyses of decision making are based on a method of problem solving which maximises positive consequences and minimises negative consequences, both long- and short-term, on the assumption that humans are basically hedonistic. In addictive decision making the reduced utility of any behaviour other than the addictive activity is a causal factor in the continuing choice of the addictive active over alternatives. In turn, as will be shown, as a direct result of increasing salience and conflict in restricting the possibility of alternative plans for reward, it increases the likelihood that yet more decisions will be made in this faulty way.

In the hedonic management model the independent variables which initiate the addictive positive feedback loops are seen as emotional (in vulnerabilities, mainly chronic dysphoria) and cognitive (mainly faulty decision making). These factors together create the initial salience of the addictive activity (make it a more easily accessible rewarding activity than any possible rival, move it further up the hierarchy of likelihood among alternative responses).

But once salience of the addictive activity is established in this way, even to a relatively small degree, several other positive feedback loops inevitably come into play, each of which in turn increases the *salience*. This salience is here taken as the major identifying feature of the phenomenon of addiction and, at least for heuristic purposes, as the prime independent variable which is affected in turn by several positive feedback loops.

One of the most important of these positive loops involves *conflict* (Orford, 1985). As the salience of the activity grows, it becomes noticed and a matter of concern to others, usually to people immediately around the potential addict. Their concern is about the harm the excessive activity may be doing to the addict and to them. Even where there is a positive addiction like jogging or transcendental meditation (Glasser, 1976), there is almost always some dispute about the extent of the behaviour and about the desirability of that extent. At the very minimum there is criticism from friends and onlookers that the jogging fanatic is missing out on a lot of *other* pleasures in life. It may be that for the addicted person him or herself there is no dispute, no concern about the excesses or about the salience, but that for the friends and relatives the behaviour is clearly excessive and they are continually in conflict with the addicted person about the extent of it.

But most often in a powerful negative addiction there is not only damage and suffering being caused to people around, but there is also an internal dispute within the addicted person him or herself about the extent of their behaviour. He or she *knows* they do it too much and however well they defend themselves against others, he or she is uneasy, dysphoric and even highly anxious about their partially suppressed self-knowledge. These conflicts increase the likelihood of further addictive activity by adding to the very dysphoria for which the addictive activity is needed to escape. They also tend significantly to reduce the range of easily accessible alternative rewarding activities open to them. For example, the drinker would sometimes enjoy a peaceful evening before the television without any drink but this is no longer open to him because his spouse, now outraged by the effects of his previous drinking, will use the occasion to attack him.

Another by-product of the addiction loop is low self-esteem. This idea is not identical with low self-efficacy which is closer to a more narrowly focused set of beliefs about the addict's ability/inability to stop. Low self-esteem is best understood (Wells & Marwell, 1976) as a more global evaluation of the self which may be a vulnerability factor present from the beginning. There is often a temporary improvement in self-esteem as the addiction gathers strength, but latterly the awareness of internal conflict and the increasing pressure on moral standards and the further loss of good relationships and esteem of others depresses it well below the initial level. This, in turn, feeds back to yet more dysphoria and yet more 'hedonic-flow problems' to be solved by crisis management and greater salience.

Once salience and conflict are established, then, especially if the addictive activity has sufficient inherent power to alter hedonic tone, *tolerance*, both psychological and physical, is developed. Tolerance and withdrawal phenomena, often mistakenly seen as central, like conflict, may be best regarded as important *by-products* of the addictive process which serve further to intensify and reinforce it. Without reference to any possible physical effects of salience, or even to the established conditioning factors in tolerance (Siegel, 1979), sustained hedonic tone achieved for long periods may be expected to produce adaptation effects (Keup, 1982). Eternal bliss is boring. Therefore more powerful stimuli are required to recapture 'that first fine rush' or the 'peak experience'. But in addition, the higher and longer the hedonic plateau has been sustained, the greater is the contrast effect in returning even to formerly mediocre levels. In some circumstances even a reduced gradient of climb in hedonic tone can seem like a reduction. When this contrast effect is added to the slow long-term build up of the rebound effect, the powerful beta opponent process (Solomon, 1977), then *not* maintaining a constant high hedonic tone has become painful. A tendency can thus be predicted for the fluctuations in hedonic tone, associated with the height of each episode of addictive activity and the contrasting depth of each withdrawal, to become greater and greater as the development of the addiction progresses. Thus, in itself, it provides a powerful additional conditioning process, teaching the addict to maintain and further develop the addictive activity (Brown, 1989). Thus there are important psychological effects of adaptation, opponent processes, and conditioning, all promoting the development of greater tolerance. In addition there are well-documented conditioning effects which promote tolerance and, for some activities involving the ingestion of substances, considerable physical tolerance phenomena (Siegel, 1975, 1979).

The growth of tolerance entails yet more time and money being spent on the achievement of the same sustained or repeatedly sought level of hedonic tone as previously. This development inevitably crowds out alternative easily accessible rewarding activities and increases salience in another positive feedback loop.

Another important by-product of the psychological process is *withdrawals*, both psychological and physical. Although the physical basis of withdrawal symptoms associated with the abrupt cessation of intake of certain substances such as alcohol and heroin is important for these particular addictive activities, there are also important *psychological* factors in the phenomena of withdrawal (Peele, 1985) common to all addictions. More recently, from the study of gambling addictions, comes a well-researched study which documents the existence of withdrawal effects following cessation of excessive gambling (Wray & Dickerson, 1981) which could be purely psychological if no physiological basis in the ingestion of substances can be pointed to. Some withdrawal phenomena may be better likened to separation within an attachment and so even to a bereavement (McAughtrie & Brown, 1988; Miller, 1986).

These withdrawal phenomena contribute to yet another positive feedback loop which, as the addiction develops, becomes one of the most important of those loops sustaining the addiction. *Relief* indulgence in the addictive activity then becomes the only way in which the painful rebound effects from the last indulgence can be offset by pleasure strong enough to overcome them temporarily. So the last-stage characteristic identifying feature of the predicament of being addicted becomes established.

All these positive feedback loops grow in power and in intensity, all have the central effect of increasing *salience* and, in turn, being strengthened because of the degree of salience, until a near total reliance on one source of rewarding activity has been developed. This phenomenon, which began with initiation, is now recognisably an 'addiction' but, although there is a process in its development, it is not necessarily a *disease* process. A more accurate description of it, which would put it in context alongside other comparable psychological phenomena, would be better conveyed by calling it a *reward specialism* or a *motivational monopoly*. The processes of this development are summarised in Figure 1.3.

Using their chosen method of maintaining high hedonic tone, the attainment of prolonged periods of bliss becomes, for a period, so reliable (almost certain) compared to anything which has been possible in the past, that the addict begins to identify an altered state of consciousness and the desirable feeling state associated with it as a

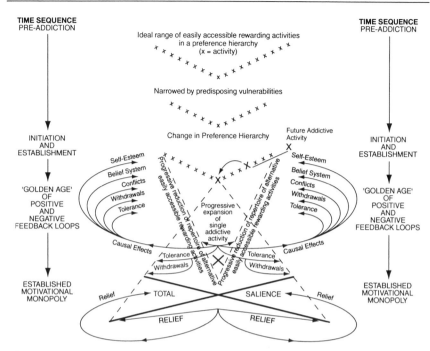

Figure 1.3. Positive feedback loops in the development of an addiction.

goal. A goal acquired in this way is accompanied by an acquired drive towards it with all the characteristics of flexible purposive behaviour. Along with the development of the skills to maintain high hedonic tone, for periods of time unprecedented in the history of the individual, goes a corresponding loss of tolerance for, or a declining ability to endure, aversive emotional states. Characteristic of the pursuit of this drive is the kind of frenzied salience of a single activity that was shown by the rats in the experiments of Olds and Milner (1954). These animals had discovered how to reward the pleasure centres of their brain directly by pressing bars and continued to do so, ignoring opportunities to eat or drink, until they dropped with exhaustion.

But even the crudest, most brutal and direct attempts to manipulate arousal using addictive activities or substances are not always sucessful, even in the short term. There are always 'bad trips', times when the gambling arousal-jag rebounds in massive anxiety, or when the alcohol-induced convivial elation turns unexpectedly to maudlin loneliness. The very unreliability of even the chosen method of mood management, superior though it is to the relatively amateur ineffectiveness and chaos of the normally conducted search for high positive hedonic tone, gives rise to an intermittent schedule of reinforcement. This makes for great resistance to extinction and a tendency to ready reinstatement, not just in gambling, as is well known, but in all addictions by their central nature.

The 'Golden Age' in the development of an addiction begins after a drive for maintenance of high positive hedonic tone has been acquired. During this time the addictive behaviour becomes increasingly skilled and hedonic tone is relatively so much more successfully maintained that the addict is prone to believe for a while that he or she has discovered the secret of eternal bliss. Like the rat with the direct link to the pleasure centres of the brain, he or she exploits the discovery to destruction. In those ways the addictive behaviour acquires a salience and begins to produce its own consequent life-problems (its 'alcohol-related problems', its severe consequences of excessive gambling) which serve to make the further manipulation of hedonic tone even *more* necessary and rewarding. This process is summarised below in the fifth basic proposition of a hedonic management model of addiction:

5.   *Development of an Acquired Drive and Increasing Salience* **An addiction is developed through a positive feedback loop involving a series of cognitive failures which lead to an acquired drive for particular feeling states as goals and to the salience of a single activity as a source of reward. Deficient self-awareness (vigilance), short-term planning and crisis management, and faulty decision making all contribute to the development of salience and consequent conflict leading to narrowing of easily accessible alternative rewarding activities. Increasing salience leads to increasing tolerance, withdrawals and relief action which in turn lead to yet greater salience.**

A NATURAL CYCLE OF EPISODES OF HIGH HEDONIC TONE WHICH PRODUCES A SERIAL

All addictions can usefully be viewed as 'serials' consisting of a series of 'episodes' (Brown, 1988). To illustrate from alcoholism, an 'episode' may be an evening's drinking or a whole six-week binge. In gambling an 'episode' may be a visit to a casino or it may be a weekend when the gambler hurries on from losses at cards to the off-track, to recoup at the casino, and back again to cards before pausing, leaving his 'scenes of action', letting the fever die down and regrouping for the next 'episode'. Such cycles are well documented for addictions to various illegal drugs (O'Doherty & Davies, 1988). Each episode represents a sustained attempt to maintain a high positive hedonic tone. It is bounded at the beginning by a belief, based on past experiential learning and sustained by a series of cognitive distortions and an organised belief system, that maintenance of hedonic tone is once again possible. It also begins with a biased anticipation, not only of how intense the positive hedonic experience will be but also of how easily it can be attained and sustained. And at the end the 'episode' is bounded by acceptance of temporary failure, perhaps by abandonment to remorse and guilt, rationalisations of what went wrong, but with a persistent underlying belief that positive high hedonic tone can be sustained more successfully some other time.

The middle of the episode itself is characterised by total orientation to the immediate present, typically to the next few minutes or, at the most, to the next few hours. The addict 'behaves like there is no tomorrow', in a partially or even fully disassociated state (Brown, 1994). They often add 'boosters' even in that state; perhaps, if a gambler, by betting particularly heavily to get an extra 'jag' even when on a sustained 'high', or, if a drug addict, by increasing the dose or mainlining to produce an extra 'rush'. Although most of the time may be spent in altered or even disassociated states, the occasional temporary threat of return 'to reality' is responded to by yet more ingenious pursuit of the well-established acquired drive to re-establish and maintain high positive hedonic tone.

To illustrate from alcohol, the drinker may, because of the biphasic nature of the effects of the drug, succeed in enjoying the high positive hedonic effects of each drink and avoiding the ensuing negative emotional rebound because he or she times and quantifies the next intake to override the rebound effects from the last. In such a way, by drinking more at the right time, he or she succeeds in staying on a high hedonic plane for hours, but, like a surf rider poised insecurely on a wave, he or she inevitably crashes on the beach in a potentiated multiple rebound state (Brown, 1989). Once again, however, the goal espoused in that state *can* be the search for the means to repeat the experience immediately and the full return to the uncontrived 'normal' state can be postponed until the 'episode' must inevitably end in misery and tears. Most relapses are such 'episodes'.

Similarly most gamblers lose during their episodes and this will usually bring about a momentary hedonic rebound. The response to this is not to walk away and face up to the total significance of the situation, with an accompanying review of the global consequences for the individual's life aims, but rather to attempt to re-establish the

high-arousal state by further 'action' in gambling. Full return to a
low-arousal non-dissociated state for any significant length of time
may only come with the end of material resources. So the gambler
gambles until the casino closes and all his or her money is gone. Even
then the 'episode' may not be finished because it may be possible to
find fresh opportunities and resources for gambling before the
current 'fever' leaves, and the full return to the 'normal' uncontrived
state that has been desperately avoided becomes finally inevitable.

Between each episode the aversive consequences of the addictive
excesses are endured in terms of physical effects, social and relationship damage, and the starting place for the next episode is prepared.
Cognitive reattribution and rationalisation rebuilds the belief in
likely success in sustaining hedonic tone next time; more material
resources are accumulated; and the acute dysphoria arising from the
consequences of the last episode makes the felt need for another
'attempt' or another 'relief', depending upon the stage of development
of the addiction, all the more intense.

Episode builds upon episode into a 'serial' in which consistent
themes of increasing loss and damage emerge, until the individual
reaches either an equilibrium in which he or she compromises
realistically and trades the limitation of some episodes, either in
extent or in number, to gain in return reduced or containable
consequences, or he or she reaches an inevitable crisis.

Especially at later stages, belief in total hedonic control and
fantastic omnipotence is liable to break down. The individual then
reindulges, although aware that he or she is buying short-term
'relief', 'escape', perhaps even sustained high positive hedonic tone,
for longer term rebound effects on 'an experiential never-never' or 'a
hedonic hire purchase scheme'.

HABIT HIERARCHIES, RITUALS, DISSOCIATED STATES, COGNITIVE DISTORTIONS AND SUPPORTING BELIEF SYSTEMS

During these serial episodes routines become established and
'overlearned', i.e. rewards associated with certain stimuli and actions
are repeatedly 'stamped in'. Increasingly potent associative bonds
between certain wholistic stimulus situations (e.g. presence of a
particular friend, certain time of day, etc.) and the performance of
the addictive activity are built up, in accordance with the well-known
and researched schedules of reinforcement and the associations of
classical conditioning. Social learning theories of addiction are

particularly useful in understanding these phenomena (Miller, 1986; Heather & Robertson, 1989; O'Brien et al., 1992).

Rituals, repeated routine series of stimuli and actions, some of which build up anticipation and arousal, and others which reduce tension (as desired), are worked out and become established during this period. For example, if the current acquired goal is a state of tension reduction, the well-known and recognised ritual acts of pipe smokers and cigarette rollers in preparing their 'fixes' are sometimes carried out deliberately and slowly. Less well known, but common to sexual addictions, are rituals building up arousal (general as well as sexual). Carnes (1989) gives examples of compulsive masturbators using certain surroundings and thought patterns, incestuous fathers and their elaborate preparations, exposers' regular routines, and the hustler's approach and cruising areas. All these are complex rituals containing a set of well-rehearsed cues which trigger arousal. Rituals managing arousal are widespread in other addictions, especially in the long middle stages of their development, although less noticeable or necessary in the latter stages when the addiction is fully established.

Dissociated states brought about at the height of intensity in the performance of the addictive activity are another feature reported across most of the field of addictions (Goodwin et al., 1969; Jacobs, 1988; Kolodner & Francis, 1993; Kuley & Jacobs, 1988; Brown, 1994). These psychological states have a quality of separateness or apartness, 'differentness' or disconnection from the normal flow of mental life. At first the dissociated state is a by-product of the addictive activity but later the addictive activity is usually used as the gateway into the dissociated state. In much the same way as the hedonic management theory suggests that particular states become acquired goals associated with addictive activity, so the dissociated state, perhaps originally the chance by-product of an attempt to attain a different pleasurable state of high hedonic tone, can, after its discovery, become the principal desired goal sought through the addictive activity. These dissociated states appear to vary from states of very high arousal and, perhaps, elation through to states of escape.

Cognitive distortions, sequences of thinking which, to an outsider, obviously rest on fallible assumptions or principles, are relatively well researched in gambling addictions (Wagenaar, 1988; Gaboury & Ladouceur, 1989; Griffiths, 1990; Brown, 1993a). Surprisingly, it is only now that they are beginning to receive the attention they deserve in the narrower field of 'substance abuse' or 'chemical dependency' (Beck et al., 1993). Excellent examples of cognitive distortions range from the biased evaluation of betting outcomes

(Gilovich, 1983), through the illusion of control (Langer, 1975), and the evolution of the belief in 'personal luck' which overrides rational calculations of odds (Keren & Wagenaar, 1985). An example from 'substance abuse' involves the abuser's belief that the abuse is an illness and therefore that cravings *must* lead to satisfaction because the abuser would not be ill if they were not 'out of control'—a typical piece of circular reasoning. Or again, the user really owes it to their best friend to take a fix with them because, if they did not, their friend would feel so lonely doing it on their own. These cognitive distortions and rationalisations mainly allow addicted persons to protect themselves against external critics of their behaviour and against their own internal conflicting doubts and anxieties about what they are doing. Individuals tend to develop their own pattern of favourite and most effective 'double thinks' to meet their own most common critical situations.

As the addiction builds up there is a gradual accretion of a supporting belief system which often persists long after the addictive activity has been abandoned. In the beginning the build-up is aided and sustained by beliefs such as: 'It is amazing what it (the addictive activity) does for me'; 'There is nothing else to do'; 'This is the best fun I know'. Later it is sustained and developed by beliefs such as: 'Drugs (or the addictive activity) are sometimes problems for some people but they will not be for me'; 'I am really quite an expert at blackjack (or the addictive activity) and I can make it work for me like these other mugs cannot'; 'I am just oversexed'; 'I have really earned this piece of action!'; 'He/she wanted it, deserved it, asked for it'. And finally it is prolonged by beliefs like: 'Just one more time won't hurt'; 'The only way I can get out of this debt is with a big win'; 'I am not a strong enough person to stop'; 'I could not endure life without (the addictive activity)' and so on. These sustaining belief systems and the crucial role they play have long been documented in sexual addictions (Carnes, 1989), more recently in gambling addictions (Walker, 1992) and are most recently and most fully set out for 'substance abuse' (Beck et al., 1993). Beck et al. were impressed by the commonality of beliefs across various types of addictions. they listed dysfunctional ideas as:

> (1) the belief that one *needs* the substance if one is to maintain psychological and emotional balance; (2) the expectation that the substance will improve social and intellectual functioning; (3) the expectation that one will find pleasure and excitement from using; (4) the belief that the drug will energise the individual and provide increased power; (5) the expectation that the drug will have a soothing effect; (6) the assumption that the drug will relieve boredom, anxiety,

tension and depression; and (7) the conviction that, unless something is done to satisfy the craving or neutralise the distress, it will continue indefinitely and, possibly, get worse.' (p. 38)

As was recognised for sexual addictions, and now in 'substance abuse', even long after the addictive activity has been abandoned, the belief system developed during its dominance may be preserved intact. This, in turn, notoriously produces a miserable sobriety among the 'dry drunks', and makes the 'recovering' but not fully recovered especially vulnerable to relapse and to the reinstatement phenomenon (see later).

This general analysis, although it bears some resemblance to social learning accounts (e.g. Marlatt, 1979), is not so much a social learning, but more an experiential- or phenomenological-learning account based upon the centrality of subjective experience and its individual interpretation. It is summarised in the sixth basic proposition of a hedonic management model of addiction set out below:

6.   *Cycles* **During the later stages of its development the engagement in the addictive activity comes in repeated cycles or in episodes which make up a serial, during which there is a build-up of (i) potent classical conditioning effects and schedules of reinforcement; (ii) rituals inducing the sought-after feeling states; (iii) dysfunctional cognitive distortions and belief systems; and, possibly, (iv) routines facilitating entry to partially or wholly dissociated states.**

FULLY ESTABLISHED ADDICTION

Although some relative success may be experienced, even from the beginning, in the maintenance of high positive hedonic tone over short and even medium terms, the human organism, is not unfortunately, 'pre-wired' (Seligman, 1970) for permanent unbroken bliss. Inevitably efforts at manipulating the hedonic system are carried to extremes—with rebound effects which are painful enough to make the further manipulation of hedonic tone not only desirable but a desperate necessity.

A fully established motivational monopoly, reward specialism or 'addiction' is reached when there are repeated episodes where tolerable hedonic tone can only be maintained by continuous (at the extreme, almost from minute to minute) manipulation of arousal through yet more of the activity. This is the stage of 'relief drinking' of the Alcohol Dependence Syndrome when (in this particular 'substance abuse' case) continuous manipulation is necessitated by physical factors in addition to psychological ones (Edwards & Gross, 1976). It is also the stage of 'relief gambling' in the final phases of Lesieur's (1979) Spiral of Options when continuous manipulation is necessitated by social and institutional pressures amounting to entrapment (Brockner & Rubin, 1985; Walker, 1992) as well as by psychological ones. It is the stage when, although positive reinforcement is still sought and occasionally obtained from the addictive activity (McAuliffe & Gordon, 1974), there is relatively little positive reinforcement left available to maintain the self-state manipulative behaviour. Indeed most drinking and gambling has lost any positive enjoyment. It is also the stage when the behaviour is most likely to be confused with a compulsion. The addictive activity is now increasingly driven by fear: fear of withdrawals; fear of the negative emotions which have been avoided for so long that tolerance to them has been reduced; and fear of the general inability to cope without recourse to the addictive activity. External restraint from the completion of the addictive activity produces intense anxiety and completion brings relief in a pattern of feeling and behaviour quite characteristic of the compulsions but without the same developmental history and aetiology.

At this stage all the classical psychological features of a fully developed addiction can be identified. These can usefully be seen as, most importantly, *salience* (Edwards & Gross, 1976), *conflict* (Orford, 1985), *relief, low self-esteem* and *relapse and reinstatement* (Edwards & Gross, 1976). (see Figure 1.4)

Salience or Precedence over Other Behaviours. The addictive activity, the drinking for example, comes to dominate all of the person's life, their thinking, their feeling and their behaviour. For the addicted person the central actions of their addiction become more important than anything else in their lives, more important than eating, sleeping or sexual satisfaction; more important than relationships. All of life revolves round the addiction. It is virtually the only source of satisfaction, of pleasure or of relief from pain.

Conflict. The addictive activity produces ill-feeling and disputes with people immediately around the addict about the harm the excessive activity may be doing to the addict and to all concerned. Alternatively, there may be an internal dispute, an approach–avoidance conflict (Orford, 1985) within the addicted person him or herself about the desirability of the extent of his or her behaviour.

Apparent Loss of control. Implicitly recognised for centuries in disease models of alcoholism, but explicitly named and studied since

Salience	The addictive activity becomes the most important thing in the person's life and dominates thinking (*preoccupations* and *cognitive distortions*), feeling (cravings), and behaviour (*deterioration of socialised behaviour*)
Conflict	Disputes about the extent of the excessive behaviour arise both between the addicted person and others around and within the addicted person themselves. Continuing conflict increases salience and the need for relief
Apparent 'Loss of Control'	Apparent inability to limit time or resources given to, or amount of, excessive behaviour, even when a decision appears to have previously been made to do so. Explainable in terms of *salience* and *relief*
Relief	At a late stage, the effects of the addictive activity are so powerful that there is a rebound effect when it ceases (withdrawals) and the only way to avoid feeling more miserable than before (to find relief) is to do it again at the earliest opportunity. *Continual choosing of short-term pleasure and relief* leads to *disregard of adverse consequences* and long-term damage which in turn increases *Salience* as the apparent need for the addictive activity as a coping strategy
Low Self-Esteem	Low global evaluation of self, including abilities, efficacy and worth.
Relapse and Reinstatement	Tendency for repeated reversions to earlier patterns of addictive behaviour to recur and for even the most extreme patterns typical of the height of the addiction to be quickly restored even after many years of abstinence or control

Figure 1.4. Common psychological components of addictions

the 1930s, the inner experience of the drinker was reinterpreted as reduced and patchy control over overwhelming cravings and urges. This was sometimes elevated into the myth of total loss of control. The 'loss of control' apparently experienced by the addict was then used as an explanation for the drinker's behaviour in an attribution of cause after the event. Loss of control was never absolute, as was demonstrated in a crucial series of laboratory experiments (Mello & Mendelson, 1965; Mello et al., 1968; Cohen et al., 1971). The patchy variations in the subjective experience of partial control are better explained in terms of lack of *easily accessible alternative activities*, cost-benefit analyses, faulty decision making (Janis & Mann, 1977) and crisis management styles of coping (Brown, 1993b), as explained above.

Relief. Has developed through the learned avoidance of rebound effects from the cessation of very strong stimulation which had major effects on hedonic tone.

The remaining important psychological features of addictions, *relapses* and *reinstatement* phenomena, do not manifest themselves until serious efforts have been made to reduce or eliminate the addictive activity. Each of these psychological features exists independently of the ingestion of any substance but, of course, can be, and often is, potentiated and intensified when a powerful mind altering chemical is involved in the addictive activity.

Other important distinguishing features of addictions which have always been accepted as major physiological features of the concept of addiction are *tolerance* and *withdrawal effects* (see Figure 1.5).

Tolerance	Increasing amounts of the addictive activity are required to achieve the former effects
Withdrawals	Unpleasant feeling states and/or physical effects when the addictive activity is discontinued or suddenly reduced

Figure 1.5. Common physical components of an addiction

Habit Hierarchies, Rituals, Dissociated States, Cognitive Distortions and Supporting Belief Systems	Increasingly potent associative bonds between certain stimulus situations and the performance of the addictive activity; repeated routine series of stimuli and actions, building up anticipation and arousal or reducing tension; states having a quality of disconnection from the normal flow of mental life; patterns of thinking that allow protection against external and internal criticism; beliefs which justify the continuance of the activity

Figure 1.6. Other psychological features of an addiction that can sometimes be identified

These physical features have an important psychological component in addition to the physical one but they have been much emphasised by those who see addictions as illnesses and the presence of withdrawal effects has been advanced as the prime criterion of the existence of an addiction.

Additionally *Habit Hierarchies, Rituals, Dissociated States, Cognitive Distortions and Supporting Belief Systems* (see Figure 1.6) will normally be identifiable at this stage.

The identifying features of the existence of an established motivational monopoly are summarised in the seventh basic proposition of a hedonic management model of addiction below:

7. ***Established Addiction* At the point of full development of an addiction a single addictive activity so dominates thinking, feeling and behaviour (i.e. has such salience) that it becomes virtually the sole source of reward and is used to maintain a near continuous subjective mood or feeling state producing mounting conflict within and without and leading to relief action to avoid withdrawals. Decisions are now made solely on a basis of extremely short-term reward or relief as mere crisis management.**

REVERSING THE PROCESS—IMPROVED HEDONIC MANAGEMENT REDISTRIBUTION AND DISPERSAL

'Treatment' or 'intervention' both initially involve some counselling on crisis management to help cope with the mounting health, social, legal and relationship problems produced by the addictive process. In the longer term 'treatment', 'intervention', and even 'recovery' without outside help, all involve a radical change in the policy and style of hedonic management.

Improved self-awareness, perhaps aided by a counsellor, begins with an increasingly full realisation of the extent of the salience of the addictive activity and of the operation of the feedback loops. Well-managed confrontation (Miller & Rollnick, 1991) of the damage to self and to relationships improves the quality of the central decision to seek behaviour change (Janis & Mann, 1977). Once such a commitment to change in the policy and style of hedonic management has been made, the reduction or, more commonly, the extinction of the addictive activity inevitably involves a period of acute and perhaps prolonged dysphoria. This may occur in a sudden collapse of the addictive way of life, a 'hedonic crash', or it may occur over a long period of 'tapering off' in a 'hedonic decline'. This initial dysphoria performs a vital function in the development of *restored tolerance of short-term dysphoria*, and attempts to avoid it by medication are usually misguided for that reason. Adaptation and comparison levels for hedonic tone must change radically.

The major work of the period of dispersal is the redistribution of the sources of pleasure. This lies in the revival of as many of the varied sources of reward in different areas of the subject's life as possible, and the establishment of new ones. If the previous repertoire of easily accessible rewarding activities is to be revived and regenerated, careful consideration and planning with a high quality of decision making must be extended to every area of the person's life—working, domestic, social and recreational, etc. Better planning for the medium- and long-term manipulation of hedonic tone will make the short-term, day-to-day, minute-to-minute, management of hedonic tone easier, and will restore the stable state of reward diversity (as opposed to specialism) or motivational pluralism.

This means that at the same time as the rewards from the addictive activity are diminishing, the rewards from a wider repertoire of easily accessible activities are growing in their place. As the redistribution of sources of reward takes place, the diminishing is bound to be faster than the replacement, and there is inevitably, as noted above, a large hedonic gap, which leaves the person with a crucial, but eventually diminishing, vulnerability to reversion to the addictive activity as the new hedonic management policy takes effect. But it is the implementation of this change of the policy and style of hedonic management, perhaps over several years, if necessary, which generates its own positive feedback loops and reverses the effects of the positive feedback loops of the earlier addiction process.

This process is illustrated diagrammatically in Figure 1.7 and summarised in the eighth basic proposition of a hedonic management model of addiction:

8.   *Redistribution and Dispersal* **Recovery is brought about through a radical change in the policy and style of management of hedonic tone. This involves (i) improved self-awareness and vigilance and a better quality of decision-making; (ii) reduction or extinction of the addictive activity along with the development of increased tolerance of short-term dysphoria; (ii) the revival and regeneration of a wide repertoire of easily accessible rewarding activities through better planning for the medium- and long-term manipulation of hedonic tone. This effects a wider dispersal of sources of reward and an improved overall rate of reward or quality of life.**

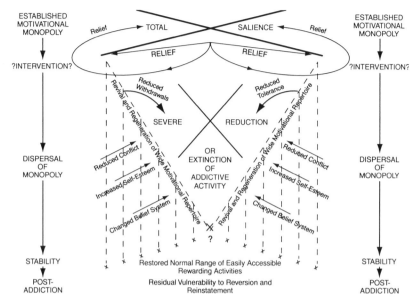

Figure 1.7. The reverse process of redistribution and dispersion of an addiction.

REVERSIONS AND RELAPSES

Once the policy commitment has been made and a change in the style of hedonic management has begun, it usually proves very difficult to implement. Not only are there failures to find easily accessible rewarding activities to replace the relative reliability of the rewards from the addictive activity, and a resulting massive increase in dysphoria, but there may also be bereavement reactions to the loss of addictive lifestyle. There is always the option available of the instant restoration of the salience of the old addictive activity, i.e. of a return or reversion to the old overlearned pattern of reward specialism or motivational monopoly.

The avoidance and management of such reversions (or relapses in the terminology of the medical model) has become recognised as a crucial issue in working with addictions (Marlatt & Gordon, 1985; Litman, 1986; Brown 1989).

From the hedonic management model it is predicted that with the implementation of new policies and style of hedonic management, the risk of reversion to the old full motivational monopoly (relapse) will decrease in proportion as the sources of reward to the person become once again more varied and dispersed, and as the overall rate of rewards from these sources rises. During the early stages of dispersal there is a well-known increased vulnerability to cross-addictions and this can also be expected to decrease as the overall quality and variety of life improves.

This process is summarised in the ninth basic proposition of a hedonic management model of addiction below:

9. *Reversion* **Throughout the process of dispersal and as it progresses the risk of reversion to the full motivational monopoly (relapse) and the vulnerability to cross-addictions decrease as the sources of reward become more dispersed and the overall rate of rewards rises.**

REINSTATEMENT PHENOMENA

Edwards, in his description of the Alcohol Dependence Syndrome (Edwards & Gross, 1977), includes as a major feature of relapse, the reinstatement effect. This is the name he gives to the rapid reinstatement of the former maximum levels of addictive activity which can immediately follow even a minor relapse. Extreme examples of this are occasionally reported, such as the gambler who, two weeks before he was about to receive recognition for 10 years total abstinence from his local group of Gamblers Anonymous, gambled again and, within a few weeks, was betting at his former levels just before he sought help 10 years earlier. Such stories are also frequent about drinkers and smokers. They require systematic investigation and verification because in many of them the time lapse is so great that there can clearly be no physiological component and it might be a better description to refer to them as examples of a reinstatement phenomenon. Explanations from cognitive psychology (Beck et al., 1993) suggest that the underpinning belief system had not changed and so had left the addict especially vulnerable to relapse. Even such an early behaviourist as Pavlov found that long after the conditioned responses had been extinguished in his dogs, flashbacks could occur and even the full conditioned reflex could be reliably and rapidly restored. Any pattern of behaviour which has been overlearned to the extent that an addictive activity usually has, would then be expected, on purely theoretical grounds, to produce the reinstatement phenomenon from time to time without any further physiological factors being necessary to the explanation.

A recognition of the existence and importance of the reinstatement phenomena is embodied in the tenth basic proposition of a hedonic management model below:

10. *Reinstatement* **After any addiction, even despite a high rate of rewards dispersed among a variety of sources and**

maintained over a long time, there always remains a residual vulnerability. Unusual cues reduce cognitive vigilance, perhaps a period of less successful hedonic management can trigger a flashback with a consequent reversion to the addictive activity, with a full and rapid reinstatement of the former overlearned pattern of reward specialism which had constituted the motivational monopoly.

THE BOUNDARIES OF THE CONCEPT OF ADDICTION

There is, sadly, often confusion, not just in the minds of educated lay persons, between *addictions* and habits, *obsessions, compulsions, attachments and dependencies*. The boundaries of the concept are more fully addressed elsewhere (Brown, 1993a). In summary (Figure 1.8), addictions can usually be distinguished from obsessions and compulsions because the former are goal-directed and the behaviour has expectancies of positive pleasure, whereas the latter are inflexible, stereotyped, do not lead to extensive action, and are experienced as involuntary, anxiety-driven and alien to the self.

Attachments, on the other hand, centre on particular *persons* and *objects*, occasionally on *ideas*, involving long-term relationships, and have virtually no adaptation or tolerance effects. Dependencies may be seen as a narrow subset of addictions referring almost exclusively to substance-based addictions and particularly to their physical aspects. The medically dominated traditional vocabulary of 'dependencies' and 'substance abuse' has distorted our perception of the central phenomena of addictions by insisting that the central processes and the

OBSESSIONS	Recurring patterns of thought that people cannot control and that distress them
COMPULSIONS	Repeated involuntary acts that the person tries to resist and feels revulsion over at the time
ATTACHMENTS	Are usually benign and constructive, centre on persons and objects, involve long-term relationships with them and do not involve increasing tolerance, relapses or withdrawal effects
DEPENDENCIES	Refer narrowly to substance-based addictions and particularly to physical aspects of them

Figure 1.8. Some problems to be distinguished from addictions.

crucially identifying phenomena of addictions are physical and physiological, when it is now emerging that just the opposite is the case. The central processes of addictions and the crucial identifying features are *psychological* phenomena and it is the physiological phenomena which are peripheral and secondary, though important.

The importance of the definition of boundaries to the concept of addiction is embodied in the eleventh basic proposition of a hedonic management model below:

11. *Boundaries and Distinctions* **Addictions are not habits, obsessions, compulsions or attachments and can be distinguished from them.**

THE PROBLEM OF VALUE IN THE CONCEPT OF ADDICTION

Glasser (1976) has outlined the concept of 'Positive Addictions'—activities, such as jogging and transcendental meditation, which produce increased feelings of self-efficacy. Other addictions, such as games and gaming (Brown, 1991; Brown & Robertson, 1993; Fisher, 1994) or 'workaholicism' do not have quite the beneficial qualities required to meet Glasser's criteria for a positive addiction, and they have a range of harmful associations, from mildly irritating to potentially serious. It was suggested (Brown, 1993a) that they could be called 'Mixed Blessing Addictions', but even the potential wreckers such as heroin, gambling and drinking are not wholly destructive. Especially in their 'Golden Age', when the individual to be addicted has learned all the skills of maximising the control and effects of his or her chosen addictive instrument for sustaining eternal high hedonic tone (Brown, 1988), addictions have several clearly positive functions. To give only two examples, they produce reliable changes of mood and subjective experience (escape from pain, boredom, etc.) and they provide positive experiences of pleasure, excitement, relaxation, etc. (Brown, 1993a). Even in the latter stages of deterioration they still, to give two examples, simplify all decisions because all decisions can be made according as to whether or not they allow of the pursuit of one single (addictive) activity or not. Further, they may, as hustling develops into a full-time activity, become a source of meaning to life and even, later, whether recovered from or not, a source of personal identity (Brown, 1993a). Clearly not even the most destructive addiction at the furthest point of the good–bad value scale is always entirely an unmixed personal disaster.

This is summarised in the twelfth and last basic proposition of a hedonic management model of addictions below :

12. *Value* Seen in their proper context as motivational monopolies or reward specialisms, addictions are almost value-free. Even the most destructive have some secondary beneficial effects. Most are mixed blessings with both valuable and undesirable consequences both socially and individually. Some positive addictions may be very constructive for individuals and societies.

THE HEDONIC MANAGEMENT MODEL OF ADDICTION

It has been argued here that there is a single core process in the development and maintenance of addictions, the continual mismanagement of the quest for happiness. According to this model, in the development of an addiction the normal functions of planning for intermediate and long-term goals that might bring satisfaction to the addicted person, and might reach and maintain tolerable levels of hedonic tone, are increasingly disrupted or become progressively deficient. The process may begin with certain personal vulnerabilities but increasingly, as it develops, it shows similar features for all people caught in the positive feedback loops. An illustrative diagram of the whole process of development and dispersal of such an addiction is given in Figure 1.9 and a summary of the basic propositions is given below:

1. *Management of Hedonic Tone* All individuals learn to manipulate their arousal, mood and experiences of subjective well-being to sustain good hedonic tone (states of relative pleasure and euphoria) for as much of the time as possible, in the normal pursuit of happiness. Some regularly reproducible feeling states become secondary goals or drives.
2. *Vulnerabilities* Personal predisposing vulnerabilities to addiction: (i) increase the individual's hedonic gap, defined as the difference between the levels of relative dysphoria they can tolerate and those they habitually experience; and (ii) narrow the range of easily accessible rewarding activities.
3. *Initiation* An addiction is initiated when there is either the gradual development or the sudden discovery of an activity which provides a relatively powerful and

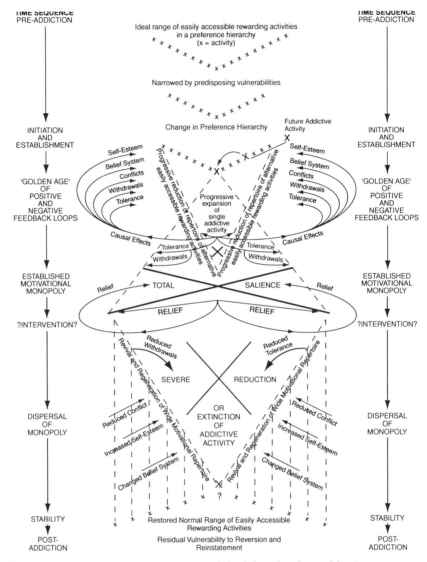

Figure 1.9. Diagrammatic summary of the lifecycle of an addiction.

effective means of manipulating hedonic tone to sustain long periods of euphoria or relief from dysphoria and so changes the preference hierarchy of the repertoire of easily accessible activities.

4. *Addictive Activity* Choice of addictive activity depends on: (i) the range of activities available in the environment, (ii) social support for that activity; (iii) inherent

properties of that activity to affect the individual's hedonic tone (e.g. through changes in arousal); and (iv) acquired skills in using that activity to manipulate hedonic tone. Activities with stronger reinforcement effects lead to faster development of addictions and a few substances have physical properties which produce steeper tolerance gradients leading to the same effect.

5. *Development of an Acquired Drive and Increasing Salience* An addiction is developed through a positive feedback loop involving a series of cognitive failures which lead to an acquired drive for particular feeling states as goals and to the salience of a single activity as a source of reward. Deficient self-awareness (vigilance), short-term planning and crisis management, and faulty decision making all contribute to the development of salience and consequent conflict leading to narrowing of the repertoire of easily accessible alternative rewarding activities. Increasing salience leads to increasing tolerance, withdrawals and relief action which in turn lead to yet greater salience.

6. *Cycles* During the later stages of its development the engagement in the addictive activity comes in repeated cycles or in episodes which make up a serial, during which there is a build-up of: (i) potent classical conditioning effects and schedules of reinforcement; (ii) rituals inducing the sought-after feeling states; (iii) dysfunctional cognitive distortions and belief systems; and, possibly, (iv) routines facilitating entry to partially or wholly dissociated states.

7. *Established Addiction* At the point of full development of a motivational monopoly or reward specialism a single addictive activity so dominates thinking feeling and behaviour (i.e. has such salience) that it becomes virtually the sole source of reward and is used to maintain a near continuous subjective mood or feeling state producing mounting conflict within and without and leading to relief action to avoid withdrawals. Decisions are now made solely on a basis of extremely short-term reward or relief as mere crisis management.

8. *Dispersal* Recovery is brought about through a radical change in the policy and style of management of hedonic tone. This involves: (i) improved self-awareness and vigilance and a better quality of decision making; (ii) reduction or extinction of the addictive activity along

with the development of increased tolerance of short-term dysphoria; (ii) the revival and regeneration of a wide repertoire of easily accessible rewarding activities through better planning for the medium- and long-term manipulation of hedonic tone. This effects a wider dispersal of sources of reward and an improved overall rate of reward or quality of life.

9. *Reversion* Throughout the process of dispersal and as it progresses the risk of reversion to the full addiction (relapse) and the vulnerability to cross-addictions decreases as the sources of reward become more dispersed and the overall rate of rewards rises.

10. *Reinstatement* After any addiction, even despite a high rate of rewards dispersed among a variety of sources and maintained over a long time, there always remains a residual vulnerability. Unusual cues reduce cognitive vigilance, perhaps a period of less successful hedonic management can trigger a flashback with a consequent reversion to the addictive activity, with a full and rapid reinstatement of the former overlearned pattern of reward specialism which had constituted the addiction.

11. *Boundaries and Distinctions* Addictions are not habits, obsessions, compulsions or attachments and can be distinguished from them.

12. *Value* Seen in their proper context as motivational monopolies or reward specialisms, addictions are almost value-free. Even the most destructive have some secondary beneficial effects. Most are mixed blessings with both valuable and undesirable consequences both socially and individually. Some positive addictions may be very constructive for individuals and societies.

Beyond the *addiction-related problems* of, for example, drinking or heroin, gambling or sex, which may confuse us because of their heavy negative-value-laden content, are a set of enduring *core characteristics of addictions*. These are now almost value-free, always present to some degree in even the most 'positive' of addictions, but still more clearly seen in the long recognised 'negative' addictions than in the others. These *core characteristics* remain salience, conflict and relief (traditionally also 'loss of control') with secondary consequences such as tolerance, withdrawal and reinstatement.

THE CONCEPT OF ADDICTION, VALUE-FREE AND EXPANDING, NOT EXPLODING

The concept of addiction has a recognisable common core distinguishable from other problem phenomena of human experience. It is also clear that not only the crude and powerful stimulants and depressants of the well-known addictive activities and substances which produce massive alterations in hedonic tone can be the instruments and vehicles of such a debasement of the normal planning and management skills of the pleasure-seeking individual. Many other leisure activities too, such as games and gaming, can be abused to gain short-term satisfactions in the same way, although not, perhaps usually, with the same spectacular effects. Thus the concept of addictions, now relatively value-free, can be studied in a much wider range of situations and functions such as gambling than in just the 'old-fashioned' negative substance-based phenomena hitherto conventionally thought of as addictions.

EXTENDING THE ADDICTION MODEL TO THE EXPLANATION OF OTHER TROUBLESOME BEHAVIOURS SUCH AS OFFENDING

Attempting to explain criminal behaviour is a notoriously unrewarding enterprise. Neither purely moral models of explanation of crime as sin, or as manifestations of evil, nor purely medical explanations in terms of loss of control and disease are at all satisfactory. The more recent attempts to explain criminal offending purely in terms of learning theory seem to many to devalue the importance of cognition, motivation and emotion in the genesis of behaviour. Addiction models of the explanation of criminal behaviour are in their early stages of development and will be lucky if their rivals do not strangle them in their cradle.

It is important first to be clear that there are many individuals who commit crimes to support and supply their addictions or as a result of their addictions. For example, patterns of offending among gamblers and some drug addicts are very similar, mostly involving crimes of property but not violence. Patterns of offending among alcohol and barbiturate addicts are more likely to involve violence to the person, perhaps without any property involvement at all (Brown, 1986). Further, there are criminals who are addicted, not to crime itself but to something else, such as drinking or gambling, but where their addiction plays no role in their offending. The only group of people we are interested in here are those who may be addicted to the particular form of their offending itself.

PREDICTING SOME IDENTIFYING FEATURES OF THOSE CRIMINAL ACTIVITIES WHICH ARE AT LEAST PARTIALLY EXPLAINABLE WITH AN ADDICTION MODEL

With such a blueprint for addictions what should we be looking for if we are trying to identify possible addictive elements in criminal offending? We can approach this question by looking at crimes and by looking at individuals (and we shall do both of these) but the best place to look is likely to be in the relationship between the individual and the crime.

Addictive Crimes?

The prime candidates for the label 'addictive crime' have been some sex offences but crimes of violence against the person have many of the features of addiction and some crimes against property must be highly suspect. The existence of sexual addictions has not yet been recognised by the American Psychiatric Association but there have been many papers about them in American psychiatric journals, sometimes whole issues devoted to the topic (e.g. the *American Journal of Preventative Psychiatry and Neurology*, **2**, 3, May 1990). Carnes (1983, 1989) attempts to examine them systematically.

Carnes (1983) sees the root of addictions in the addict's belief system and he sees the addictive experience as going through a four-step cycle which intensifies with each repetition. The steps in the cycle are:

(1) preoccupation—the trance or mood wherein the addict's mind is completely engrossed in thoughts of sex (2) ritualisation—the addict's own special routines which lead up to the sexual behaviour (the ritual intensifies the preoccupations, adding arousal and excitement) (3) compulsive sexual behaviour—the actual sexual act, which is the end goal of the preoccupation and ritualisation (sexual addicts are unable to control or stop this behaviour) (4) despair—the feeling of utter hopelessness addicts have about their behaviour and their powerlessness'.

The pain the addicts feel at the end of the cycle can be numbed or obscured by the sexual preoccupation which re-engages the addiction cycle. (p. 9)

Although Carnes perceives the addiction through a very medicalised belief system, it is also fully recognisable in terms of the Hedonic Management model.

Carnes (1989) attempts to distinguish phases in the development and expression of the sexual addiction:

Level One includes behaviour that is perceived in our culture as acceptable. These behaviours include masturbation, heterosexual relationships, homosexual relationships, pornography and prostitution.

Level Two specifies sexual behaviour that is generally regarded as nuisance behaviour. These behaviours include exhibitionism, voyeurism, transvestism, bestiality, indecent phone calls and indecent liberties.

The risk of arrest does add excitement for the addict who finds that the exhilaration of the illicit in Level One behaviour is not enough.

Level Three includes sexual behaviour that is dangerous, abusive or life threatening. These behaviours include incest, child molestation, sexual abuse of vulnerable adults and rape. (pp. 79–82)

Although Carnes is careful to point out that these levels do not necessarily indicate progressive stages of addiction, he maintains that it is possible to escalate through the levels as the addiction grows.

Here is a description from Carnes (1983) of the voyeur:

As with most addicts, the voyeur is sustained by excitement. He waits in a trance-like state, with energies focused in the waiting. Totally absorbed, the addict loses all contact with reality, save for focus of the addiction. Cares, worries, deadlines, and responsibilities are, for a blessed moment, suspended. The mood-altering qualities of the experience are enhanced by the intrusive, the stolen, the illicit parts of the behaviour. Objectively the voyeur could go to the local topless bar and see more with less risk and discomfort. He could have sex with someone who wants to have sex with him. Or he could pay for sex. But it is not the same. The excitement of the illicit victimisation is rooted in the addict's anger. Breaking the rules is a way to retaliate for hurts, real and imagined. (pp. 40–41)

This combination of sexual excitement and ego-enhancing self-assertion in the release of previously inhibited anger and the breaking of rules seems to be a powerful mood-elevating factor in more minor breaches of conventional moral codes by both sexes and in more serious sexual crimes also.

Marques and Nelson (1989) equate reoffending with relapse in an addiction model. A number of studies in reoffending provide evidence which can be used to support the addiction relapse model. For example 77% of rapists reported feeling frustrated, depressed, angry or rejected prior to their attacks (Queens Bench Foundation, 1976), and 75% of a mixed group of sex offenders had experienced a negative emotional state prior to their crimes (Pithers et al., 1983). There appeared to be a common sequence in this group prior to their offences which consisted of: (i) a stressful situation and inability to cope effectively; (ii) anger, anxiety and frustration; (iii) beginning to fantasise about performing a deviant sexual act; (iv) thoughts or actual plans of action; (v) action. This pattern follows the Marlatt and Gordon (1985) model of relapse in addictions very closely. One study of serial sadistic sexual offenders (MacCulloch et al., 1983) describes typical processes surrounding reoffending which are open to explanation by an opponent-process model of fantasy advanced for gambling addictions (Brown, 1989). This is in accord with the relapse management work in sexual addictions reported more generally by Laws (1989).

The emotional experiences accompanying acts of violence without apparent extraneous motivation have never been adequately investigated but they may have recurrent effects on the mood of some perpetrators. The element of challenge and arousal in some crimes of breaking and entering may also have effects on the perpetrator's mood or his or her ability to escape. There is a need for extensive use of the type of study that Fransella and Adams (1965) conducted with the repertory grid technique on the emotional experience of a fire raiser, establishing the content and meaning of the experience for the offenders. Other, more obvious, offences with possible mood-changing effects discussed later in this book, include 'joy-riding'.

Addictive Offenders?

Addiction factors in offending are likely to belong neither to a particular class of crimes nor to a particular class of individuals, but rather to be a part of the way an individual relates to their crime and the role it plays in their life. The most obvious features of the individual's relationship with their crime might be predicted from a hedonic management model of addiction to be:

1. *Specialisation in a single offence* or a narrow range of similar offences. It is unlikely that anyone can be addicted to crime as a whole or to a range of criminal activities which may be expected to provide widely differing subjective emotional experiences.
2. *Individual vulnerabilities* of the person involved similar to those identified for addictions—for example poor relationships, and a restricted range of easily accessible rewarding activities.
3. *Powerful emotional reaction* experienced by the individual in association with the criminal act which is mood-changing—colloquially a strong 'buzz' for the individual.

4. *Increasing salience of the criminal activity* so that, even when it is not being committed, it is being planned or fantasised about and all of life, thinking, feeling and behaviour is dominated by and organised around the next opportunity to offend.

5. *Positive feedback loops* promoting increasing and repeated offending, like conflict narrowing the range of easily accessible alternative rewarding activities, tolerance escalating the risks to be taken to achieve the same escape, withdrawals leading to restlessness and irritability when offending is not possible, and relief offending arising out of the need to block despair and guilt from the last offence by beginning preoccupation with the next.

6. *Cycles of criminal activity*—corresponding to cycles of need to use the criminal activity to manage hedonic tone within the offender.

7. *Low self-esteem*—usually accompanied by subjective descriptions of loss of control, unsuccessful attempts to cut down offending or embrace total abstinence.

8. *Rituals before or after offending*—series of routines or chains of stimuli and responses/actions which seem to build up or break down arousal.

9. *Disconnection from normal flow of mental life*—offence is committed in a 'time capsule' apart from ordinary life.

10. *Pattern of reoffending which looks like relapse* in the addictions, i.e. involves fantasies stimulated by relapse provoking situations which become progressively more extreme and dominant as the offence is approached.

11. *Occasional reinstatement phenomena*—even after many years of remission a rapid reversion to the frequency and intensity of offending which was characteristic of offending at its height perhaps many years before.

IMPLICATIONS FOR CUSTODIAL CARE

An individual offender who displays all of these features in their relationship to their criminal offending is likely to be better understood, and therefore helped to reduce or cease offending, by applying an addiction model to their custodial care. In the population of offenders, one wholly addicted to their pattern of crime may be an extreme example and therefore a relatively rare individual. But a wide range of those in custodial care may display several of these identifying features of an addictive relationship with their offending, and some of them may be to some extent helped if they are treated as having *an addictive element* in in their offending.

Applying an addiction model may involve any one or all of: (i) improving self-awareness of the addictive processes governing their offending (especially the positive feedback loops that may operate through fantasy); (ii) using motivational interviewing techniques (Miller & Rollnick, 1991) to improve the quality and basis of their commitment to cease offending through supporting self-confrontation of the damage to self, to others, and to relationships; (iii) improving tolerance for dysphoria; (iv) training and counselling in the avoidance of reversions to the addictive pattern of activity and in coping with them if and when they occur (Marlatt & Gordon, 1985; Wanigaratne et al., 1990); (v) reviving and regenerating the previous repertoire of easily accessible rewarding activities and generating new ones (including better medium- and long-term planning for good hedonic tone). Additional suggestions are to be found in the work with addiction models of sexual offending (Laws, 1989).

It will be obvious that, although many of these intervention initiatives can be started while the offender is still in custody, the crucial assistance is likely to be in a period of aftercare or rehabilitation of indefinite length following release. The end must be the establishment of a well-distributed pluralistic range of easily accessible rewarding activities which yield a high rate of reward, i.e. a general improvement in the subjective quality of life 'going straight'.

REFERENCES

American Psychiatric Association (1994). *Diagnostic and Statistical Manual of Mental Disorders, Fourth Edition.* Washington, DC: American Psychiatric Association.

Anderson, G. & Brown, R. I. F. (1984). Real and laboratory gambling, sensation seeking and arousal. *British Journal of Psychology,* **75**, 401–410

Apfel, R. J. & Sifneos, P. E. (1979). Alexithymia; Concept and Measurement. *Psychotherapy and Psychosomatics,* **32**, 180–190.

Apter, M. J. (1982). *The Experience of Motivation : The Theory of Psychological Reversals.* London: Academic Press.

Armour, D. H., Polich, J. M. & Stambul, H. B. (1978). *Alcoholism and Treatment.* New York: Wiley.

Bandura, A. (1986). *Social Foundations of Thought and Action: A Social Cognitive Theory.* Engelwood Cliffs, NJ: Prentice-Hall.

Beck, A. T., Wright, F. D., Newman, C. F. & Liese, B. S. (1993). *Cognitive Therapy of Substance Abuse.* New York: Guilford Press.

Bejerot, N. (1972). *Addiction: An Artificially Induced Drive*. Springfield, IL: Charles C. Thomas.

Bejerot, N. (1975). The biological and social character of drug dependence. In K. P. Kisker, J. E. Meyer, C. Muller & E. Stromgren, (Eds), *Psychiatrie der Gegenwart, Forshung und Praxis*, Vol. III, 2nd edn. Berlin: Springer-Verlag.

Brockner, J. & Rubin, J. Z. (1985). *Entrapment in Escalating Conflicts: A Social Psychological Analysis*. New York: Springer-Verlag.

Brown, R. I. F. (1986). Arousal and sensation seeking components in the general explanation of gambling and gambling addictions. *International Journal of Addictions*, **21**, 1001–1016.

Brown, R. I. F. (1987). Pathological gambling and associated patterns of crime: Comparisons with alcohol and other drug addictions, *Journal of Gambling Behavior*, **3**, 98–114.

Brown, R. I. F. (1988). Reversal theory and subjective experience in the explanation of addiction and relapse. In M. J. Apter, J. M. Kerr & M. Cowal, *Progress in Reversal Theory*. Amsterdam: North-Holland (Progress in Psychology Series).

Brown, R. I. F. (1989). Relapses from a gambling perspective. In M. Gossop (Ed.), *Relapse and Addictive Behaviour*. London: Croom Helm.

Brown, R. I. F. (1991). *Games and Gaming as Addictions*. In M. J. Apter & J. N. Kerr, *Adult Play*. London: Routledge.

Brown, R. I. F. (1993a). Some contributions of the study of gambling to the study of other addictions. In W. R. Eadington & J. A. Cornelius (Eds), *Gambling Behavior and Problem Gambling*. Reno NV: University of Nevada.

Brown, R. I. F. (1993b). Planning deficiencies in addictions from the perspective of reversal theory. In J. H. Kerr S. Murgatroyd & M. J. Apter (Eds), *Advances in Reversal Theory*. Amsterdam: Swets and Zeitlinger.

Brown, R. I. F. (1993c). El papal de la activacion, distorsiones cognitivas y busqueda de sensaciones en las addictiones la juego. *Psicologia Conductual*, **1**, 375–388.

Brown, R. I. F. (1994). Dissociation Phenomena Among Normal and Addicted Gamblers. Paper presented at the 18th International Conference on Gambling and Risk Taking, Las Vegas, June 1994.

Brown, R. I. F. & Robertson, S. (1993). Home computer and video game addictions in relation to adolescent gambling: Conceptual and developmental aspects. In W. R. Eadington & J. R. Cornelius (Eds), *Gambling Behaviour and Problem Gambling*. Reno NV: University of Nevada.

Carnes, P. (1983). *Out of the Shadows: Understanding Sexual Addiction*. Minneapolis, MN: Compcare.

Carnes, P. (1989). *Contrary to Love: Helping the Sexual Addict*. Minneapolis, MN: Compcare.

Cleckley, H. (1964). *The Mask of Sanity*. Saint Louis, MO: C. V. Moseby.

Cohen, M., Liebson, I. A., Faillace, L. A. & Speers, W. (1971). Alcoholism: Controlled drinking and incentives for abstinence. *Psychological Reports*, **28**, 575–580.

Commission on the Review of National Policy Towards Gambling in America (1976). Washington, DC: United States Government Printing Office. (Stock No. 052–003–00243–4).

Davies, J. B. (1992). *The Myth of Addiction: Application of the Psychological Theory of Attribution to Illicit Drug Use*. Reading: Harwood Academic.

Dickerson, M. G. & Adcock,S. G. (1987). Mood, arousal and cognitions in persistent gambling: Preliminary investigations of a theoretical model. *Journal of Gambling Behavior*, **3**, 3–15.

Edwards, G. & Gross, M. M. (1976). Alcohol dependence: Provisional description of a clinical syndrome. *British Medical Journal*, **1**, 1058–1061.

Eysenck, M. W. (1982). *Attention and Arousal: Cognition and Performance*. Berlin: Springer.

Fisher, S. E. (1994). Identifying video game addiction in children and ɛdolescents. *Addictive Behaviours*, **14**, 21–28.

Fransella, F. & Adams, B. (1965). An illustration of the use of repertory grid technique in a clinical setting. *British Journal of Social and Clinical Psychology*, **5**, 51.

Frith, C. D. (1971). Smoking behaviour and its relation to the smoker's immediate experience. *British Journal of Social and Clinical Psychology*, **10**, 73–78.

Gaboury, A. & Ladouceur, R. (1989). Erroneous perceptions and gambling. *Journal of Social Behavior and Personality*, **4**, 411–420.

Gilovich, T. (1983). Biased evaluation and persistence in gambling. *Journal of Personality and Social Psychology*, **22**, 228–241.

Glasser, W. (1976). *Positive Addictions*. New York: Harper and Row.

Goodwin, D. W., Crane, J. B. & Guze, S. B. (1969). Phenomenological aspects of the alcoholic 'blackout'. *British Journal of Psychiatry*, **115**, 1033–1038.

Greaves, G. (1974). Towards an existential theory of drug dependence. *Journal of Nervous and Mental Diseases*, **155**, 363–365.

Griffiths, M. (1990). The cognitive psychology of gambling. *Journal of Gambling Studies*, **6**, 31–42.

Hare, R. D. (1970). *Psychopathy: Theory and Research*. New York: Wiley.

Heather, N. & Robertson, I. (1989). *Problem Drinking, 2nd edn.*. London: Oxford University Press

Jacobs, D. F. (1988). Evidence for a common dissociative reaction among addicts. *Journal of Gambling Behavior*, **4**, 27–37.

Jaffe, J. H. (1990). Trivialising dependence. *British Journal of Addiction*, **85**, 1425–1427.

Jaffe, J. H. (1992). Current concepts of addiction. In C. P. O'Brien & J. H. Jaffee, *Addictive States*. New York: Raven Press.

Janis, I. L. & Mann, L. (1977). *Decision Making: A Psychological Analysis of Conflict, Choice and Commitment*. New York: Free Press.

Keren, G. & Wagenaar, W. A. (1985). On the psychology of playing blackjack: Normative and descriptive considerations with implications for decision theory. *Journal of Experimental Psychology: General*, **114**, 133–158.

Kerr, J. H., Frank-Regan, E. & Brown, R. I. F. (1993). Taking risks with health. *Patient Education and Counselling*, **22**, 73–80.

Keup, W. (1982). Pleasure-seeking and the aetiology of dependence. In M. M. Glatt & J. Marks (Eds), *The Dependence Phenomenon*. Lancaster: MPT Press.

Kolodner, G. & Francis, R. (1993). Recognising dissociative disorders in patients with chemical dependency. *Hospital and Community Psychiatry*, **44**, 1041–1043.

Kuley, N. B. & Jacobs, D. F. (1988). The relationship between dissociative-like experiences and sensation seeking among social gamblers. *Journal of Gambling Behavior*, **4**, 197–207.

Ladouceur, R. & Gaboury, A. (1988). Effects of limited and unlimited stakes on gambling behavior. *Journal of Gambling Behavior*, **4**, 119–126.

Langer, E. J. (1975). The illusion of control. *Journal of Personality and Social Psychology*, **32**, 311–328.

Laws, R. (Ed.) (1989). *Relapse Prevention with Sex Offenders*. New York: Guilford Press.

Leary, K. & Dickerson, M. G. (1985). Levels of arousal in high and low frequency gamblers. *Behaviour Research and Therapy*, **23**, 635–640.

Lesieur, H. R. (1979). The compulsive gambler's spiral of options and involvement. *Psychiatry*, **42**, 79–87.

Lindstrom, L. (1992). *Managing Alcoholism; Matching Clients to Treatments*. Oxford: Oxford University Press.

Litman, G. K. (1986). Alcoholism survival: The prevention of relapse. In W. R. Miller & N. Heather (Eds), *Treating Addictive Behaviors*. New York: Plenum.

Lumley, M. A. & Robey, K. J. (1995). Alexithymia and pathological gambling. *Psychotherapy and Psychosomatics*, **63**, 201–206.

Marks, I. (1990a). Behavioural (non-chemical) addictions. *British Journal of Addictions*, **85**, 1389–1394.

Marks, I. (1990b). Reply to comments on 'behavioural (non-chemical) addictions'. *British Journal of Addictions*, **85**, 1429–1431.

Marlatt, G. A. (1979). Alcohol use and problem drinking: A cognitive-behavioural analysis. In P. C. Kendall & S. D. Hollon, *Cognitive-Behavioral Interventions: Theory, Research and Procedures*. New York: Academic Press.

Marlatt, G. A. & Gordon, J. R. (Eds) (1985). *Relapse Prevention: Maintenance Strategies in the Treatment of Addictive Behaviors*. New York: Guilford Press.

Marques, K. & Nelson, C. (1989). Understanding and preventing relapse in sex offenders. In M. Gossop (Ed.), *Relapse and Addictive Behaviour*. London: Tavistock/Routledge.

McAughtrie, L. & Brown, R. I. F. (1988). Addiction recovery as bereavement and as liberation. In W. R. Eadington (Ed.), *Research in Gambling: Proceedings of the Seventh International Conference on Gambling and Risk Taking*. University of Nevada, Reno.

McAuliffe, W. E. & Gordon, R. (1974). A test of Lindesmith's theory of addiction: The frequency of euphoria among long term addicts. *American Journal of Sociology*, **79**, 795–840.

MacCulloch, M. J., Snowden, P. R., Wood, P. J. W. & Mills, H. E. (1983). Sadistic fantasy, sadistic behaviour and offending. *British Journal of Psychiatry*, **143**, 20–29.

Mello, N. K. & Mendelson, J. H. (1965). Operant analysis of drinking habits of chronic alcoholics. *Nature*, **206**, 43–46.

Mello, N. K., McNamee, H. B. & Mendelson, J. H. (1968). Drinking patterns of chronic alcoholics: Gambling and motivation for alcohol. *Psychiatric Research Report No. 24*. Washington, DC: American Psychiatric Association.

Milkman, H. B. & Sunderworth, S. (Eds) (1987). *Craving for Ecstasy: The Consciousness and Chemistry of Escape*. Lexington, MA: D. C. Heath.

Miller, W. (1986). Individual outpatient treatment of pathological gambling. *Journal of Gambling Behavior*, **2**, 95–107.

Miller, W. R. & Heather, N. (Eds) (1986). *Treating Addictive Behaviours: Processes of Change*. New York: Plenum Press.

Miller, W. R. & Rollnick, S. (1991). *Motivational Interviewing: Preparing People to Change Addictive Behaviour*. New York: Guildford Press.

Mischel, W. (1973). Towards a cognitive social learning reconceptualisation of personality. *Psychological Review*, **80**, 319–324.

Morris, W. N. & Reilly, N. P. (1987). Towards the self-regulation of mood: Theory and research. *Motivation and Emotion*, **11**, 215–249.

Nemiah, J. C. (1977). Alexithymia: Theoretical considerations. *Psychotherapy and Psychosomatics*, **28**, 199–206.

Newton, T. L. & Contrada, R. J. (1994). Alexithymia and repression: Contrasting emotion-focused coping styles. *Psychosomatic Medicine*, **56**, 457–462.

O'Brien, C. P., Childress, A. R., McLellan, A. T. & Ehrman, R. (1992). A learning model of addiction. In C. P. O'Brien & J. H. Jaffe (Eds), *Addictive States*. New York: Raven Press.

O'Doherty, F. & Davies, J. B. (1988). Life events, stress and addiction. In S. Fisher and J. Reason (Eds), *Handbook of Life Stress, Cognition and Health*. Chichester: Wiley.

Olds, J. & Milner, P. (1954). Positive reinforcement produced by electrical stimulation of septal areas and other regions of rat brain. *Journal of Comparative and Physiological Psychology*, **47**, 419–427.

Orford, J. (1985). *Excessive Appetites: A Psychological View of Addictions*. Chichester: Wiley.

Peele, S. (1980). Addiction to an experience : A social-psychological-pharmacological theory of addiction. In D. J. Lettieri, M. Sayers & H. W. Pearson, *Theories on Drug Abuse: Selected Contemporary Perspectives*. National Institute on Drug Abuse Monograph, No. 30, DHSS Publication Number (ADM) 84–967.

Peele, S. (1985). *The Meaning of Addiction: Compulsive Experience and its Interpretation*. Lexington MA: Lexington Books.

Pinard, L, Negrete, J. C., Annable, L. & Audet, N. (1996). *American Journal on Addictions*, **5**, 32–39.

Pithers, W. D., Marques, J. K., Gibat, C. C. & Marlatt, G. A. (1983). Relapse prevention with sexual aggressives: A self-control model of treatment and maintenance of change. In J. G. Greer & I. R. Stuart (Eds), *The Sexual Aggressor: Current Perspectives on Treatment*. New York: Van Nostrand Reinhold.

Polich, J. M., Armour, D. J. & Braiker, H. B. (1980). *The Course of Alcoholism: Four Years After Treatment*. Santa Monica, CA: Rand Corporation.

Queens Bench Foundation (1976). *Rape: Prevention and Resistance*. San Francisco, CA: Queens Bench Foundation.

Rotter, J. B. (1982). *The Development and Application of Social Learning Theory: Selected Papers*. New York: Preager.

Rotter, J. B., Chance, J. E. & Phares, E. J. (1972). *Applications of a Social Learning Theory of Personality*. New York: Holt, Rinehart and Winston.

Roy, A., Adinoff, B., Roehrich, L., Lamparski, D., Custer, R., Lorenz, V., Barbaccia, M. Guidotti, A., Costa, E. & Linnoila, M. (1988). Pathological gambling : A psychobiological study. *Archives of General Psychiatry*, **45**, 369–373.

Russell, J. A. (1980). A circumplex model of affect. *Journal of Personality and Social Psychology*, **39**, 1161–1178.

Russell, J. A. & Mehrabian, M. A. (1975). The mediating role of emotions in alcohol use. *Journal of Studies in Alcohol*, **29**, 355–363.

Russell, J. A. & Mehrabian, A. (1977). Evidence for a three factor theory of emotions. *Journal of Research in Personality*, **11**, 273–294.

Russell, J. A. & Ridgeway, D. (1983). Dimensions underlying children's emotion concepts. *Developmental Psychology*, **19**, 795–804.

Seligman, M. E. P. (1970). On the generality of the laws of learning. *Psychological Review*, **77**, 406–418.

Siegel, S. (1975). Evidence from rats that morphine tolerance is a learned response. *Journal of Comparative and Physiological Psychology*, **89**, 498–506.

Siegel, S. (1979). The role of conditioning in drug tolerance and addiction. In J. D. Keehn (Ed.), *Psychopathology in Animals: Research and Treatment Implications*. New York: Academic Press.

Solomon, R. L. (1977). An opponent-process theory of acquired motivation: The affective dynamics of addiction. In J. D. Maser & M. E. P. Seligman (Eds), *Psychopathology: Experimental Models*. San Francisco, CA: Freeman.

Thayer, R. E. (1989). *The Biopsychology of Mood and Arousal*. New York: Oxford University Press.

Von Neumann, J. & Morgenstern, O. (1944). *Theory of Games and Economic Behaviour*. Princeton, NJ: Princeton University Press.

Wagenaar, W. A. (1988). *Paradoxes of Gambling Behaviour*. Hove: Lawrence Erlbaum Associates.

Walker, M. B. (1992). *The Psychology of Gambling*. Oxford: Pergamon.

Wanigaratne, S., Wallace, W., Pullin, J., Keaney, F. & Farmer, R. (1990). *Relapse Prevention for Addictive Behaviours: A Manual for Therapists*. Oxford: Blackwell Scientific.

Watson, D. & Tellegen, A. (1985). Toward a consensual structure of mood. *Psychological Bulletin*, **98**, 219–235.

Weil, A. (1972). *The Natural Mind*. New York: Houghton Mifflin.

Weiner, B. (1993). *Human Motivation: Metaphors, Theories, Research*. Newbury Park, CA; Sage.

Wells, L. E. & Marwell, G. (1976). *Self Esteem: Its Conceptualisation and Measurement*. Beverly Hills, CA; Sage.

Witman, G. W., Fuller, N. P. & Taber, J. I. (1987). Patterns of polyaddictions in alcoholism patients and high school students. In W. R. Eadington (Ed.), *Research in Gambling: Proceedings of the Seventh International Conference on Gambling and Risk Taking*. University of Nevada, Reno.

Wray, I. & Dickerson, M. G. (1981). Cessation of high frequency gambling and 'withdrawal' symptoms. *British Journal of Addictions*, **76**, 401–405.

Yochelson, S. & Samenow, S. E. (1976). *The Criminal Personality*. Vol. 1. *A Profile for Change*. New York: Jason Aronson.

Zuckerman, M. (1979). *Sensation Seeking: Beyond the Optimum Level of Arousal*. Hillsdale, NJ: Lawrence Erlbaum.

CHAPTER 2

Crime and Emotion Control

Derek Roger

Department of Psychology, University of York

INTRODUCTION

Attempting to explain the motivation for sadistic sexual crimes, MacCulloch et al. (1983) suggested that these were driven by 'internal circumstances'—sadistic fantasies that are progressively elaborated into behavioural trials, which lead eventually to committing the offence itself. Commenting on this and other papers, Prentky et al. (1989) argue that the compulsive fantasising provides an explanatory model for seemingly unmotivated sexual crimes, and these authors point to a wealth of experimental evidence which demonstrates the role of fantasy in deviant sexual behaviour (e.g., Abel & Blanchard, 1974).

Fantasy no doubt plays an important role in normal sexuality as well, and other factors must contribute to the development of deviant fantasies and eventual pathological behaviour. For example, more than half of the subjects studied by MacCulloch et al. led such impoverished social lives that vicarious gratification through fantasy and behavioural try-outs were their only source of sexual arousal, and the authors point to a variety of negative childhood experiences which might have contributed to this later social inadequacy. However, it is fantasy which provides the private world in which to experiment with behaviour, and the more the cognitive fantasies are rehearsed, the more power they acquire (Prentky et al., 1989).

Violent imagery often features prominently in fantasies associated with sexual crime, and aggression is thought to be a major motiva-

Addicted to Crime? Edited by J.E. Hodge, M. McMurran and C.R. Hollin.
© 1997 John Wiley & Sons Ltd.

tional factor in sex offending, particularly in the case of rape (Hollin, 1989). This is not to suggest that rapists are necessarily a homogeneous group—as Hollin has pointed out, there is evidence for subgroups within the overall classification of rapists. Anger is nonetheless reported as being associated with the offence by 94% of rapists and by almost 90% of sex offenders generally (Pithers et al., 1988). Anger in turn may arise as a result of other social or psychological circumstances, and Finkelhor (1986) has suggested that stress contributes to sex offending, perhaps by serving a disinhibitory function. Indeed, Pithers et al. note that almost half of a sample of paedophiles they studied experienced marked anxiety prior to offending, with a substantial proportion reporting feelings of depression.

Responding to these findings, Hollin (1989) has emphasised the need for further research on the predispositional and social factors which may contribute to sex offending, but a major obstacle to this work has been the lack of a satisfactory theoretical model to guide the choice of candidate factors. Measures of extraversion, neuroticism and psychoticism derived from the Eysenck Personality Questionnaire (EPQ—Eysenck & Eysenck, 1975) have been used to obtain profiles from various offender groups (see for example McGurk & McDougall, 1981), but the results have been inconclusive, in part because the scales themselves are compromised by serious psychometric shortcomings. Rocklin and Revelle (1981) confirmed long-standing concerns over the equivalence of extraversion scales from the EPQ and the earlier Eysenck Personality Inventory (EPI—Eysenck & Eysenck, 1964) by showing that the impulsivity component of EPI extraversion was absent from the corresponding EPQ scale. Impulsiveness is widely acknowledged to be the most important factor contributing to the arousal model upon which extraversion theory is based (Revelle et al., 1980), and Roger and Morris (1991) have demonstrated that impulsiveness on the EPQ is represented by a small number of items appearing in an extremely heterogeneous collection of subscales comprising the EPQ psychoticism factor.

The role of individual differences in sex offending has thus remained unclear, and more importantly, the research has failed to provide an adequate basis for the development of treatment or training programmes. Although sex offender reconviction rates may be no greater than for other types of crime in the short term, the long-term risk of reconviction remains high (Soothill, 1986), and there is an urgent need for a systematic evaluation of the effectiveness of treatment regimes. This chapter describes a new approach to sex offender treatment based in part on emotion and emotion control strategies, using an adaptation of a programme which developed from a series of studies investigating the role of emotion control in stress responses.

In the context of stress, the training programme has emphasised the maladaptive consequences of rehearsing or ruminating on emotionally upsetting events (Roger, 1992). However, individuals may ruminate about desired events as well as distressing ones, which may be particularly important in relation to sex offending. As was pointed out earlier in this chapter, deviant fantasies may offer vicarious gratification prior to behavioural try-outs and eventual offending (Prentky et al., 1989). The reinforcing effect of perseverative rumination on desired events thus offers an explicit link with the model of crime as addiction, since habitual fantasised gratification in these cases serves to sustain and strengthen the emergence of deviant behaviour. By contrast, conventional desensitisation treatment procedures assume that repeated revision of events will reduce their emotional impact, but desensitisation presupposes that the target behaviour is distressing, such as anxiety or fear.

EMOTION CONTROL AND STRESS

Stress is widely thought to contribute to both mental and physical illness, but direct experimental evidence for the link with physical illness in particular was inconclusive. Subsequently, a number of authors suggested that moderator variables such as personality might be involved, serving either to augment or to attenuate individual responses to events, and there has been some empirical support for this hypothesis. Kobasa et al. (1982), for example, devised a composite measure of 'hardiness' which included an internal locus of control, and found that hardiness had a significant buffering effect against stress. However, other studies have failed to confirm the relationship between personality and coping: Denney and Frisch (1981) predicted that neuroticism would contribute to stress by facilitating emotional arousal, but the interactive effects of neuroticism and life events in predicting outcomes were non-significant.

The equivocal findings reported in these and other studies may have resulted from psychometric shortcomings in the scales themselves, a problem which was referred to earlier with regard to the EPQ. Furthermore, the scales may be measuring constructs which are actually unrelated to stress. This has proved to be true in the case of the Repression-Sensitization (R-S) Scale (Byrne et al., 1963), which was proposed as a measure of emotional response style. Repressors are said to experience particularly high levels of physiological arousal in response to stress, while paradoxically reporting little overt indication of emotional upset (see e.g. Scarpetti, 1973). The implications for research on stress are clear, but the validity of the repression-sensitisation construct has been questioned in a number of subsequent papers (for example, Budd & Clopton, 1985), and factorial validation of the R-S Scale has shown that it is primarily a measure of the sociability component of extraversion, with only a handful of items relating specifically to emotional style (Roger & Schapals, 1996).

These inconclusive findings do not necessarily undermine the importance of emotional inhibition in determining how effectively people are able to cope. Indeed, the problems with repression-sensitisation have more to do with psychometric than theoretical issues. However, other factors are likely to play a role as well, and while repression-sensitization focused particularly on the expression or inhibition of emotion, our own work at the University of York has emphasised the extent to which emotional upset continues to be rehearsed or ruminated upon after the event. As early as 1982, Cameron and Miechenbaum had noted that 'the habit of mentally rehearsing failures and concurrently engaging in self-denigrating thoughts might interfere with at least some dimensions of the unwinding process' (p.702), and there are certainly strong theoretical grounds for incorporating the rehearsal construct in stress research. As has been pointed out, rehearsal may play an equally important role in a model of crime as addiction—for example, by sustaining deviant fantasies prior to sex offending. The research programme on emotion control at York has shown in addition that emotional inhibition serves to exacerbate the effect of rumination on stress, and these ideas suggested that an integrative approach based on the effects of both inhibition and rumination may be relevant to the view of crime as addictive behaviour.

THE CONSTRUCTION AND VALIDATION OF THE EMOTION CONTROL QUESTIONNAIRE

The research commenced with the construction of an instrument for assessing emotional response style entitled the Emotion Control Questionnaire (ECQ—Roger & Nesshoever, 1987; Roger & Najarian, 1989). The ECQ comprises four discrete scales: Rehearsal, Emotional Inhibition, Aggression Control, and Benign Control. As the names imply, Rehearsal assesses the tendency to rehearse or ruminate on emotionally upsetting events, while Emotional Inhibition provides an index of the suppression of emotion. Benign Control (so named to distinguish it from the aggressive content of the third scale) is strongly inversely correlated with measures of impulsivity, and there is a modest but significant correlation between it and Aggression Control (Roger & Nesshoever, 1987). Benign Control and Aggression Control thus appear to form part of the extraversion constellation, and are statistically independent of the first two scales. Rehearsal and Emotional Inhibition are in turn relatively orthogonal to one another, which allows subjects to be drawn from quadrants in tests of independent and interactive effects.

Theoretically, the implication of emotion control for stress is that the inhibition of emotion, particularly when accompanied by the tendency to ruminate on emotionally upsetting events, will result in the prolongation of defensive physiological arousal. During the 'fight-or-flight' response, catecholamine levels are elevated by the activation of the sympathetic adreno-medullary axis, resulting in rapid accelerative changes in the respiratory and cardiovascular systems. These changes are adaptive in the short term, but prolonged arousal exerts a significant physiological strain on the organism. Fight-or-flight also stimulates the pituitary-adrenocortical system to secrete corticosteroids, including cortisol. Cortisol has a number of functions, among them the regulation of inflammation, but in the long term cortisol impairs immune function by suppressing the production of leukocytes, sensitised lymphocytes and antibodies (Asterita, 1985). Sustained provocation of the hypothalamic-pituitary-adrenal system through chronic over-arousal thus provides a clear mechanism for linking stress and illness, and it is important to bear in mind that all of these physiological processes are mediated by cognitive processes such as emotional inhibition and rumination.

The effects of emotion control on physiological responses have been demonstrated in two studies. In the first (Roger & Jamieson, 1988), stress was manipulated primarily by performance on a competitive task, and the dependent variable was heart-rate recovery time following completion of the task. In addition to the ECQ, all subjects completed the Eysenck Personality Inventory (EPI—Eysenck & Eysenck, 1964), which provides measures of both extraversion and neuroticism. For the analyses, extraversion was further broken down into impulsivity and sociability, and neuroticism into hypochondriasis and social sensitivity (see Roger & Nesshoever, 1987). The results of this study, which were subsequently replicated on other samples, were conclusive: there were no significant effects for the EPI factors, and only Rehearsal from the ECQ correlated significantly and positively with heart-rate recovery times.

For the second study (Roger, 1988), a sample of student nurses from the nursing school at the York District Hospital gave urine samples on two occasions: immediately after completing a nursing examination known to provoke considerable apprehension, and again two weeks later. The samples were assayed for free cortisol, and an index was derived from the difference in cortisol levels from the first to the second sample, expressed as a proportion of the second sample 'baserate'. After partialling out the effects of minor infections, examination results and intervening life events, Rehearsal was again significantly correlated with cortisol elevations. The EPI was included in this study, but as with the heart rate experiment, neither extraversion nor neuroticism were related to cortisol secretion. However, Emotional Inhibition showed some relationship to the cortisol index in this study, and subsequent unpublished findings from pooled analyses of these and other data have shown that high scores on both Emotional Inhibition and Rehearsal result in a stronger relationship with arousal indices than either scale separately.

THE EMOTION CONTROL TRAINING PROGRAMME

The experimental work with the ECQ indicated that emotion control, particularly when it involves emotional inhibition and rehearsal, is significantly related to physiological indices of delayed recovery from stress. The question which then arose was whether or not adaptive emotion control strategies could be acquired through training, and the development of a training programme commenced in 1987. Much of the initial work was carried out in collaboration with the North Yorkshire Fire Service and the North Yorkshire Police Force. The training emphasised individual differences which served to moderate the impact of stress, and the theoretical foundation of the programme widened as new components were added.

The programme now includes three 'dimensions of control' relating to personality: emotion control, perceived control and intensity control. Perceived control (or locus of control) describes the tendency to attribute control either to the individual (internality), or to fate, chance or powerful others (externty). A number of studies have suggested that internality might act as a 'buffer' against stress (see e.g. Kobasa et al., 1982), but the personality predisposition also interacts with the nature of the events, so that the buffering effects of having an internal locus of control are compromised when the individual has to deal with a disproportionate number of uncontrollable events (Meadows, 1989). Intensity control refers to the stimulus intensity modulation model of individual differences (Roger & Raine, 1984), which argues that differences in basal arousal are determined by central augmenting or reducing processes. These processes account for differences in the need for stimulation, and although their direct implications for stress are relatively small, their importance for offender behaviour in particular lies in the link between lower baserate cortical arousal and impulsiveness.

The role of social support networks is included in the programme, and the degree of social support available to trainees is assessed during follow-up. Social supports provide the opportunity for the expression of emotion, and are thus important buffers against stress (Cohen & Wills, 1985). The programme also includes a measure of coping style, the Coping Styles Questionnaire (CSQ—Roger et al., 1993). The CSQ assesses coping styles in four primary dimensions of Detachment, Rational Coping, Emotional Coping and Denial, and although the findings are as yet unpublished, maladaptive coping (emotional and denying styles) has been shown to be predictive of a higher incidence of illness and poorer adjustment to emotionally demanding situations. The programme uses a variety of questionnaires to assess the personality components, both initially and as an index of change during follow-up.

The programme is modular, allowing presentation over several sessions if necessary. The aim of the training is to identify individual strengths and weaknesses in cognitive and emotional functioning, and to offer specific strategies for modifying behaviour based on the experimental work with the dimensions-of-control model. The programme is accompanied by a feedback pack and an audio tape which describes attentional control and relaxation techniques. Pilot studies have indicated that the benefits of the programme extended beyond individual stress management to include wider social and job networks, and further validation work has shown a variety of benefits, including enhanced job satisfaction and reduced absenteeism, many of which have been sustained over quite prolonged follow-up periods (see Roger & Hudson, 1995).

EMOTION CONTROL AND OFFENDER BEHAVIOUR

In an early model of the relationship between emotion control and offender behaviour, Megargee (1966) argued that individuals who 'internalise' emotional conflict have higher thresholds for the expression of aggressive behaviour, and may be predisposed to engage in less frequent but much more violent outbursts than those who are emotionally expressive. Although McGurk and McGurk (1979) were able to distinguish controlled from undercontrolled inmates using the Undercontrolled Personality Scale (UPS), empirical tests of this hypothesis have yielded equivocal findings (Fisher, 1970). Other personality dimensions which have been investigated in relation to offender behaviour are the EPI and EPQ scales of extraversion, neuroticism and psychoticism (for example, McGurk & McDougall, 1981), but the results have again tended to be inconclusive.

Despite these discouraging findings, emotion control has continued to be linked to offender behaviour in a variety of ways. For example, as Pithers et al. (1988) and Finkelhor (1986) have pointed out, stress and aggression control may both show significant associations with sexual offences, and Prentky et al. (1989) have argued that obsessive rumination may provide a central explanatory mechanism in sex offending. Indeed, the repression and rehearsal of emotion is likely to be involved in the whole cycle of offending, from fantasy through to the offence itself.

The first study of the role of the ECQ scales in offender behaviour (Roger & McEwan, 1987) used a sample of young offenders from HM Youth Custody Centre, Deerbolt, County Durham. The subjects were 86 young offenders with a mean age of 18.37 years, and serving a mean sentence length of 15.89 months. In addition to the ECQ, the analyses included the number of previous violent convictions, previous convictions before and after 16th birthday, minor reports and Governor's reports, and staff ratings derived from comments regarding manageability while in the Centre.

A manipulation check showed that, as expected, Governor's Reports and the manageability index were significantly correlated. The correlation between the number of previous convictions after 16th birthday and number of previous violent convictions was also significant, as was the correlation between number of convictions before 16th birthday and manageability. In view of the postulated role of impulsivity in determining arousal-seeking behaviour (Revelle et al., 1980), it had been expected that the Benign Control scale from the ECQ would be particularly strongly implicated in offender behaviour, with Aggression Control also expected to be involved. Amongst the ECQ scales, however, the only significant correlation was between Rehearsal and Governor's reports.

Further analyses showed that neither Governor's reports nor the manageability index were significantly correlated with minor reports.

Minor reports do not constitute serious breaches of discipline, and a trainee with frequent minor reports would not necessarily be regarded by staff as unmanageable or receive a high number of Governor's reports. However, the fact that minor reports and Governor's reports are statistically independent indicates that they may be measuring individual differences in frustration tolerance. Individuals with low thresholds may thus be reported frequently for reacting to relatively trivial disciplinary demands, while those with high thresholds may correspond to the emotional 'internalisers' described earlier, who typically display less frequent but much more violent outbursts. In relation to the ECQ scales, the internalisers might be expected to obtain higher scores on Rehearsal and Emotional Inhibition.

To examine this question in more detail, young offenders were selected from the sample to form two groups. The first comprised trainees who had incurred three or more Governor's reports but less than three minor reports ($N = 12$), while the second group included those trainees who had three or more minor reports but less than three Governor's reports ($N = 10$). The groups were then compared on each of the four ECQ scales, and the results showed that the groups did indeed differ significantly on Rehearsal, with those low on Governor's reports but high on minor reports obtaining higher mean scores than those in the opposite quadrant. There were no significant effects for Emotional Inhibition, but the findings from this first experiment suggested that 'overcontrol' might best be explained in terms of Rehearsal. There were also no significant effects for Benign Control, which was surprising, since impulsiveness is thought to be the basis for arousal-seeking behaviour and might thus be expected to play an important role in an addictive model of criminal behaviour. These preliminary findings suggest that Rehearsal may be as important a factor as impulsiveness in determining offender behaviour.

The role of emotion control in offender behaviour was further explored in a second study (McDougall et al., 1991), which attempted to identify the emotion control strategies associated with an offender population by comparing groups of offenders rated as angry or non-angry. The study formed part of a larger project aimed at evaluating anger control training programmes for offenders (McDougall, 1990), where it was noted that the emotional states of anger, hostility and aggression are not always clearly differentiated. Howells (1988), for example, attempted to distinguish them by describing anger as a subjective state of emotional arousal, hostility as an attitude or a longer-term negative evaluation of people or events, and aggression as overt behaviour involving harm to another person. However, aggression is not always the behavioural expression of anger or hostility—Blackburn (1985), for example, draws a distinction between incentive-motivated aggression, where the aggression is secondary to some other goal, and annoyance-motivated aggression, which serves directly to reduce an aversive emotional state.

Further problems have arisen over the use of personality scales to identify the emotion control strategies associated with violent or aggressive behaviour. The Hostility and Direction of Hostility Questionnaire (HDHQ—Caine et al., 1967), for example, has been used extensively in prisons, but scores on the HDHQ correlate poorly with overt hostile behaviour (Oldham et al., 1976). In the study by McDougall et al., three instruments were used: the State–Trait Anger Scale (STAS—Spielberger et al., 1983), the Special Hospitals Assessment of Personality and Socialisation (SHAPS—Blackburn, 1982) and the ECQ. The STAS yields scores on both state and trait dimensions, but since the study was designed to assess underlying predispositional components of anger, only the trait–anger scores were used. The SHAPS was constructed for use with British institutionalised populations, and in addition to aggression, hostility and anxiety, the scale includes scales to assess extraversion, shyness, depression, tension, psychopathic deviance, impulsivity and lying (i.e. 'faking good').

The participants in the study were 40 male young offenders from a long-term young offender unit, with an average sentence length for the sample as a whole of just over four years. The subjects were selected on the basis of assessments of anger control problems by the Senior Officer in charge of an accommodation wing in the institution. This was the normal route for referring inmates for anger control training, and half of the sample were judged to have problems with anger control; the other half had no problems and served as controls. Mean ages and average sentence lengths were comparable in both groups, and different types of offence were approximately equally represented.

In addition to the STAS, SHAPS and ECQ, a behavioural index was compiled from the number of times each offender had been placed on Governor's report. Not all the offences for which offenders are 'put on report' can clearly be attributed to anger, but no attempt was made in the study to differentiate between types of Governor's report. Finally, all subjects' anger behaviour was rated independently by officers responsible for their welfare, using four-point scales ranging from 'hardly ever' to 'very often' in response to items such as 'loses his temper when criticised' and 'gets into arguments with other inmates'. Ratings were unavailable for five inmates, and since evaluations by personal welfare officers do not normally form the basis for referrals for anger control training, the ratings were used only for subsidiary analyses.

There were 15 dependent variables in the study, comprising the 10 SHAPS scales, the 4 ECQ scales, STAS Trait Anger, and Governor's reports. The mean scores for the experimental and control groups on each of the variables are displayed in Table 2.1.

The scores for the two groups were compared by means of one-way analyses of variance, and the results showed that four of the dependent variables discriminated significantly between them: ECQ Rehearsal, ECQ Aggression Control, SHAPS Aggression and Governor's reports. However, in view of the number of simultaneous analyses which were performed on the data, those comparisons which exceeded the 1% level of significance should be regarded as the more reliable; these were for ECQ Rehearsal and for SHAPS Aggression.

The angry/non-angry classification of the offenders and their anger behaviour ratings were significantly correlated, and analysis of variance based on the rating data confirmed the results obtained from

Table 2.1. Mean scores for the non–angry and angry groups on the 15 dependent variables

		Groups	
		Non–angry	angry
SHAPS:	Aggression	17.80	22.90
	Hostility	18.95	20.00
	Anxiety	23.65	23.65
	Extraversion	24.56	27.65
	Shyness	7.25	6.95
	Depression	9.45	10.05
	Tension	9.80	10.40
	Psychopathic Deviance	27.20	28.40
	Impulsivity	20.35	22.90
	Lie	4.80	4.15
ECQ:	Rehearsal	2.70	5.10
	Emotional Inhibition	4.65	4.85
	Aggression Control	4.80	3.25
	Benign Control	3.05	2.75
STAS:	Trait Anger	23.00	25.95
GOVERNOR'S REPORTS:		1.05	3.95

From: McDougall (1990).

the angry/non-angry classifications: subjects with high or low ratings were significantly discriminated by ECQ Rehearsal, SHAPS Aggression and Governor's reports, although the F ratio for STAS trait anger was also significant for the rating scale analyses. Rehearsal also correlated significantly with the SHAPS tension scale, described by Blackburn (1982) as a measure of somatic tension resulting from worry. The correlation with Rehearsal is thus consistent with the earlier findings relating the ECQ scales to prolonged physiological recovery times. The results also indicate that rehearsing or ruminating about upsetting events may generate somatic tension, which may be reduced by engaging in emotionally expressive behaviour such as aggression. The relief from tension may in turn reinforce the use of aggression amongst these individuals. The findings argue for training in emotion control strategies rather than anger control, using programmes which would include relaxation techniques to reduce somatic tension as well as training in reducing inhibition and rumination.

EMOTION CONTROL AND SEX OFFENDING

Cumulatively, the results of the experiments reported so far indicate that emotion control, especially in the form of rehearsing or ruminating on emotionally upsetting events, plays a pivotal role in determining a wide variety of behaviour. Furthermore, the training programme based on emotion control strategies has been shown to enhance motivation and satisfaction at work and to improve adjustment and coping skills generally. It is also clear that emotion control has significant implications for sex offending, both in terms of stress management and in the reinforcement of the cycle of offending provided by obsessive fantasies.

However, while poor control over emotional impulses is implicit in many of the theoretical models of sex offending, there have been few systematic investigations of the role which it might play. The cycle of fantasy, try-out and offence which characterises sex offending suggests a clear link with models of crime as an addictive behaviour, and the findings from previous studies of both normal and offender populations suggested that the training programme developed at York might offer the opportunity to interrupt the cycle by offering alternative strategies to inhibition and rumination. A programme of research aimed at evaluating an emotion control training regime amongst sex offenders was initiated in 1991, funded by the Home Office Research and Planning Unit, and the preliminary results will be discussed in this section.

The study was carried out amongst inmates of HMP Wakefield. The prison is a top security unit, with the majority of inmates serving long sentences for serious crimes. Sex offences feature prominently, either explicitly or implicitly; indeed, it has been suggested that there is at least some sexual component in up to 70% of the offences for which the inmates have been convicted. For the pilot study, however, it was felt that participants on the programme should not be identified within the prison system as falling into the particular category of sex offenders, and of the 18 inmates in the sample, the offence was explicitly sexual in 9 cases, with most of the remainder convicted of murder. The overall mean age of the sample was 33.4 years.

The programme used in the pilot study was adapted from the procedure which had been used previously. A battery of questionnaires comprising the four scales from the ECQ and three coping scales from the CSQ (Emotional Coping, Rational Coping, and Denial) was completed on two occasions, the first prior to participating in the training and the second approximately six weeks later. All participants also completed a self-report follow-up questionnaire approximately two months after completing the programme. Various exercises were used on the programme to train participants in disengaging attention from emotional preoccupations and in using rational rather than maladaptive strategies. The programme was accompanied by an audio tape of the attention control exercise and the relaxation procedure, which the participants listened to in their own time during the follow-up period.

The programme itself was delivered to small groups of between three and five inmates in a series of three consecutive sessions, each lasting about 90 minutes. The tapes were handed out after the first session, and the prisoners were also offered the opportunity to be seen individually after completing the second batch of questionnaires. All participants took up the offer, and the questionnaire results were discussed with them at these sessions. This allowed a full debriefing on the study as well as providing a wealth of anecdotal evidence which has subsequently been incorporated into the development of the final programme.

For the analysis of the data, the scores on the ECQ and CSQ scales for the first and second administrations were compared by means of correlated t-tests. Each of the offenders served as their own control in the within-subjects design, and the mean scores are shown in Table 2.2.

The trends in the data are clear, with reductions in Rehearsal, Emotional Coping and Avoidance Coping and increases in control

Table 2.2. Mean scores on the primary dependent variables at first and second administration

	First administration	Second administration	t value
ECQ			
Rehearsal	16.94	13.78	1.89 ($p < 0.10$)
Emotional Inhibition	6.83	6.78	0.10 N.S.
Aggression Control	8.06	8.78	1.01 N.S.
Benign Control	5.83	7.28	2.06 ($p < 0.10$)
CSQ			
Rational Coping	11.11	13.56	2.43 ($p < 0.03$)
Emotional Coping	24.89	21.00	2.74 ($p < 0.02$)
Avoidance Coping	8.94	7.56	1.65 N.S.

Table 2.3. Endorsement frequencies on the feedback questionnaire

1. What was your general impression of the course?

very good	good	fair	poor
8	7	4	0

4. Have the points made in the course come to mind since?

very often	quite often	sometimes	never
6	9	5	0

5. Have you put any of the advice offered into practice?

very often	quite often	sometimes	never
6	6	8	0

6. When you did practise the advice given did you feel a reduction in stress?

definitely	sometimes	not really	haven't practised
9	8	2	0

10. (iii) Did you feel less stressed after practising (the tape–recorded exercise on attentional control)?

definitely	a bit	not much	not at all
9	6	3	0

11. (i) Did (the deep relaxation tape) help you to relax?

definitely	a bit	not much	not at all
9	8	1	0

Note: Item numbers refer to the original questionnaire. The figures are based on returns from a sample ranging from 18 to a total of 21 subjects; three of the 21 submitted incomplete returns on the other questionnaires, and they were omitted from the statistical analyses reported in Table 2.1.

over expressed hostility (Aggression Control), impulsiveness (Benign Control) and Rational Coping. The contrasts were statistically significant for Emotional Coping and Rational Coping from the CSQ, and approached significance for the Benign Control and Rehearsal scales from the ECQ.

What these findings suggest is that the emotion control training package will produce positive changes in attitudes, with a general shift towards more adaptive coping styles and a reduction in both emotional rehearsal and impulsiveness. The inclusion of impulsivity in the findings is particularly encouraging in the context of the model of crime as addiction. Impulsiveness is thought to provide a physiologically-based explanation for arousal-seeking behaviour (Revelle et al., 1980), but Benign Control had not featured in the findings from the earlier Roger and McEwan (1987) study. Furthermore, these results were supported by the self-report data obtained from the feedback questionnaire administered two months after completing the training. For the follow-up assessment, the most relevant items from the original questionnaire were 1, 4, 5, 6, 10 and 11, and the response frequencies to these items are shown in Table 2.3.

GENERAL CONCLUSIONS

The programme of research on emotion control was originally aimed at uncovering individual differences which might serve to augment or attenuate the intensity with which people responded to stress. Following the programme through from its inception, the findings from the various studies showed, firstly, that emotion control constructs could be measured reliably, and that they were systematically related to physiological indices of stress-related arousal. This was particularly true of the tendency to rehearse emotionally upsetting events and to inhibit the emotion which accompanied these events. Secondly, the studies showed that a training programme based on emotion control strategies could successfully be implemented in the general population, and that the benefits of the training included a reduction in illness and absenteeism and an enhanced sense of well-being.

A number of authors have indicated a link between stress, emotion control and offender behaviour, and the final series of studies investigated the role of emotion control amongst prison inmates. The results of the first experiments showed that both Rehearsal and Aggression Control scores from the ECQ could distinguish reliably between inmates identified as either having or not having behavioural problems. This work then led to the development of an emotion control training programme adapted for use in prisons, and a pilot study was carried out amongst sex offenders. These preliminary data indicated a significant improvement in emotion control and coping styles amongst trainees, and in the light of the results the programme was refined for the main study which is currently under way.

The cumulative results of these investigations suggest that the programme has considerable potential benefit in the prison service. The interval between training and assessment was comparatively brief in the pilot work, but the earlier studies in the normal population have indicated a substantial conservation of the effects, even over periods of up to 18 months. The sample was also comparatively small, which may account in part for the failure to obtain any effects for the Emotional Inhibition scale from the ECQ. However, the main study is designed to include a much larger sample as well as samples of matched, untrained controls. The York Coping Styles Questionnaire has since been modified to include an additional adaptive style, Detachment, and inmates will also be assessed on actual behaviour rather than relying solely on self-assessed change. Neither the pilot nor the main study address the much wider issue of whether or not the training will affect recidivism rates. However, the results obtained so far suggest that the programme could have significant effects on behavioural control within the prison system, and its effectiveness would probably be enhanced by combining it with related training programmes which are already in operation.

Finally, the results of the studies reported here have important implications for the theoretical model of crime as addictive behaviour. This is particularly true in the findings from the Rehearsal scale of the ECQ, which measures the tendency to ruminate on emotion. Rehearsal offers an explicit mechanism for linking stress and illness, but is also implicated in offender behaviour. The ECQ scale focuses primarily on negative emotion, but in the context of sex offending, rumination generally can be seen as a cognitive behaviour which offers vicarious gratification prior to actual behavioural try-outs of offences. As Prentky et al. (1989) pointed out, the more cognitive fantasies are rehearsed the stronger they become, and once offending has started rehearsal may then serve to sustain the desire for engaging in further deviant behaviour. Some support for the role of impulsiveness (ECQ Benign Control) was also found in the studies reported here, though the findings were less clear than those for Rehearsal. It is hoped that the main study will provide further confirmation of these findings.

REFERENCES

Abel, G. G. & Blanchard, E. B. (1974). The role of fantasy in the treatment of sexual deviation. *Archives of General Psychiatry*, **30**, 467–475.

Asterita, M. F. (1985). *The Physiology of Stress*. New York : Human Sciences Press.

Blackburn, R. (1982). The Special Hospitals' Assessment of Personality and Socialisation (SHAPS) and the Personality Deviation Questionnaire (PDQ). London: Unpublished manuscript, Park Lane Hospital.

Blackburn, R. (1985). Cognitive-behavioural approaches to understanding and treating aggression. Paper presented at the Second Leicester Conference on Forensic Psychology: Clinical Approaches to Aggression and Violence, Leicester, September.

Budd, E. C. & Clopton, J. R. (1985). Meaning of the Repression-Sensitization Scale. *Journal of Clinical Psychology*, **41**, 63–68.

Byrne, D., Barry, J. & Nelson, D. (1963). Relationship of the revised Repression-Sensitization Scale to measures of self description. *Psychological Reports*, **13**, 323–334.

Caine, T. M., Foulds, G. A. & Hope, K. (1967). *Manual of the Hostility and Direction of Hostility Questionnaire (HDHQ)*. London: University of London Press.

Cameron, R. & Meichenbaum, D. (1982). The nature of effective coping and the treatment of stress related problems: A cognitive-behavioral perspective. In L. Goldberger & S. Bernitz, *Handbook of Stress*. New York: Free Press.

Cohen, S. & Wills, T. A. (1985). Stress, social support, and the buffering hypothesis. *Psychological Bulletin*, **98**, 310–357.

Denney, D. R. & Frisch, M. B. (1981). The role of Neuroticism in relation to life stress and illness. *Journal of Psychosomatic Research*, **25**, 303–307.

Eysenck, H. J. & Eysenck, S. B. G. (1964). *Manual of the Eysenck Personality Inventory*. London: Hodder and Stoughton.

Eysenck, H. J. & Eysenck, S. B. G. (1975). *Manual of the Eysenck Personality Questionnaire*. London: Hodder and Stoughton.

Finkelhor, D. (1986). *A Source-Book on Child Sexual Abuse*. Beverly Hills, CA: Sage.

Fisher, G. (1970). Discriminating violence emanating from overcontrolled versus undercontrolled aggressivity. *British Journal of Social and Clinical Psychology*, **9**, 54–59.

Hollin, C. R. (1989). *Psychology and Crime: An Introduction to Criminological Psychology*. London: Routledge.

Howells, K. (1988). The management of angry aggression: A cognitive-behavioural approach. In W. Dryden & P. Trower (Eds), *Developments in Cognitive Psychotherapy*. London: Sage.

Kobasa, S. C., Maddi, S. R. & Kahn, S. (1982). Hardiness and health: A prospective study. *Journal of Personality and Social Psychology*, **42**, 168–177.

MacCulloch, M. J., Snowden, P. R., Wood, P. J. W. & Mills, H. E. (1983). Sadistic fantasy, sadistic behaviour and offending. *British Journal of Psychiatry*, **143**, 20–29.

McDougall, C. (1990). Anger control. Unpublished DPhil thesis, University of York.

McDougall, C., Venables, P. & Roger, D. (1991). Aggression, anger control and emotion control. *Personality and Individual Differences*, **12**, 625–629.

McGurk, B. J. & McDougall, C. (1981). A new approach to Eysenck's theory of criminality. *Personality and Individual Differences*, **2**, 338–340.

McGurk, B. J. & McGurk, R. E. (1979). Personality types among prisoners and prison officers—an investigation of Megargee's theory of control. *British Journal of Criminology*, **19**, 31–49.

Meadows, M. (1989). Life experience and health. Unpublished DPhil thesis, University of York.

Megargee, E. I. (1966). Undercontrolled and overcontrolled personality types in extreme anti-social aggression. *Psychological Monographs*, **80**, whole no. 611.

Oldham, H., McGurk, B. & Magaldi, R. (1976). *Hostility and Assaultiveness*. DPS Report (Series 1, 7). London: Home Office.

Pithers, W. D., Kashima, K. M., Cumming, G. S. & Beal, L. S. (1988) Relapse prevention. In A. C. Salter (Ed.), *Treating Child Sex Offenders*. London: Sage.

Prentky, R. A., Burgess, R. N., Rokous, B. A., Lee, A., Hartman, R. N., Ressler, R. & Douglas, J. (1989). The presumptive role of fantasy in serial sexual homicide. *American Journal of Psychiatry*, **146**, 887–891.

Revelle, W., Humphreys, M. S., Simon, L. & Gilliland, K. (1980). The interactive effects of personality, time of day, and caffeine: A test of the arousal model. *Journal of Experimental Psychology*, **109**, 1–31.

Rocklin, T. & Revelle, W. (1981). The measurement of extraversion. *British Journal of Psychology*, **20**, 279–284.

Roger, D. (1988). The role of emotion control in human stress responses. Paper presented at the Annual Conference of the British Psychological Society, Leeds University, April.

Roger, D. (1992). The development and evaluation of a work skills and stress management training programme. British Psychological Society Annual Conference, Scarborough, UK, April.

Roger, D. & Hudson, C. (1995). The role of emotion control and emotional rumination in stress management training. *International Journal of Stress Management*, **2**, 119–132.

Roger, D. & Jamieson, J. (1988). Individual differences in delayed heart-rate recovery following stress: The role of extraversion, neuroticism and emotional control. *Personality and Individual Differences*, **9**, 721–726.

Roger, D., Jarvis, G. & Najarian, B. (1993). Detachment and coping: The construction and validation of a new scale for measuring coping strategies. *Personality and Individual Differences*, **15**, 619–626.

Roger, D. & McEwan, A. (1987). *The role of emotion control in the behaviour of young offenders: A preliminary study*. Research Report, Department of Psychology, University of York.

Roger, D. & Morris, J. (1991). The internal structure of the EPQ scales. *Personality and Individual Differences*, **12**, 759–764.

Roger, D. & Najarian, B. (1989). The construction and validation of a new scale for measuring emotion control. *Personality and Individual Differences*, **10**, 845–853.

Roger, D. & Nesshoever. (1987). The construction and preliminary validation of a scale for measuring emotional control. *Personality and Individual Differences*, **8**, 527–534.

Roger, D. & Raine, A. (1984). Stimulus intensity control and personality: A research note. *Current Psychological Research and Reviews*, **3**, 43–47.

Roger, D. & Schapals, T. (1996). Repression-sensitization and emotion control. *Current Psychology*, **15**, 30–37.

Scarpetti, W. L. (1973). The repression-sensitization dimension in relation to impending painful stimulation. *Journal of Consulting and Clinical Psychology*, **40**, 377–382.

Soothill, K. (1986). Is treatment necessary? The analysis of long-term change without specific intervention. In P. Pratt (Ed.), *Issues in Criminological and Legal Psychology No. 8, Sexual Assessment: Issues and Radical Alternatives*. Leicester: The British Psychological Society.

Spielberger, C. D., Jacobs, G., Russell, S. and Crane, R. S. (1983). Assessment of anger: the State–Trait Anger Scale. In J. Butcher and C. D. Spielberger (Eds), *Advances in Personality Assessment*. Hillsdale, NJ: Lawrence Erlbaum.

CHAPTER 3

Addiction to Violence

John E. Hodge

Rampton Hospital

> where sits our sulky, sullen dame
> gathering her brows like gathering storm,
> nursing her wrath to keep it warm

> ('Tam o' Shanter', Robert Burns)

This quotation from Burns may seem at first sight to have little relevance to a chapter on addiction to violence. This may be so. However, it provides one of the most evocative pictures of impending violence (verbal or physical) to be found in any literature. In fact, it seems likely that Burns must have had some personal experience to be able to describe this so well.

If we examine the quotation more closely, however, it seems clear that Tam's wife (to whom the quotation refers) is clearly devoting a fair amount of time to planning this violence. It seems likely that this is not the first time and that there is an element of repetition involved, and although she is 'sulky' and 'sullen', we can almost experience the underlying satisfaction she feels as she 'nurses her wrath' probably by rehearsing and fantasising what she is going to say or do to Tam when he gets home (unfortunately we never find out: Tam gets diverted along the way by a scantily-dressed young lady).

In this vignette, it is easy to accommodate Tam's behaviour as potentially addictive ('bowsing at the nappy', and 'getting fou and

Addicted to Crime? Edited by J.E. Hodge, M. McMurran and C.R. Hollin.
© 1997 John Wiley & Sons Ltd.

unco happy'—i. e. drinking strong ale and getting merry and drunk'). However, his wife's behaviour which is equally repetitive, deliberate (though probably also demonstrating some element of 'loss of control'), is not. Yet there are many commonalities between the two sets of behaviour. Both behaviours are salient (in that the participants spend a lot of time engaged in the behaviour); both are repetitive; both escalate over time; and both have strong emotional impact. Could these behaviours be described as 'addicted'?

ADDICTION

Our concept of addiction is changing. The idea that addiction or 'addictiveness' is a property of *substances* is losing ground. While it is clear that much addictive behaviour relates to substances, such as alcohol and certain drugs, there is increasing consensus that addiction can be demonstrated where no substance is involved—e.g. gambling, exercise, sexual behaviour (Orford, 1985). Non-substance-based theories of addiction are beginning to appear in the literature. Peele (1985) has developed the concept of addiction to an *experience*, which the individual wants to repeat. This *experience* may be the result of drug action, but also could stem from other sources. In slight contrast, Brown (1986, chapter 1 this volume) perceives addiction to be an active strategy which the individual uses to manipulate their emotional well-being. For most of us, this process of ensuring our personal well-being involves a wide range of strategies. However, where addiction becomes an issue, the individual narrows the focus to a small number of (apparently) highly effective strategies. Again, these narrow strategies can involve the use of substances, but can also involve other behaviours (e.g. gambling, rock climbing, golf). Thus, for Brown, the primary characteristics of addictive behaviour are:

- *salience*
- *relief*
- *tolerance*
- *withdrawals*
- *conflict*
- *reinstatement after abstinence*

While these modern theories of addiction are still controversial, they have the advantage that they explain some aspects of addiction much better than biological theories: for example, reinstatement after long-term abstinence, and addictive behaviour in the absence of an addictive substance are easier to accommodate within Brown's model.

However, the notion of an 'addiction to violence' seems alien even given these modern perspectives on addiction. It is perhaps difficult to accept that there may be people for whom violence becomes a central (salient) feature of their lifestyle to the extent that they seek it out and suffer some kind of 'withdrawal' or 'abstinence' effects when they are denied the opportunity for violence.

On the other hand, we accept the view that violence-seeking can be a social event and a major (salient) activity of delinquent gangs. We have become used to newspaper headlines of 'MINDLESS VIO-LENCE' in relation to apparently motiveless attacks on strangers by individuals or small groups of young men.

'Hooliganism' is well established as a phenomenon which, on occasion, is deliberately planned by groups of young men who attend soccer matches in order to participate in a violent event. Kerr (1988) has analysed soccer hooliganism within the context of reversal theory (Apter, 1982) and suggests that it is a form of delinquent behaviour driven by the search for excitement.

We have also long accepted the idea that a small number of individuals have an unhealthy interest in violence. The well-estab-lished concept of sado-masochism refers to individuals whose sexual behaviour involves elements of violence, sometimes extreme violence. We also recognise the existence of serial rapists and serial murderers. In the case of the last, the motivation for the extreme violence involved is not always clear.

There are few occasions in the current literature where the concept of addiction is directly paired with that of violence. Clearly, if 'addiction' is to have any explanatory value in the phenomenology of violence, we are likely to find evidence of addictive processes in individuals who repeatedly commit acts of violence over significant periods of time. These repeated acts of violence should be difficult to explain in terms of what we currently see as 'normal' motivations for violence such as anger, instrumental explanations (e.g. robbery), cultural traditions, sport, military action, or self-protection. In fact, it is likely that we would be looking for evidence of repeated acts of violence in which the violence itself appears to be the desired outcome, or at least the function served by the violence is not obvious. Obviously, this does not entirely rule out some of the 'normal' explanations of violence. However, even 'normal' violence may be excessive or in some ways unusual, as where excessive violence is used within the context of a robbery or a sporting event.

This chapter will selectively review the literature on repetitive violence and in the process examine the circumstances and precursors associated with this phenomenon. Later, it will examine more closely what we mean by 'addiction' and develop ideas and hypothesis about the processes by which violence may become addictive. At this stage in our knowledge, we can do little more than try to identify the appropriate questions rather than make any serious attempts to answer them.

REPETITIVE VIOLENCE

In the large literature examining the nature and precursors of violence, recent attention has focused primarily on two factors: personality disorder and childhood physical and sexual abuse. The psychological literature on personality disorder and violence has been dominated by two main camps. The work of Robert Hare (e.g. Hare & Hart, 1993) in developing the Psychopathy Checklist has created a useful tool for risk assessment and the prediction of later violent behaviour. However, Hare's approach rests on the original description of psychopathy by Cleckley (Cleckley, 1976) and is essentially atheoretical and categorical. It tells us little about the *functions* of violence for the perpetrators.

British research in this field has been dominated by Ronald Blackburn who has developed a personality dimension concept of psychopathy, focusing mainly on the clinical arena for his research (Blackburn 1989, 1993). This style of personality research focuses on the traits or dispositions of individuals which describe their stable patterns and behaviour. While it is by no means impossible that an addictive process may come to be seen or represented as a trait or disposition, it is very difficult to determine the converse, i.e. whether a trait or disposition has come about by an addictive process. In our search for a possible addictive aspect of violence we must focus, to a degree more than is common in the literature on personality, on the *functions* that a stable pattern of behaviour (such as violence) may have for the individual.

The other main factor identified in the literature on violence is childhood physical and/or sexual abuse. There is a general belief that physical and sexual abuse in children leads to the victims themselves becoming violent. However, the evidence for this belief (usually described as the 'Cycle of Violence') is equivocal (Blackburn, 1993).

Studies of violent adults indicate that a high proportion have experienced physical and/or sexual abuse as children. For example, Kellert and Felthous (1985), in a study of violent adult criminals, found an association between childhood cruelty towards animals and violent family backgrounds with parental abuse and alcoholism.

Dutton and Hart (1992) in a review of Canadian prisoners, found that men who had been abused as children were three times more likely than non-abused men to engage in violent acts as adults, while Araji and Finkelhor (1986) found that many child sex offenders had themselves been victims of molestations as children. Similarly, in a study of serial murderers, Stone (1994) found that the background of serial killers is typically one of severe abuse and neglect. Again, Kroll et al. (1985) found that amongst alcoholic men, adulthood violence was associated with physical abuse as children rather than the abuse of alcohol *per se*. Control samples of alcoholics not abused as children showed much less violence.

Similarly, cohort studies have demonstrated a link between childhood abuse and childhood aggression (e.g. Hoffman-Plotkin & Twentyman, 1984). Dodge et al. (1990) in a study of 309 4-year-old children indicated that physical abuse is a risk factor for later aggressive behaviour, and Widom (1989b) also demonstrated that findings from a cohort study showed that being abused or neglected as a child increased the likelihood of delinquency, adult criminal behaviour and violent criminal behaviour. In a study examining the symptoms resulting from physical and sexual abuse of children, Goodwin (1988) noted a high instance of aggression in these children, while a study by Burgess et al. (1987) showed that among young people who had been sexually abused for more than a year, some sort of aggressive behaviour was inevitable and most victims perpetrated violence on other people.

However, the evidence is not clear cut. Many violent offenders have no childhood history of abuse. Araji and Finkelhor (1986) found only about 50% of their child sexual offenders had themselves been victims of sexual abuse while Stone (1994) in his study of 42 serial murderers found that about one-third had suffered from neither parental neglect nor abuse.

Overall there is consistent evidence that violent adults have often been abused as children. However, it has become recognised that only a relatively small proportion of abused children later themselves become abusers or violent offenders. Kaufman and Zigler (1987) found that about 30% of abused children were likely to become abusers themselves, while Widom has found the majority of abused children do not go on to become violent offenders (Widom, 1989a). In her cohort study, Widom (1989b) found only a small effect in men and no significant effect in women.

It seems therefore, that while many violent adults have been abused as children, most abused children do not become violent adults. This bears a remarkable similarity to the relationship between alcohol and violence. Again, many violent acts are committed under the influence of alcohol, but most people who drink alcohol do not commit violence (Hodge, 1993).

Advocates of the 'Cycle of Violence' have tended to focus on social learning theory as an explanation of the development of violence in previously abused children. This suggests that victims model their behaviour on that of their parents and abusers. However, social learning theory would probably predict that a higher proportion of abused children than is actually the case would later become violent. One of the problems in this literature of course is that there is no generally agreed description or definition of what constitutes 'abuse'. This problem is confounded by the fact that most researchers have to rely on self-report data, sometimes for events which may have happened many years ago. These issues make it very difficult to compare between studies and to ensure that equivalent populations are being compared. It may be that a certain threshold of abuse may have to be reached before long-term effects begin to become apparent. Alternatively, it may not be the abuse itself which leads to problems, but a secondary factor *associated* with abuse which is responsible.

Goodwin (1988) found that many children suffering significant abuse demonstrated symptoms of post-traumatic stress disorder (PTSD). She found that many children who had suffered significant parental abuse demonstrated anxiety, compulsive repetitions, sleep disturbances, and depression. The occurrence of these symptoms of PTSD also seemed to be associated with higher levels of aggression in these children. There is therefore a possible link between PTSD and childhood aggression. There is also a clear link between aggressive behaviour in children and later adulthood violence (Farrington, 1989). It may be then that it is PTSD that acts as a mediating factor in the development of long-term aggression in abused children. This link between PTSD and violence also emerges from the literature on studies of American veterans of the Vietnam war.

American veterans of the Vietnam war were not the first soldiers to develop PTSD. However, there do seem to be some aspects of this war which made it even more traumatic for the participants than other conflicts prior to that date. The average age of American soldiers was under 20 years, lower by about six years than the average age in World War II. The nature of the conflict itself, that of guerrilla warfare, was very different to formal battles in that it was continuous, insiduous, and extremely difficult to distinguish friends and foes. These conditions, together with the lack of support given to many veterans on their return the United States, seem to have led to very high levels of diagnosed PTSD. Higgins (1991) offers figures which suggest that about one-quarter of returning Vietnamese veterans experienced some symptoms of post-traumatic stress disorder. There has been considerable research, mainly through the American Veterans Association, on the problems experienced by the Vietnam veterans after the return to America.

A number of papers have examined the relationship between PTSD and criminal behaviour in Vietnam veterans. Wilson and Zigelbaum (1983), in a questionnaire study of 114 Vietnam veterans, found violent criminal acts to be positively correlated with the severity of PTSD and the intensity and duration of combat experience. They found no relationship between the criminal acts and pre-morbid personality traits. Solursh (1988, 1989) found clear evidence of a range of post-traumatic stress disorder symptoms in a sample of 100 veterans. Their symptoms included depression and suicide attempts, flashbacks and nightmares, substance abuse and interpersonal problems and almost all showed a post-war history of fascination with weapons and of seeking fights. Again he found little evidence of any pre-military tendency to violence. McFall et al. (1992) found 11% of a sample of veterans seeking help for substance abuse had significant combat PTSD symptoms which included 'difficulty in controlling violent tendencies'.

These studies have not been without their critics and a number of investigations have failed to find relationships between combat-related post-traumatic stress disorder and violent behaviour. For example, Shaw et al. (1987), in a study comparing Vietnam veterans who had committed offences against a community sample of Vietnam veterans, found that the prevalence of PTSD was roughly the same in both samples. These authors suggested that there was a higher level of antisocial personality disorder in the prison sample and concluded that although combat exposure may lead to the development of aggressive tendencies, PTSD is not an important cause of violent crime. However, this study was relatively small scale and a much larger scale epidemiological study of Vietnam veterans, the National Veteran Readjustment Study (Kulka et al., 1990) found that male Vietnam veterans with PTSD reported a much higher rate of violence in the preceding year than their non post-traumatic stress disorder counterparts—13.3 acts of violence as compared to 3.5. Many of these acts of violence occurred within the family setting. Although earlier reports of the violence of Vietnam veterans suggested a close relationship to combat exposure, Lasko et al. (1994) found that later aggression in war veterans was associated with PTSD itself and could not be explained by the amount of combat exposure. Two variables have been identified which may be relevant to the *severity* of PTSD in war veterans. Although previous studies had indicated no association with pre-military adjustment, Zaidi and Foy (1994) found that 45% of veterans with post-traumatic stress disorder had previously experienced abusive physical punishment during childhood. These authors found a positive correlation between childhood physical abuse history and the severity of combat-related PTSD. The other factor influencing the severity of PTSD veterans seems to have been whether or not they participated in war zone abusive violence or atrocities. Hiley-Young et al. (1995) found that participation in atrocities or war zone abusive violence predicted post-military violence but was not clearly associated with pre-military factors. Glover (1988) found that veterans who had participated in atrocities had developed particularly severe symptoms of PTSD unless they developed effective cognitive strategies to minimise their guilt, such as viewing their victims as subhuman (Glover, 1985).

It seems fairly clear therefore that there is a relationship between symptoms of PTSD (at least those relating to a violent experience) and the later perpetration of violence. This relationship was examined more closely in a criminal population by Collins and Bailey (1990). Aware of the evidence emerging from the Vietnam veteran studies and of some of the controversy surrounding it, these authors wished to look at the relationship between PTSD and violence in a population where the PTSD was not combat-related. They also wished to make some attempt to tease out issues of causality in the relationship between the two factors.

Collins and Bailey studied 1140 recently imprisoned males in North Carolina. They found that 2.3% (26) of their sample met the strict diagnostic criteria for PTSD. However, they also found an additional 70% of the sample reporting one or more *symptoms* of post-traumatic stress disorder, but not reaching the full diagnostic criteria. Of those reaching the full criteria for diagnosis of PTSD, only one-third reported their symptoms to be combat-related. In this small group, they found that prisoners diagnosed as suffering from PTSD were much more likely to have been in prison for a serious violent offence, to have a history of arrest for serious violent offences, or to have had an arrest for violence in the year before their present imprisonment. When they broadened their analysis to include those with at least some presenting symptoms, they also found a significant positive relationship between the number of PTSD symptoms and current imprisonment for a serious violent offence (homicide, rape or assault) or an arrest in the last year for a violent offence. The more PTSD symptoms reported the more likely it was that individuals were imprisoned or had been recently arrested for these types of offences.

These results have two implications. First, making use of a categorical approach to PTSD, that is using it as a diagnosis only after certain rigid criteria are met, may mean that important relationships are being missed. Second, it appears possible that there may be a graded effect of PTSD on behaviour such that less severe manifestations of the disorder may have lesser effects on behaviour. It may be important therefore to have ways of measuring the severity of PTSD when looking for its impact on behaviour.

Collins and Bailey went one stage further in their research and attempted to ascertain the temporal sequence in the relationship between PTSD symptoms and violent behaviour. Of those prisoners reporting one or more symptoms of PTSD and who had at least one arrest for violence (80 men), 85% reported that their first symptom of PTSD occurred either in the same year as or in the year preceding their arrest. Collins and Bailey suggest that this supports the view that PTSD may be causally related to the occurrence of violence. This finding may be particularly important when taken with research which suggests that the perpetration of violence can also lead to symptoms of PTSD in the perpetrator. Collins and Bailey (1990) found that 15% of their sample initially experienced PTSD symptoms *after* their violence. Hiley-Young et al. (1995) suggest that studies of veterans who had *engaged in atrocities* during the Vietnam war found that they often presented with extreme PTSD symptoms and were particularly at risk for later violent behaviour. Similarly, Kruppa et al. (1995) found clear evidence of PTSD in violent offenders, the disorder having been triggered by their own offences. If PTSD is causal to later violence, then this creates the possibility that for some people, the PTSD following their own violence may lead to further episodes of violence.

POST-TRAUMATIC STRESS DISORDER AND ADDICTION TO VIOLENCE

If PTSD is implicated in later violent behaviour, how does this fit in with the concept of *addiction* to violence? Explanations other than addiction to account for this relationship are possible. Social learning theory explanations seem unlikely since only a small proportion of childhood victims of abuse later become violent, and since the later violence of Vietnam veterans seems to be linked to PTSD, rather than to participation in combat *per se* or to training for combat. However, revenge against, for example, men, women, society, government, and/or those in authority, may be a possible explanation for this relationship. This hypothesis is supported by some descriptive reports of abused children and of Vietnam veterans as being very angry and explosive (Goodwin, 1988; Boman, 1986). It is in fact highly possible that for many victims of abuse or participants in war, revenge is a cogent and major issue. It is also possible that the emotional chaos associated with PTSD in itself leads to a greater tendency for impulsive behaviour and explosive violence. These explanations have a great deal of face validity, but do not explain some of the behaviour of people exposed to traumatic violence.

In his two papers studying PTSD in Vietnam veterans, Solursh (1988, 1989) found that almost all his sample experienced flashbacks and nightmares that related to their experiences of combat. As expected, these symptoms were described as frightening. However, 94% of the veterans referred to in these studies also described the nightmares and flashbacks as 'exciting', 'powerful' and 'a high' even while at the same time they were describing the experience of considerable fear. Often the flashbacks and nightmares were reported as being followed by a depressed and unpleasant mood, *although occasionally they could be followed by a relaxed and calm state.* Descriptions of these experiences by the veterans themselves, liken them to that of *'taking cocaine'*, and *'addiction to adrenalin'*, and a *'rush'* (experience produced by the injection of heroin). Despite their clear attraction to their experiences, Solursh's veterans paid a price of loneliness, depression, anxiety, helplessness, feelings of guilt and lack of control; indeed, many veterans were described as loners or agoraphobic, and substantial numbers abused alcohol.

Associated with these unexpected reactions to their PTSD symptomatology, the veterans also supported their memories and flashbacks by compulsively keeping weapons close by, engaging in hunting or re-enacting combat scenes, and actively seeking fights, apparently in an attempt to recreate the emotional experience of combat. Solursh described the syndrome as 'Combat Addiction' and commented that a therapeutic approach based on the assumption that the PTSD symptomatology was aversive to the veterans would be unlikely to be successful. Many veterans would be unwilling to give up their symptoms. It is noticeable that Solursh was unable to find any evidence of pre-military adjustment problems in his sample.

Similarly, Nadelson (1992) described five Vietnam veterans who experienced positive excitement when reviving memories of mortal risk and killing. He claimed that these five individuals were representative of a much larger group and presented considerable case material that clearly demonstrates the conflict experienced by these veterans in recognising their attachment to the power and thrill of combat and killing, while at the same time recognising this attachment to be alien. Again the veterans used words such as *'addictive'*, *'rush'*, *'out of control'*, and again, according to Nadelson, all these veterans stated that they had had a normal childhood with little evidence of abuse, poverty, conflict with their parents, violence or delinquency. All the veterans experienced problems on their return from Vietnam with two out of the five having frequent clashes with the police. All had found establishing relationships with others, particularly women, very difficult and expressed their attachment to violence with confusion, shame and often anger.

How are we to understand these veterans' contradictory reactions to their experiences? They certainly meet the criterion of Peele's (1985) theory of addiction in that their subjective experiences are ones which the individual wishes to repeat. However, this consideration does not greatly further our understanding of why the individual may wish to repeat them. If we examine these experiences within Brown's Hedonic Management Model of Addiction then their attachment to these experiences becomes more easily explained (Brown, 1986; Chapter 1 this volume).

Brown's model classifies addictions within a motivational framework. He argues that most human activity is generally geared towards the management of hedonic tone, that is, optimising subjective feelings of pleasure and well-being. This is normally achieved by a wide range and variety of strategies which manage hedonic tone by lowering and raising arousal levels. Thus, activities which are successful in achieving effective management are reinforced. Addiction occurs when the majority of available strategies are no longer effective in maintaining hedonic tone and the individual has focused down to either a single or a very narrow range of strategies. The individual becomes more and more preoccupied with their core strategy to the detriment of all the others.

In the case of the Vietnam veterans described above, they describe their experiences of nightmares and flashbacks using words such as *'power'*, *'control'*, and *'thrill'*; clearly these are words which relate to arousal level and also to hedonic tone. It seems possible that the experience of the intense environmental stimulation of combat, coupled with the feelings of power and control which occurred for many in combat situations, have become predominant in these individuals' attempts to experience pleasure and manipulate hedonic tone.

A similar argument is put forward in relation to multiple murderers by Gresswell and Hollin in Chapter 5 in this volume. They suggest that some multiple murderers can become addicted to their fantasies of homicide because these fantasies are rewarded by experiences of sexual pleasure, feelings of power and control, and that they provide escape from adverse experiences. Their suggestion parallels a finding by McCulloch et al. (1983) who found 13 out of a series of 16 sadistic sex offenders to have engaged in fantasy, planning, and 'behavioural try-outs' of their offences prior to actually committing the offences. It seemed this group of sex offenders demonstrated many of the features of addiction described by Brown: that is, the six characteristics of addictive behaviour mentioned earlier—*salience, relief, tolerance, withdrawals, conflict and reinstatement after abstinence*. These sex offenders spent a great deal of time engaging in their fantasies, which were obviously very powerful in manipulating hedonic tone (*salience*). McCulloch et al.'s paper does not give any indication of the fantasies achieving *relief* but they clearly demonstrated a form of *tolerance* since they eventually required behavioural try-outs to enhance the experience originally obtained by the fantasies alone. Of course, these sex offenders also demonstrated *relapses* in that many were multiple offenders. This particular group of offenders did not particularly demonstrate the other elements of addiction, i.e. *conflict* or *withdrawal*, but there is some evidence in the literature for some serial offenders to experience these phenomena as well (See Gresswell & Hollin, Chapter 5; Drukteinis, 1992).

In the case of the Vietnam veterans, clearly their nightmares and flashbacks were highly *salient* to them in that many of them spent considerable time engaged in these and they were very powerful in manipulating hedonic tone. (They experienced them as '*addictive*'.) Indeed, it is possible that their tendency to be loners was brought about by their desire not to be interrupted by others as they relived their memories and experiences. Some veterans experienced *relief* Solursh (1989) described the veterans in his studies as sometimes achieving a *relaxed and calm state* after experiencing their nightmares and flashbacks (although usually it was a depressed low mood). There is no direct evidence of the veterans developing *tolerance* to their flashbacks and nightmares unless their enthusiasm for weapons, hunting, re-enacting combat experiences and actively seeking fights may be an indication of their dissatisfaction with the levels of excitement produced by their memories and flashbacks alone. That some of them experienced *conflict* is amply demonstrated in Nadelson's (1992) description of the five veterans in his study who experienced shame and guilt as well as enthusiasm for their memories of killing in combat. As yet I have not found any evidence in the literature that the veterans experienced any *withdrawals* after treatment of their PTSD symptomatology. However, in the literature available to date there is a general agreement that Vietnam veterans with PTSD are extremely hard to treat and in some cases are reluctant to enter treatment. Likewise, I have found no evidence as yet of any phenomenon which might be viewed as *reinstatement after abstinence.*

It is clearly possible, therefore, that the attraction that some Vietnam veterans have to their symptoms of PTSD may be similar to the behaviour of addicts. This state of affairs may well translate into violence by their attempts to re-experience the 'high' of combat and through the power and control over themselves and others which it provided for them.

However, while this explanation may account for the addiction to trauma or violence of some Vietnam veterans, it does not as yet explain the violence of abused children or indeed of some adults who have been subject to abuse. While the majority of the surviving Vietnam veterans were *perpetrators* as well as victims of violence, abused children and adults are clearly only *victims* of violence. Despite this fundamental difference, however, there are a few indications that the outcome may be the same, regardless of whether the experience is that of being a victim of violence or a perpetrator of violence. Pizzey (1974), who ran a refuge for battered wives and children, described some women who seemed to *seek out* violent relationships and who appeared to need 'to live on an adrenalin high'. Hanks and Rosenbaum (1977) in a study of battered women, suggested that some abused women helped to 'ignite' violence by seeking out relationships similar to those of their mothers. Adshead (1994), in a study of women referred to a Department of Forensic Psychiatry, found that a high proportion of her sample of 16 women described experiencing some form of thought or impulse to harm others. In three cases this experience involved complex visual fantasies of harming others: there is a parallel here to descriptions of Vietnam veterans being preoccupied with violent fantasies (Feldmann, 1988). The majority of the women in Adshead's sample had a history of sexual and/or physical abuse as children and half of them had suffered physical or sexual abuse as adults. Ten of the sample had at least one charge of previous assault but their case notes indicated a large amount of violence not reported to the police. In fact all but one of the sample had committed acts of violence towards others. Adshead's sample were not diagnosed as having PTSD, but she compares their symptoms to those of patients with this diagnosis. In fact, most of these women were diagnosed as borderline personality disorder; a diagnosis which may overlap considerably with that of chronic PTSD (Gunderson & Sabo, 1993). Hodge (1992) has also argued that PTSD may underlie the English legal classification of 'Psychopathic Disorder'.

Adshead's report is unclear with respect to visual flashbacks but eight of the women experienced 'voices' (either in their own voice or in that of an abuser from childhood) giving commands or urging action: 'At least two of the women found their fantasies, thoughts, visions or voices arousing and exciting if not frankly sexual' (Adshead, 1994, p. 239).

It seems possible therefore that some victims of childhood or adulthood abuse may well display some of the phenomena associated with PTSD in Vietnam veterans. Evidence for this hypothesis is currently very sparse. Victims of child or adult abuse who later commit violent offences tend to be labelled as 'personality disordered' rather than as suffering from PTSD. This latter diagnosis tends to be reserved for victims of violence or disaster and for Vietnam veterans. Clearly, however, there are many parallels in the experiences and behaviour of those labelled as suffering from *posttraumatic stress disorder* and those with *personality disorder* label although the two groups are perceived very differently by professionals. The major common factor, however, may be different manifestations of PTSD.

How many people are affected in this way is impossible to tell at present. The literature is very vague as to the proportions of Vietnam veterans who find their symptomatology exciting and powerful. Solursh (1989) found that most of his veterans described their experiences in this way, but other studies appear to find smaller proportions of veterans who actively seek and engage in their symptomatology (Glover, 1988). There is so far very little evidence of victims of childhood and adult abuse behaving in this way, although Adshead's sample of women referred to a forensic clinic do show some similarities to the veterans in their fantasies. However, Adshead provides no indication of how close these fantasies were to the original traumatic experiences.

CONCLUSION

I hope that this chapter has demonstrated that addiction to violence may be a real phenomenon for some people. While the focus has been on this addiction occurring through PTSD symptomatology, it is more than likely that other routes into this addiction may exist. Films and television provide many examples of relatively powerless individuals gaining power over their 'enemies'. Any individual with a low threshold for violence could easily understand this message. Indeed, there does seem to be some anecdotal evidence that some acts of extreme violence have been modelled on violent films such as *Clockwork Orange*.

It is less easy to understand people becoming addicted through being victims of violence as, for example, suggested by Pizzey (1974) with regard to battered wives. However, it may be that the heightened arousal, awareness and hypervigilance which would accompany being the victim of a violent act may be a desirable hedonic state for some people, despite how it is achieved. If this is so, it may be possible that they attempt to achieve this hedonic state by placing themselves at risk for revictimisation.

Clinically, the implications of addiction to violence are considerable. 'Addiction' is a well-researched phenomenon. While it is certainly true that we are nowhere near being able to confidently claim a 100% success rate, treatment effectiveness is certainly improving with many 'packages' and strategies becoming well established and available—for example, 'relapse prevention' (Marlatt & Gordon, 1985) and 'motivational interviewing' (Miller, 1983). The application of these packages to sex offenders has already begun (Pithers, 1990; Mann & Rollnick, 1996). It is possible that they may be also appropriate to some violent offenders. Treatment strategies developed for one type of addictive behaviour have generally been found to be useful for others. Perhaps equally importantly however, a study of the ways in which violence becomes addictive may advance our knowledge about *addictions* in general and so contribute to their overall management and treatment.

It seems unlikely that Tam O'Shanter's wife was addicted to perpetrating violence on her husband. It seems more likely that she was just angry. However, is it possible that anger itself could become addictive? Anger is a powerful emotional experience which will impact on hedonic tone. While to most people it is experienced as aversive, some people appear to get considerable satisfaction from ruminating over past slights and insults and fantasising about how they will achieve revenge on the perpetrator. For those people who find themselves powerless to affect events, perhaps anger provides the same feelings of power and control as we have discussed earlier in this chapter.

In the meantime, as far as we know, Tam got away from the witches and, we assume, eventually arrived home to meet with a stormy reception.

REFERENCES

Adshead, G. (1994). Damage: Trauma and violence in a sample of women referred to a forensic service. *Behavioural Sciences and the Law*, **12**, 235–249.

Apter, M. J. (1982). *The Experience of Motivation*. London & New York: Academic Press.

Araji, S. & Finkelhor, D. (1986). Abusers: A review of the research. In D. Finkelhor (Ed.), *A Sourcebook on Child Sexual Abuse* (pp. 89–118). Beverly Hills, CA: Sage.

Blackburn, R. (1989). Psychopathy and personality disorder in relation to violence. In K. Howells & C. R. Hollin (Eds), *Clinical Approaches to Violence* (pp. 179–208). Chichester: Wiley.

Blackburn, R. (1993). *The Psychology of Criminal Conduct*. Chichester: Wiley.

Boman, B. (1986). Combat stress, post-traumatic stress disorder, and associated psychiatric disturbance. *Psychosomatics*, **27**, 567–573.

Brown, R. I. F. (1986). Arousal and sensation seeking components in the general explanation of gambling and gambling addictions. *International Journal of Addictions*, **21**, 1001–1016.

Burgess, A. W., Hartman, C. R. & McCormack, A. (1987). Abused to abuser—antecedents of socially deviant behaviours. *American Journal of Psychiatry*. **144**, 1431–1436.

Cleckley, H. (1976). *The Mask of Sanity*, 6th edn. St Louis, MO: Mosby.

Collins, J. J. & Bailey, S. L. (1990). Traumatic stress disorder and violent behavior. *Journal of Traumatic Stress*, **3**, 203–220.

Dodge, K. A., Bates, J. E. & Pettit, G. S. (1990). Mechanisms in the cycle of violence. *Science*, **250** (4988), 1678–1683.

Drukteinis, A. M. (1992). Serial murder—the heart of darkness. *Psychiatric Annals*, **22**, 532–538.

Dutton, D. G. & Hart, S. D. (1992). Evidence for long-term, specific effects of childhood abuse and neglect on criminal behaviour in men. *International Journal of Offender Therapy & Comparative Criminology*, **36**, 129–137.

Farrington, D. P. (1989). Early predictors of adolescent aggression and adult violence. *Violence and Victims*, **4**, 79–100.

Feldmann, T. B. (1988). Violence as a disintegration product of the self in posttraumatic stress disorder. *American Journal of Psychotherapy*, **42**, 281–289.

Glover, H. (1985). Guilt and aggression in Vietnam veterans. *American Journal of Social Psychiatry*, **59**, 15–18.

Glover, H. (1988). Four syndromes of post-traumatic stress disorder: Stressors and conflicts of the traumatized with special focus on the Vietnam combat veteran. *Journal of Traumatic Stress*, **1**, 57–78.

Goodwin, J. (1988). Post traumatic symptoms in abused children. *Journal of Traumatic Stress*, **1**, 475–488.

Gunderson, J. & Sabo, A. (1993). The phenomenological and conceptual interface between borderline personality disorder and PTSD. *American Journal of Psychiatry*, **150**, 19–27.

Hanks, S. E. & Rosenbaum, C. D. (1977). Battered women: A study of women who live with violent alcohol-abusing men. *American Journal of Orthopsychiatry*, **47**, 291–306.

Hare, R. D. & Hart, S. D. (1993). Psychopathy, mental disorder and crime. In S. Hodgins (Ed.), *Mental Disorder and Crime*. Newbury Park, CA: Sage.

Higgins, S. A. (1991). Post-traumatic stress disorder and its role in the defense of Vietnam veterans. *Law and Psychology Review*, 15, 259–276.

Hiley-Young, B., Blake, D. D., Abueg, F. R., Rozynko, V. & et al. (1995). Warzone violence in Vietnam: An examination of premilitary, military, and postmilitary factors in PTSD in-patients. *Journal of Traumatic Stress*, 8, 125–141.

Hodge, J. E. (1992). Addiction to violence: A new model of psychopathy. *Criminal Behaviour and Mental Health*, 2, 212–223.

Hodge, J. E. (1993). Alcohol and violence. In P. Taylor (Ed.), *Violence and Society* (pp. 127–137). London: Royal College of Physicians.

Hoffman-Plotkin, D. & Twentyman, C. T. (1984). A multi-modal assessment of behavioural and cognitive deficits in abused and neglected preschoolers. *Child Development*, 55, 794–802.

Kaufman, J. & Zigler, E. (1987). Do abused children become abusive parents? *American Journal of Orthopsychiatry*, 57 86–192.

Kellert, S. R. & Felthous, A. R. (1985). Childhood cruelty toward animals among criminals and noncriminals. *Human Relations*, 38, 1113–1129.

Kerr, J. H. (1988). Soccer hooliganism and the search for excitement. In M. J. Apter, J. H. Kerr & M. P. Cowley (Eds), *Progress in Reversal Theory* (pp. 223–230). Amsterdam: Elsevier Science B.V. (North-Holland).

Kroll, P. D., Stock, D. F. & James, M. E. (1985). The behaviour of adult alcoholic men abused as children. *Journal of Mental and Nervous Disease*, 173, 689–693.

Kruppa, I., Hickey, N. & Hubbard, C. (1995). The prevalence of post traumatic stress disorder in a special hospital population of legal psychopaths. *Psychology, Crime and the Law*, 2, 131–141.

Kulka, R. A., Schlenger, W. E., Fairbank, J. A., Hough, R. L., Jordan, B. K., Marmar, C. R. & et al. (1990). *Trauma and the Vietnam War Generation*. New York, NY: Brunner/Mazel.

Lasko, N. B., Gurvits, T. V., Kuhne, A. A., Orr, S. P. & et al. (1994). Aggression and its correlates in Vietnam veterans with and without chronic posttraumatic stress disorder. *Comprehensive Psychiatry*. 35, 373–381.

Mann, R. E. & Rollnick, S. (1996). Motivational interviewing with a sex offender who believed he was innocent. *Behavioural and Cognitive Psychotherapy*, 24, 127–134.

Marlatt, G. A. & Gordon, J. R. (Eds) (1985). *Relapse Prevention*. New York: Guilford Press.

McCulloch, M. J., Snowden, P. R., Wood, P. J. W. & Mills, H. E. (1983). Sadistic fantasy, sadistic behaviour and offending. *British Journal of Psychiatry*, 143, 20–29.

McFall, M. E., Mackay, P. W. & Donovan, D. M. (1992). Combat-related posttraumatic stress disorder and severity of substance abuse in Vietnam veterans. *Journal of Studies on Alcohol*, 53, 357–363.

Miller W. R. (1983). Motivational interviewing with problem drinkers. *Behavioural Psychotherapy*, 11, 147–172.

Nadelson, T. (1992). Attachment to killing. *Journal of the American Academy of Psychoanalysis*, 20, 130–141.

Orford, J. (1985). *Excessive Appetites: A Psychological View of Addictions*. Chichester: Wiley.

Peele, S. (1985). *The Meaning of Addiction: Compulsive Experience and its interpretation.* Lexington, MA: Lexington Books.

Pithers, W. D. (1990). Relapse prevention with sexual aggressors: A method for maintaining therapeutic gain and enhancing external supervision. In W. L. Marshall, D. R. Laws & H. E. Barbaree (Eds), *Handbook of Sexual Assault: Issues, Theories and Treatment of the Offender* (pp. 343–361). New York: Plenum Press.

Pizzey, E. (1974). *Scream Quietly or the Neighbours Will Hear.* Harmondsworth: Penguin Books.

Shaw, D. M., Churchill, C. M., Noyes Jr, R. & Loeffelholz, P. L. (1987). Criminal behaviour and post-traumatic stress disorder in Vietnam veterans. *Comprehensive Psychiatry,* **28**, 403–411.

Solursh, L. P. (1988). Combat addiction Post-traumatic Stress Disorder re-explored. *Psychiatric Journal of the University of Ottawa,* **13**, 17–20.

Solursh, L. P. (1989). Combat addiction: Overview of implications in symptom maintenance and treatment planning. *Journal of Traumatic Stress,* **2**, 451–462.

Stone, M. H. (1994). Early traumatic factors in the lives of serial murderers. *American Journal of Forensic Psychiatry,* **15**, 5–26.

Widom, C. S. (1989a). The cycle of violence. *Science,* **244**, 160–166.

Widom, C. S. (1989b). Does violence beget violence? A critical examination of the literature. *Psychological Bulletin,* **106**, 3–28.

Wilson, J. P. & Zigelbaum, S. D. (1983). The Vietnam veteran on trial: The relation of post-traumatic stress disorder to criminal behaviour. *Behavioural Science and the Law,* **1**, 69–83.

Zaidi, L. Y. & Foy, D. W. (1994). Childhood abuse experiences and combat-related PTSD. *Journal of Traumatic Stress,* **7**, 33–42.

PART II

Application

CHAPTER 4

Addiction Models of Sexual Offending

Gail McGregor

Bamburgh Clinic, Newcastle upon Tyne

and

Kevin Howells

Edith Cowan University, Western Australia

INTRODUCTION

The clinical application of theoretical constructs and models from the field of substance addiction to a range of presenting problems and symptoms is increasingly common. Such models have been transplanted from the field of chemical addiction to more general human behaviours such as exercise (Sacks & Sachs, 1981; Davis & Tunks, 1991), sexuality (Levine & Troiden, 1988) and love (Sacks & Sachs, 1981), to specific clinical symptoms and psychopathology such as eating disorders (Harris et al., 1980; Wilson 1991), and gambling (Orford, 1985) and more recently to the field of sexual offending (Laws, 1989; Pithers, 1990).

This development has resurrected disputes as to the relative importance of medical, psychological and social factors in contributing to an understanding of individual differences and psychopathology. There has been an increasing use of treatment approaches taken

Addicted to Crime? Edited by J.E. Hodge, M. McMurran and C.R. Hollin.
© 1997 John Wiley & Sons Ltd.

from the addictive behaviours field with the range of problem behaviours described above. The validity of transposing constructs for substance addiction to other problem behaviours has received little scrutiny in the literature.

In this chapter the appropriateness of using models of addiction (e.g. the classical 'disease' model and the cognitive—behavioural model) to understand sexual offending will be discussed and the implications of this practice for the development of appropriate disposal and management strategies for sexual offenders considered. The degree of commonality between substance addiction and sexual offending will be considered in terms of the aetiology, co-occurrence and maintenance of behaviour patterns. The extent to which an addiction model can adequately account for what we know about sexual offending will be considered. The implications of an addiction model for the treatment of sexually abusive behaviours will be compared with other influential models of sexual offending. Finally, specific areas in which addiction models have been applied to the assessment and treatment of sexual offenders will be reviewed with particular reference to the relapse prevention components included in many current treatment programmes.

MODELS OF ADDICTION

Although ideas from a variety of addiction models appear to inform a large number of current treatment programmes available for sexual offenders, it is empirically unclear whether chemical dependencies traditionally considered within an addictions framework and sexual offending are linked in terms of their aetiology, maintenance and modification. Two prevalent current models of addiction—the disease model and the cognitive-behavioural model—will be reviewed in terms of their applicability to sexual offending.

The Disease Model of Addictions

Early work on addictions was based on a 'disease' model, the main tenet of which emphasises a genetic or biological predisposition towards a particular substance (see Chapter 1). This predisposition leads to increased consumption of that substance, tolerance to it and withdrawal stress if such consumption is withheld. The notion of a progression from initial consumption to craving and eventual uncontrolled use is implicit since the disease process is seen as causing a disability which prohibits the expression of control over intake. If the link between behaviour and chemical substances is accepted, then the model provides a framework for understanding at least some aspects of the sexual offence process.

Predisposition

A particular difficulty in applying such concepts to the notion of sexual offending stems from the assumption that an individual may be biologically predisposed to certain behaviour as well as to chemical agents.

The early work of Seligman (1970) on the concept of the 'preparedness' of certain non-sexual behaviours and Groth's (1978) work on individual predisposition to sexual contact with children, in the case of 'fixated paedophiles' may be helpful in explaining the eventual acting out of this interest by some individuals. Marshall and Barbaree (1990) postulated a theory of sexual violence which stresses the importance of biological predispositions towards such behaviour. These authors describe two features of such a predisposition. Firstly, the neural and hormonal mechanisms which mediate both sexual and aggressive responses are seen as virtually identical, thus making it difficult to separate the expression of these impulses. Secondly, males are seen as having a biological sex drive which is relatively non-specific. From Marshall and Barbaree's perspective, males are faced with two tasks in development: (i) to learn to inhibit aggression in a sexual context, and (ii) to change the age of desired sexual partners throughout development. Sexual offending can occur because sex and aggression have not been sufficiently differentiated (in rape offences) or because the individual has failed to acquire socially inculcated rules about the age appropriateness of sexual partners (in child sexual abuse).

Increased Consumption

As applied to sexual offending, the disease model would predict that, over time, more frequent and intense forms of contact would be sought, with a loss of interest in other forms of activity and increased psychological distress in the absence of sexual contact with children, or other forms of sexual aggression. Indeed, a number of studies have indicated that sexual offending can become a high-frequency behaviour of this sort. Abel et al. (1987) studied the self-reports of 561 non-incarcerated offenders who had been guaranteed confidentiality. A total of over one-quarter of a million completed assaults were disclosed. However, significant differences were found between offenders which suggests that the relationship between the urge to offend and the assaults themselves is complex. This issue will be discussed further in a later section. Fisher and Thornton (1993) discussed the differences between discrete groups of offenders, namely those for whom offending occurred at a very high rate (often described as having an addictive pattern) and those for whom offending is a low-frequency behaviour.

Tolerance

The disease model suggests that, over time, particular environmental and internal cues (or conditioned stimuli) which are temporally associated with chemical ingestion of a substance (the unconditioned stimulus) come to elicit conditioned responses opposite in direction to the original, unconditioned response. This classical conditioning model indicates an anticipative, conditioned compensatory response (CCR) as the body's attempt to maintain balance by counteracting the drug's primary effect. This CCR becomes stronger with increased pairings of the conditioned stimulus and the unconditioned stimulus, and hence the drug effect becomes progressively weaker, producing a tolerance effect and stimulating a further increase in consumption. We are aware of no current research which has similarly examined physiological responses to offending (other than penile tumescence measures, summarised for example by Laws & Marshall, 1991; Quinsey & Earls, 1990) in order to demonstrate such a tolerance effect. Indeed, there would be ethical problems in attempting to do so.

However, if this addiction model is applied to sexual offending then there is an implication of a tolerance effect in respect of the offence-related behaviour. In this case, internal and environmental cues for offending such as fantasy, pornography or environmental cues associated with previous offending episodes would be seen as conditioned stimuli while the offending itself may be seen as the unconditioned stimulus. The model would therefore predict a subsequent compensatory response (CCR) which would inhibit or limit the offending response. It may be argued, for example, that we should see increased victim empathy and reduced cognitive distortion (as a means of psychologically counteracting the effects of offending). At a behavioural level, many offenders do note that fantasy or actual offending may provoke negative feelings. However, such reactions more often lead to subsequent offending as a means of ameliorating this negative mood state, than to a spontaneous reduced likelihood of offending due to increased victim empathy. Clinical evidence indicates that increased frequency and/or severity of offending is also mediated by an ability to overcome psychological and other blocks to offending.

This suggests a more complex psychological rather than a physiological tolerance effect and a limited application of traditional disease models to offending behaviour. The implications of such a model for overcoming psychological tolerance to offending are very different from those involved in the treatment of chemical addictions or dependency. If one assumes a shared form of aetiology for sexual offending and addiction to chemical substances, then the treatment process may be viewed as involving an approach similar to the 12-step programme introduced by Alcoholics Anonymous and subsequently applied to other behaviours viewed within an addictions framework (Bell & Khantzian, 1991).

Withdrawal

Following increased tolerance and loss of control over substance intake the disease model hypothesises a period of physiological adaptation of the body to the substance. If access to this substance is then denied a readjustment phase is entered, during which the body must readapt to functioning without the chemical agent. This is seen as producing a characteristic and time-limited set of symptoms associated with the body's response to the absence of the substance. Although there is some anecdotal information from offenders on psychological conflict and 'cravings' during offence-free intervals there is little empirical evidence for this as a biological response. Indeed the 'cravings' described by some sex offenders are most usually precipitated by some negative life event and consequent aversive emotional reaction rather than being consistently present throughout the whole of the offence-free period.

However, although offenders may indicate increased 'grooming' behaviour prior to the offence, there is often no indication that the 'withdrawal' is particularly aversive. Indeed, clinical observation would suggest that for some individuals it may be viewed as arousing, exciting or challenging in itself. The model would imply an eventual disorder of control leading to the seeking of uncontrolled contact as a result of an 'uncontrollable urge'. Such terms are sometimes used by sex offenders but ethical problems arise in using such concepts due to the risk of reinforcing the offenders' lack of acceptance of responsibility for their behaviour.

Orford (1985) argues against the continued acceptance of what he terms 'excessive appetitive behaviours' as diseases, and argues that a better understanding of such problem behaviours can be produced by the synthesis of a range of theoretical approaches based on work with individual excessive appetites such as drinking, drug use, eating, gambling and sexual behaviour. Similarly, Davies (1992) highlights the role of psychological mediators such as attributions, decisions and expectations in understanding substance addiction. When considering sexual offending it is clear that a disease model alone is insufficient wholly to explain the problem.

Cognitive-Behavioural Model of Addiction

The cognitive—behavioural model of addictive behaviours differs from the disease model in the emphasis placed on psychosocial influences in addition to biological vulnerabilities. Addictive behaviours are viewed as merely a subset of general behaviours which are modified and regulated by those variables encompassed by learning theory and in particular operant learning theory (Orford, 1985). The role of cognitive variables is of particular importance. This model does not assume an inevitable loss of control over behaviour or a progression to a disease state. However, a number of the other concepts inherent in the disease model are present in a modified form.

Within a learning theory framework, cravings are not assumed to have a merely physiological basis and are explained with reference to learned expectations and conditioned responses. With reference to substance abuse it is suggested that the reingestion of a particular substance following an abstinent interval is mediated by the expectation of consequences, in terms of both positive and negative reinforcement. Bandura (1977) noted that the expectation of reinforcement is often as powerful, if not more potent, than the actual reinforcement itself. The expectation of and desire for reinforcement is seen as being labelled by the individual as a craving, highlighting the role of both physiological and cognitive mediators. The role of antecedents in controlling subsequent behaviour is also emphasised.

Orford highlights the value of an 'adaptive' approach to addictions in which addictive behaviour is viewed as a response to pre-existing environmental, physiological, situational or dispositional stress. The behaviour is seen as the individual's attempt to cope with such stress. The cognitive-behavioural model thus provides a framework for understanding the high frequency of self-reports of negative emotional states as 'triggers' for sexual offending. The importance of offending behaviour as a negative reinforcer, enabling the offender to escape or completely avoid unpleasant emotional states, is emphasised. Such avoidance conditioning may increase the likelihood of reoffending and explain persistent offending. The offence itself can be seen both as intrinsically rewarding and as a means of reducing preceding psychological distress.

However, this approach does not fully explain the progressive nature of substance addiction and some sexual offence patterns, nor does it explain the relative difference in the impact of predisposing factors at different stages in the move towards uncontrolled use. Orford (1985) suggests that three features of operant learning theory are of specific value in explaining 'the insidious development of strongly habitual appetitive behaviour' (p. 175):

(a)   the relatively stronger influence of intermittent, as opposed to continual, reinforcement in shaping and maintaining behaviour;
(b)   the notion that certain behaviours gradually become increasingly probable (rather than one set of behaviours or responses immediately replacing others);
(c)   the importance of immediate (and usually positive) rather than more distant (and usually negative) consequences in shaping addictive behaviour—termed the *gradient of reinforcement*.

Such features are useful in explaining aspects of the development of a habitual pattern of offending. Clinical experience suggests that for many sex offenders the effects of intermittent engagement in offending behaviour are particularly powerful. For some individuals the interval between offences, in which fantasy and grooming for the next offence occur, serves to heighten their interest in abusive rather than appropriate sexual behaviour—although there may be periods during which both types of contact are sought. In addition, the expectation of immediately reinforcing consequences of offending are often described by offenders as constituting an 'uncontrollable urge'. This is acted upon in spite of knowledge of the negative consequences such as damage to the victim, precipitation of lowered mood, disclosure and legal proceedings. Such potential inhibitors may be ignored by means of cognitive distortions.

Orford also describes an early 'learned appetite' theory of sexual motivation by Hardy (1964) in which repeated, emotionally positive sexual experiences are recognised as important determinants of sexual preference. The repetition of these experiences may facilitate an increased range of cues which elicit a sexual response and a strengthening of certain associations, rather than others, with sexual satisfaction. This is similar to McGuire's theory of the masturbatory conditioning of sexual preference (McGuire et al., 1965).

Withdrawal or abstinence stress is seen as being conditioned in a similar manner, with withdrawal symptoms being specifically elicited by situations previously associated with substance use. A relapse, or return to substance use, serves to relieve these symptoms and is conditioned by the negative reinforcement principle earlier described. This theory has been further refined (Teasdale, 1973, cited in Orford, 1985) such that generalised anxiety (often indistinguishable from the effects of substance withdrawal) becomes associated with substance-use environments. The cognitive-behavioural model suggests that a range of environmental, affective and physiological cues associated with prior substance use can become conditioned stimuli which may have effects similar to those of the substance itself. The presence of such conditioned cues is suggested to motivate the person to engage in the substance abuse behaviour, even after a considerable period of abstinence, by signalling the likelihood of reinforcement following the behaviour. The development of such signals for a range of behaviours is well documented and examples include the sensory associations with smoking or alcohol consumption and the excitement of the gambling environment. Similarly, the importance of offence-related sexual fantasies, pornography use, planning and rehearsal of offending as cues for further sexual assaults is clear within this framework. Indeed, for some individuals, the pre-offence grooming of persons and environments may be seen to be as challenging and arousing as the actual offence.

Although valuable in explaining a range of behaviours observed in substance abuse and sexual offending, early learning theory models do not fully explain the role of cognitive processes in the development and maintenance of such behaviours (Stermac et al., 1990). The importance of social expectations and attributions in determining behaviour have been increasingly recognised (Fisher & Howells, 1993). A range of studies have demonstrated the effect of cognitive and affective mediators on sexual behaviour and aggression (Knopp, 1984; Quinsey & Earls, 1990). The improved understanding of the role of these factors has had a significant influence on the therapeutic interventions developed for a range of clinical problems such as anxiety and stress (Meichenbaum, 1977), anger (Novaco, 1975) and eating disorders (Wilson, 1991). Treatment approaches for sexual aggression have had a similar history, with early treatments placing increased, or exclusive, significance on behavioural techniques such as fantasy or arousal modification and masturbatory reconditioning. As knowledge of the range of factors motivating different forms of sexual offending has increased, so current treatment methods place far greater emphasis on cognitive techniques such as altering patterns of distorted thinking, attitudes and perceptions and increasing victim empathy. This has led to the increased use of group-based rather than individual treatment programmes. Such programmes are informed by cognitive theory relating to attitude formation and maintenance, problem solving, attributional processes and behavioural theory relating to the modification of interpersonal behaviour, skills training and the modification of deviant arousal patterns (Laws & Marshall, 1991). In summary, psychological principles governing a wide range of both 'normal' and deviant thoughts, feelings and behaviours are being used in many current treatment programmes. This suggests that while the cognitive-behavioural model of addictions is useful in furthering understanding of some aspects of sexual offending it is not sufficient either to explain completely the range of sexually assaultive behaviour or to fully direct treatment approaches.

Cognitive-Behavioural Model—Summary

The cognitive-behavioural model appears to be more congruent with the existing knowledge about sexual offending in the following areas:

(a) It gives greater emphasis to the importance of psychosocial learning processes and developmental issues. This is consistent with the more recent models of a range of sexual offence behaviours which seek to integrate biological, developmental, relationship and cognitive variables in order to explain and indicate treatments for such behaviours (Marshall & Barbaree, 1990).

(b) The cognitive-behavioural model does not imply eventual loss of control as does the disease model.

(c) The cognitive-behavioural model gives more attention to the role of cognitive factors, and such factors have been shown to be important for sexual offences, hence the frequency with which they are addressed in treatment. The literature on treatment outcome indicates that cognitive-behavioural approaches have been shown to be relatively effective in treatment (Marshall et al., 1991). As part of the emphasis on cognitive factors, the cognitive-behavioural model explains the withdrawal effects in terms of expectations, rather than physiological cravings.

(d) The cognitive-behavioural model takes a broader account of the influences on sexual-offending behaviour, including descriptions of important emotional states, environmental triggers and physiological cues, particularly sexual arousal.

CO-OCCURRENCE OF SEXUAL OFFENDING AND OTHER ADDICTIVE BEHAVIOURS

Research on substance addictions has demonstrated a degree of co-occurrence between a range of addictions within individuals. With regard to sexual offending, investigations of substance abuse and offending have not generally demonstrated such a co-existence within an addictions framework. Although a range of sexually inappropriate behaviours may be evident in the history of offenders, these tend to be viewed as evidence of a behavioural progression rather than as separate addictive behaviours. Fisher and Howells (1993) also indicate difficulties in assuming homogeneity across a range of sexual offending categories, and they highlight functional differences between offenders in terms of the needs served by the behaviour for each individual.

At the present time the results relating to the co-occurrence of substance abuse and sexual offences are unconvincing. Glueck (1956, cited in Rada, 1978), noted the almost total lack of use of narcotics amongst sex offenders and more recent work has concluded that there is little evidence to support an aetiological association between the use of drugs and the commission of sexual offences. Thus, there is little evidence to support the view that an underlying 'addiction-proneness' may explain both substance use and sexual offending.

Similarly, although alcohol often plays a significant role in the commission of sexual offences the results of available studies on the co-occurrence of alcoholism and sexual offences do not provide support for a view of these as manifestations of a common underlying addiction process. Indeed, other models (Finkelhor, 1984) would suggest that alcohol use by offenders may reflect a deliberate or unconscious learning process by which the individual overcomes internal inhibitions against offending. Although alcohol is encountered frequently as a reason by which offenders themselves explain their actions, there is relatively little research evidence to support a generally higher rate of diagnosed alcoholism in sexual offenders as opposed to other offender groups. Studies have varied in the importance given to alcohol either in causing or in influencing sexual offending.

Alcoholism and alcohol abuse have been considered as an important determinant of future reoffence risk in both rapist (Rada, 1975) and child molester groups (Maletzky, 1991). Marques and Nelson (1989) describe a study of 168 incarcerated sexual offenders undergoing assessment for inclusion in a treatment programme. Of this total, 60% reported a significant history of alcohol and/or drug abuse at some point in their lives and 70% of these reported alcohol consumption at the time of the index offence. However, significant differences were identified among particular subgroups of offenders such that rapists were found to highlight alcohol use or substance use as linked with offending relatively more often than the child molester sample, again highlighting significant differences between subgroups of offenders.

Marques and Nelson indicate that these figures may also be overestimates due to the importance of alcohol to the offenders themselves as a justification or rationalisation for their behaviour. It is of note that this study is reliant upon the self-report of the offenders rather than a more objective assessment or diagnosis of alcohol or substance use. They commented on the significant discrepancies in prevalence rates of alcoholism cited in studies involving sexual offenders.

There are a number of difficulties in comparing studies of the co-occurrence between sexual offending and substance addiction. These relate to methodological differences in the definitions used to describe various disorders and also to different theoretical assumptions about the role of substances in either *influencing* or *causing* offending.

In summary, while the co-occurrence of other addictive behaviours with sexual offending has been noted, it has not been demonstrated that this results from any underlying biological processes. Even if it can be shown that there is a statistical association between sexual offending and other addictive behaviours, this may be better explained in terms of, for example, a disinhibition effect whether cognitively or physiologically mediated.

DIFFICULTIES IN APPLYING ADDICTION MODELS TO SEXUAL OFFENDING

Functional similarities between substance abuse and other disorders are not sufficient to describe the disorders as addictions and the overuse of such terminology may lead to the overemphasising of similarities and the deemphasising of differences.

Disease models and cognitive-behavioural models of sexual offending have differing functions and consequences. In some ways the disease model has some positive consequences for the treatment of sexual offenders. As Orford (1985) points out, individuals who have developed excessive appetites may be seen as less responsive to normal constraints and controls, and therefore can be legislatively viewed as having a diminished level of responsibility to some extent.

Clearly, there are dangers in overusing the disease model to the point at which the sense of personal responsibility for behaviours is substantially impaired. On the other hand, sexual interests and preferences are not easily changed by a simple act of will and an appreciation of this may lead to a more helpful approach to perpetrators, allowing legislative changes which recognise the need for the direction of individuals to treatment settings, rather than to purely custodial environments.

> Disease models are now retarding our understanding. They put too great a weight upon the experience of clinical cases and insufficient upon the far more numerous incidence of troublesome appetitive behaviour in the general population. They have elevated the role of expert, particularly medical, help out of all proportion to its real significance, and they have over-emphasised the one factor of altered biological response, or 'physical addiction', and have hence neglected the psychological mechanisms involved in the development of strong attachment to appetitive activity. (Orford, 1985, p, 323)

Davies (1992) has produced a penetrating analysis of the concept of addiction. The term addiction is often used as follows:

1. 'Addiction' tends to imply a *state* which is different from the state of being 'normal', though as Davies suggests, the components of the state are a mystery. The supposed addicted state is suggested to interfere with or remove the capacity for voluntary behaviour.
2. Davies points out 'addictions' tends to be used in a *categorical* rather than a quantitative way.
3. The term addiction often implies 'disease' which in turn is thought to disrupt integrated and purposive behaviour patterns. Studies of sexual offending suggest the offending behaviour is often purposeful, planned and integrated.

Mechanisms of craving and withdrawal are crucial to addiction models Davies points out that the notion of *craving* implies that the person does not simply *want* but *has to have* something. Davies argues, plausibly, that the state of *craving* is simply an attribution of an internal state to explain the desire to engage in or repeat an activity, rather than an 'autonomous force whose power cannot be resisted' (Davies, 1992, p. 51). The issue of whether behaviour is or is not under voluntary control has crucial implications for the development of treatment programmes. Davies sees 'craving' as reflecting a particular attribution and suggests it refers not to a biological process but to recollections that an experience was pleasurable the last time it occurred plus the hope that it might happen again. This is a more useful account for understanding and managing sexual offending.

In relation to *withdrawal* Davies notes that even for substance addictions withdrawal often has no simple relationship to biological processes. The nature of withdrawal experiences depends greatly on a range of situational and cognitive factors. 'The idea that addiction is a state in which the driving force for autonomic action becomes lost to the individual, and is taken over by craving, an irresistible psychological force fuelled by inevitable and excruciating withdrawal symptoms, is untenable...' (Davies, 1992, p. 55).

While it is clear that concepts from the addictions field continue to have a major impact on our understanding and management of the problem of sexual offending (Laws, 1994), it is useful to consider other theoretical constructions of sexual offending at this point.

OTHER MODELS OF SEXUAL OFFENDING

A number of theoretical models have been applied to the problem of sexual offending. The problem in comparing such models arises from differences in definition of offending, categories of different offences and attempts to distinguish discriminating features of different offences versus those dealing with a variety of intrapersonal qualities of offenders themselves, in addition to environmental explanations. Psychodynamic, biological and behavioural and social learning theories have been proposed for a range of sexually unusual behaviours and sexual offences including child sexual abuse, rape and exhibitionism (Rada, 1978; Ellis, 1989; Lanyon, 1991) and constitute too large a field to be reviewed here. Instead the most common models influencing clinical practice with sexual offenders will be briefly discussed.

Offender Characteristics

A range of investigators have attempted to produce typologies of offenders which relate to the behaviours in which they engage. The most common distinction which has been made with reference to sexual offenders against children has been that of enduring preference. A number of subtypes of offenders have been distinguished, for example by Cook and Howells (1981), which reflect either a fixed and enduring sexual preference for children or a more situational pattern of offending within the context of an established preference for adult partners. The latter type of offenders have been considered to be more situationally vulnerable to engaging in behaviour with children in response to either sexual or non-sexual life problems. Some

differences in offence patterns in different subgroups of offenders
have been highlighted, including adolescent offenders (Ryan, 1987).

Similar typologies have been suggested for rape offenders with adult
victims. A number of subgroups of rape offenders have been suggested,
including those who engage in behaviour as a result of sadistic
interests and pleasures, those engaging in behaviour within the
context of more general criminal activities, those engaging in behaviour in group situations, and those motivated by anger responses.

Offender Characteristics — Summary

Although there have been such attempts to identify subclasses of
offenders, it would seem clear that in terms of characteristics,
offenders may be viewed as having a range of developmental and
psychosocial problems to a greater extent than the normal population
regardless of the specific offence type (Marshall & Eccles, 1991;
Fisher & Howells, 1993). This lack of homogeneity and the subsequent identification of important subtypes of offenders mitigates
against a unitary addiction model of offending and suggests that
further work is needed in order to clarify further the mechanisms
underlying different patterns of offence behaviour.

Offence Characteristics

A number of researchers have attempted to examine the nature of the
pattern of offending behaviour itself and to define specific features
which suggest an increasing engagement in offending behaviour. The
work of Wolf (1984) in relation to adult sexual offenders has proved
influential in examining repetitive patterns of offending. In this
respect Wolf's work provides an integration of offender characteristics
and impact on behaviour patterns. Wolf suggests that following
personal victimisation, an acceptance of abusive behaviour as a
means of improving personal control is formed and this belief system
is seen as an important causal factor in the onset of offending.
Subsequently, a pattern may be established in which offending
becomes more frequent and important for the individual, leading to a
'cycle of offending'. It is easy to link such concepts of a cycle of
behaviour with the characteristics of addictive behaviour previously
described and cyclical or 'transitional stage' models have been applied
to other addictive behaviours (Orford, 1985).

Models incorporating a cyclical formulation of offending have been
influential in determining treatment for adult offenders. They
originate from an earlier use of the concept in relation to cognitive-

behavioural dysfunction cycles in treatment work with adolescent sexual offenders (Lane & Zamora, 1984). A number of different stages in offending are identified by Lane and Zamora, including factors relevant to pre-offence, actual offence and post-offence stages. The pre-offence stage is considered to be triggered by factors such as self-esteem threats, social anxiety and expectation of rejection leading to social avoidance as a coping mechanism. Fisher and Howells (1993) also note the importance of social difficulties as triggers for the offence cycle. Social or relationship difficulties may have a specific effect upon self-esteem, triggering a range of dysfunctional beliefs culminating in offending. The means by which such beliefs influence behaviour have received increasing research attention. This concept again has its roots within the field of addictions where the concept of '*apparently irrelevant decisions*', now referred to as '*seemingly unimportant decisions*', is seen to influence this progression through stages of an addictive or offending cycle (Pithers, 1989, 1990; Nelson & Jackson, 1989).

Offence Characteristics—Summary

1. It would appear that the literature on sex offending refers to at least two types of behaviour: repetitive behaviour and 'one-off' situational offending (Fisher & Thornton, 1993). Addiction models appear to be relevant only to enduring, repetitive offending. However, there is some controversy as to whether apparent one-off offences are simply an early manifestation of a pattern of repetitive offending. It is unlikely that a resolution of such a debate is possible without studies incorporating longer-term follow-up periods.

2. For those engaging in repetitive sexual abuse behaviours, education about the concept of offence cycles is a primary focus of treatment. After long-term social and personal effectiveness problems, the offence is likely to provide the offender with rewarding consequences which were perceived as previously unattainable and which may serve as one of a number of factors which increase the chances of the behaviour being repeated. However, the validity of the transfer of this cyclical concept from an addiction to an offending field has received little empirical evaluation.

FINKELHOR'S FOUR PRECONDITIONS MODEL

In addition to the idea of offence cycles, another prevalent theoretical model of offending is Finkelhor's (1984) Four Precondition Theory of sexual abuse. Developed following earlier work on the nature and extent of sexual victimisation of children, this model has had a significant impact on the development of treatment services, not only within its original context of both intra- and extrafamilial child sexual abuse, but also in programmes relating to other types of offences. In defining the four conditions which must be present in order for child sexual abuse to occur, the model has succeeded in integrating motivational or causal theories with treatment implications and goals. This has had a further important impact in providing a means of monitoring change in behaviour and thinking and thereby providing therapists with a means of evaluating the efficacy of treatment programmes. Such causal factors relate not simply to the offender, but also to the significant others in the lives of offenders and their victims, in addition to specific environmental features which permit offending to occur.

The Four Precondition Theory was developed from a review of then current factors, relating to families, victims and offenders, which had been suggested to contribute to sexual abuse. Factors seen as motivating offenders included the meaning of children to them, the processes by which sexual arousal becomes associated with children rather than being expressed in more appropriate ways, and the cognitive mechanisms which mediate the offenders' control over their impulses. Finkelhor then went on to suggest a staged process in which the above factors could be integrated with other psychosocial influences to explain the individual's process of offending. The similarity of this model to issues of offence cycles and what Orford (1985) has referred to as transitional stages in the development of addictive behaviours will be noted. Evidence for the precondition model which has been published since 1984 has recently been reviewed by Howells (1994).

Finkelhor identified four preconditions for the occurrence of child sexual abuse, namely: (i) the motivation to sexually abuse; (ii) the ability to overcome internal inhibitions against acting on the motivation; (iii) the ability to overcome external blocks against offending; and (iv) the ability to overcome or undermine the child's resistance. This model is one of the few available which can accommodate a range of sexually abusive behaviours towards children (and arguably also sexually aggressive behaviour in other contexts, such as against other adults) and also which can be translated into a plan for the assessment and supervision of offenders. Finkelhor suggests that all of these preconditions must be fulfilled before sexual abuse will occur.

Motivation to Sexually Abuse

Finkelhor described three components of this motivation which explain the process by which this motivation develops, in the context of the individual's past experiences.

Emotional Congruence

This incorporates the notion that sexual activity with children serves some important emotional need in the offender. Clinical examples include the need to feel powerful and controlling (often easier to achieve through relationships with children); to increase self-esteem generally, to overcome personal trauma through repetition or identification with the aggressor or arrested emotional development in the offender. Howells (1979) has provided some evidence that offenders do, in fact, view children as less personally threatening than adults. Previous work on the incidence of sexual abuse consistently indicates a higher rate of personal victimisation experiences in offender samples as compared to the general population (Finkelhor, 1984).

Sexual Arousal

An individual may become motivated to engage in sexual contact with children by means of a sexual arousal mechanism in which children are viewed as a source of sexual gratification (permanently or temporarily). Much of the work in this area has included studies of the sexual arousal patterns of various types of offenders at various stages in assessment or therapy and in a range of psychological mood states. This has been done by means of the computer-assisted measurement of changes in penile volume in response to exposure to a variety of stimuli (for example, preferred partners, type of sexual activity or offence), known as penile plethysmography (PPG). However, the results have often been conflicting. Some studies appear to have demonstrated a higher level of sexual arousal to children in extrafamilial child abusers as compared to 'normal' groups (Abel et al., 1981), while others have demonstrated a perhaps surprisingly high rate of response to children even amongst such 'normal' groups in laboratory measures. The studies by Marshall et al. (1986, 1988) would suggest that rather than a higher response to children, child sex offenders may instead show a marked reduced arousal response to adults and some differences in offence patterns depending on victim gender preference. A conditioning model has been hypothesised to explain sexual interest in children resulting from the pairing of child-centred fantasy material with arousal and orgasm during masturbation (McGuire et al., 1965). Similarly, a de-sensitisation or modelling process has been suggested to explain the development of deviant arousal patterns in those with personal victimisation experiences, although this does not account for the significant numbers of offenders who do not have such histories.

There is also an increasing body of evidence suggesting that such deviant arousal responses are formed at an earlier age than was previously supposed. Abel et al. (1987) found that 58% of their sample of 400 sex offenders attending an outpatient facility had developed a deviant arousal response, which was related to their later offending, prior to 18 years of age. Similar findings have been reported for incarcerated samples of both child abusers and adult rapists (Longo & Groth, 1983). Marshall et al. (1991) noted that in their sample of 129 child molesters attending a community assessment and treatment service, support for adolescent development of deviant interest was found, although only 21.7% of the total number indicated that such fantasies preceded their first offence (and 47.3% denied ever having experienced child-related fantasies). Although PPG measures were used to provide empirical measurement of current sexual arousal patterns, clearly there are difficulties in retrospectively describing onset of deviant interest based only on offenders' self-reports.

Blockage

Finkelhor suggests that for some offenders alternative and more acceptable means of achieving sexual gratification are unavailable or may be less rewarding. Individuals may encounter developmental difficulties leading to a failure to form adequate peer relationship skills. In a review of work on the social relationships of offenders, Fisher and Howells (1993) conclude that deficits in self-perception and in actual social competence are frequently important triggering factors for offending, in both child sex offenders and rapist groups.

Even where initial relationship-forming skills are present, offenders may encounter difficulties in maintaining satisfactory adult relationships which may make them more likely to engage in inappropriate contact with children. Bownes (1993) studied 74 recently sentenced sexual offenders within the Northern Ireland prison system and found that 81% had a current adult heterosexual relationship, with only 18% of the sample having had little or no adult sexual experience. He reported a prevalence of 62% for current relationship and/or marital dysfunctions and noted that this was a higher proportion than that found in the general population, using similar measures. A prevalence of specific sexual dysfunction of 57% was recorded and this is again higher than rates quoted for non-offender samples. No significant difference between groups of incest, rape and extrafamilial child sex offenders were noted in terms of overall pattern. However, higher dissatisfaction rates were associated with increased use of violence during the index offence and the number of previous offences, and a similar association was noted for sexual dysfunction and degree of injury inflicted. Bownes notes that victim reports also indicate that offender sexual dysfunction during the assault was not uncommon.

In identifying these three components of motivation, Finkelhor noted that these are not in themselves preconditions and acknowledged that, although in many cases elements of each are present, there are also a number of offenders for whom only a subset of these components appears to be important. He further described the particular combination of these elements as having consequences for the victim gender preference, strength and duration of the impulses experienced by the offender. Treatment goals would address the individual motivational characteristics of a particular offender in order to decrease the level of interest in abusive sexual contact and would include methods designed to increase social and relationship skills, coping with aversive emotional events, behavioural techniques to modify deviant arousal patterns and possible marital/relationship counselling.

Overcoming Internal Inhibitions

Being motivated to engage in abusive behaviour is not seen as sufficient for it to be acted upon due to the inhibiting influence of social, legal and cognitive constraints. Thus, offenders must develop ways of disabling these in order to carry out an assault. A range of disinhibitors has been suggested which include personal character-istics of offenders (such as mental illness or organic damage, use of alcohol or other disinhibitory substances) and sociocultural influ-ences such as social tolerance of behaviour, influence of pornography and weak sanctions against offenders (Lanyon, 1991).

However, it is of note that such substances, while having a physiologically disinhibiting effect also serve to provide the offender with a means of understanding the cause of his offending without reference to his underlying motivation. More attention has recently been directed towards these particular cognitive mechanisms, or cognitive distortions, which may be viewed as a means of overcoming internal inhibitions. Salter (1988) has identified a number of aspects of offender denial which serve to minimise the offender's responsibility or place this onto the victim, in order to justify and excuse their behaviour.

Overcoming External Inhibitors

In addition to the above 'intrapsychic' preconditions Finkelhor describes a number of factors external to the offender which will determine whether or not an offence will occur. Some important external blocks include the level and quality of supervision a child receives from others and environmental/situational constraints serving to deny opportunities for offending. It is apparent clinically that most offenders do not simply engage in opportunistic offending but may expend considerable effort in creating situations in which offending is possible by the targeting and grooming of not only their victims but also their families and environments. Again, such concepts are relevant to other types of sexual offences such as rape or exhibitionism.

Overcoming the Resistance of the Child

The last precondition indicates the range of methods used by offenders in overcoming the resistance of their victims. It is clear that this stage does not refer simply to the immediate use of physical force during the actual assault but to a variety of 'grooming' behaviours used to facilitate offending. Offenders may spend large amounts of time preparing the victim for abuse in both intrafamilial and extrafamilial contexts. Finkelhor posited that certain victim characteristics are more likely to be targeted by offenders in order to facilitate offending. Specific factors such as emotional insecurity, lack of sexual awareness and unusually trusting relationships are highlighted in addition to a range of coercive methods.

Finkelhor Precondition Model—Summary

The above model is one of the most influential multi-factorial theories currently informing clinical practice. Despite its original focus on contact sexual offences against children the model appears to have a wider applicability and to encompass individual, environmental and situational factors in understanding offending. The role of external factors in influencing behaviour is also gaining wider interest within the addictions field, although until relatively recently addiction models were unable to encompass these areas.

However, there appear to be a number of differences between the Finkelhor model and the Addiction model:

1. Although both theories address biological factors to some degree, the treatment of biological factors is very different in each theory. The Finkelhor model does not view biological variables as necessarily pathological, but rather as normal physiological processes subject to faulty learning. This framework has been further expanded by Marshall and Barbaree (1990) in their 'Integrated theory of offending' in which sociocultural, biological, situational and developmental factors are combined to explain the aetiology of male sexual aggression. Finkelhor places greater emphasis on biological factors as having a role, for example, in the disinhibition of deviant impulses (Precondition 2). This disinhibition could be the product of the biological effects of alcohol or of organic dysfunction. Where substance use is implicated in the Finkelhor model, it is not seen as reflective of an addiction process. The emphasis is more on the means by which individuals overcome inherent inhibitions about sexual offending.
2. The Finkelhor model does not emphasise the uncontrollability of sexual behaviour, as would an addiction model, although there is a recognition that distorted thinking may lead the individual offender to believe that their behaviour stems from an 'uncontrollable urge'. Thus, the reality of the mechanisms prompting offending is viewed as different to the explanations offered by offenders in most cases.
3. In its focus on the role of cognitive mediators of behaviour, the Finkelhor model would appear to be closer to the cognitive-behavioural addiction model, than to the disease model. Both have the advantage of allowing these mediators to become a direct focus of therapy by increasing the offender's acceptance of responsibility for the control of future behaviour.
4. The emphasis in the Finkelhor model on external factors in the situation (external inhibitors and victim factors) is much more congruent with the cognitive-behavioural framework with its emphasis on expectations and perceptions of the environment and the victim.
5. Although sexual arousal is emphasised by Finkelhor as an important aspect of motivation, it is only one of three forms of motivating factor that are emphasised and indeed the model specifies that the deviant sexual arousal is not a necessary condition for deviant sexual behaviour.

6. The Finkelhor theory allows for low-frequency deviant sexual behaviour, which contrasts with addiction models which tend to stress the constant continual nature of the addictive process. This is consistent with the information provided by Fisher and Thornton (1993) which lends further support to the generally accepted view that sexual offending is not a unitary phenomenon.

7. Both models give some weight to the 'blocking' of appropriate, alternative responses to the problem behaviour. However, neither specifies in detail whether this is a cause or an effect. It is clear that for a number of offenders, once the deviant behavioural response is introduced there may be less motivation to seek more appropriate outlets.

8. A major feature of the Finkelhor account is the importance of victim resistance factors. There would seem to be no parallel for this factor in the addiction models. It is possible to speculate that similar processes may be involved in the means by which addicts may overcome obstacles to their continued use of the addictive substance. However, this may be seen as more akin to the third precondition (that of overcoming external inhibitors) than to the process by which offenders overcome the resistance of the actual victim during abuse. There would seem to be no real parallel for this aspect of sexual offending within an addictions framework. Current models of sexual offending emphasise the often prolonged interaction between the offender and the potential victim as a means by which the latter's submission is produced by the former. There is no equivalent social process involved in addictive behaviours in terms of the interaction between the addict and the substance itself.

It would appear then that the current addiction models are insufficient wholly to explain either the heterogeneity of sexual offending behaviour and offenders or the complete process of offending. The Finkelhor model would appear more able to explain these factors. However, the contribution of certain concepts from the addictions field has been significant in the development of more comprehensive treatment packages. One key example of the enrichment of treatment programmes by reference to an addictions framework is given by the considerable importance ascribed to *Relapse-Prevention* work within current treatment programmes.

TREATMENT IMPLICATIONS OF THE ADDICTION MODEL OF SEXUAL OFFENDING—THE RELAPSE PREVENTION MODEL

Considerable attention has been given in recent years, often in response to the theoretical models described above, to treatment methods aimed at helping an individual to interrupt an offence cycle or to stop offending. However, although such approaches may achieve positive short-term results, studies of recidivism or reconviction rates appear to indicate little cause for long-term optimism in respect of maintenance of change. This has led to further work aimed at improving offenders' self-control in the longer term. One of the most effective treatment components in helping tackle this problem has been the inclusion of *relapse-prevention* components in treatment programmes.

The concepts of relapse prevention were first applied within the context of addictive behaviours in order to address similar maintenance problems in the treatment of alcoholism, substance abuse, smoking and eating disorders (George & Marlatt, 1989). In view of the apparent commonalities between these addictive behaviours and sexual offending (e.g. the presence of immediate gratification and delayed negative consequences, high personal and social sanctions against the behaviour, and difficulties in maintaining treatment effects), the relapse-prevention elements of cognitive interventions, education and behavioural skills training were included in sex offender programmes (Pithers et al., 1983). However, Marshall et al. (1991b) argue that inclusion of the relapse-prevention components need not imply acceptance of an addiction model of sexual offending *per se*. They highlight the importance of the offender viewing the prevention of further offending as achievable and under their own control rather than as an uncontrollable urge.

Pithers (1988) cites Marlatt (1982) as defining the intervention as involving an analysis of precursors to past relapse, skills training to help the offender predict and avoid future risk situations, the development of effective coping methods, and finally the lessening of the abstinence-violation effect surrounding lapses. Pithers et al. (1983) modified the programme for application with sexual offenders. A number of assumptions about the similarities between sexual offending and other addictive behaviours are made, as previously described, such that similar therapeutic techniques are employed.

The model suggests that change is maintained by offenders until a high-risk situation is encountered which threatens their self-control. By using an adaptive coping response progress continues and the risk of relapse is reduced. However, an unsuccessful attempt at coping is likely to produce feelings of helplessness and poor expectation of future success. Pithers et al. (1988, 1989, 1990) state that if such psychological reactions are elicited in an environment which contains cues associated with previous offending then a relapse is triggered, particularly in the context of an expectation of the previous immediate rewards associated with offending. A distinction is made between a behavioural 'lapse' and a full relapse. The former is viewed as the initial occurrence of the precursors of sexual assault. These are considered to follow a predicted sequence from affect to fantasy, distorted thinking, planning and final enactment of behaviour. In this context, a lapse would be identified as the return of offence-related sexual fantasies whereas a relapse would be a further offence, with the transition being mediated by the abstinence-violation effect.

The aim of the relapse-prevention strategy is for the offender to develop skills which will allow him to halt this sequence at the earliest possible point. Indeed, the approach also involves the identification of factors preceding an offender's entry into a high-risk situation. This point has been considered essential by Marshall et al. (1990) who criticised Pithers' definition above of a lapse as being too narrow. While cautioning against trivialising the impact on future victims of a single reoffence, Marshall et al. also discriminate between such an event and a return to pre-treatment offending frequency. They argue that it is important for the offender to believe that it is possible to prevent future reoffending regardless of which stage of the process they have reached. Determinants of relapse or 'cues' are seen as including affective (negative emotional states), cognitive (including distorted thinking and seemingly unimportant decisions) and behavioural (including the use of disinhibiting substances or entry into a high-risk situation) events, all of which may become the focus for specific skills training and rehearsal. Such approaches are outlined in more detail by Laws et al. (1989). The client is taught to reduce the probability of offence-related affects, cognitions and behaviours recurring and to deal adaptively with them if they do recur.

Pithers (1990) has further expanded his use of relapse-prevention components and distinguishes between 'internal management' and 'external community supervision' with the latter providing a network of informed community supervisors to monitor the offender's functioning (including partners, families, friends and work colleagues in addition to professionals). Such approaches have been successfully incorporated into a number of US and Canadian programmes (Maletzky, 1991) and are becoming increasingly prevalent in Britain (Beckett et al., STEP Project, 1994).

Efficacy of Relapse Prevention Treatment

There have been relatively few attempts to investigate the impact of relapse-prevention components on treatment outcome. This is perhaps not surprising given the difficulty in evaluating differential outcomes of specific treatment components in general. Difficulties relating to definitional differences, offence and offender characteristics, duration and context of treatment provision, are only some examples of problems faced by researchers. However, further to their earlier review of treatment outcome indicating the efficacy of group-based cognitive-behavioural treatments (Marshall et al., 1991c), Marshall and Pithers (1994) attempted to investigate the contribution of relapse-prevention components. They examined a number of treatment facilities, including institutional programmes without relapse prevention; those with internal management components; those with both internal and external management; and community programmes with and without relapse-prevention elements. In spite of major difficulties in making meaningful comparisons between such widely differing programmes, it was concluded that the inclusion of Relapse Prevention elements generally increases the efficacy of treatment programmes.

SUMMARY

In this chapter we have reviewed addiction models and their application to the field of sexual offending. The conceptual difficulties with the concept of addiction have been discussed. The disease model of addiction (Wilson, 1991; Orford, 1985) has a number of features, including notions of predisposition, increased consumption, tolerance and withdrawal. We have argued that, despite superficial similarities between the behaviours, the assumption that the mechanisms underlying such processes are identical in the case of substance use and sexual offending is problematic. While some authors (Marshall & Barbaree, 1990) have discussed the possible import of biological predispositions in aggressive male sexual behaviour this has been in the context of environmental and socialisation processes. Similar limitations are encountered in attempting to view sexual offending within the simply physiological framework of increased consumption, tolerance and withdrawal. We have argued that certain predictions of the disease model are not borne out in relation to sexual offending and indeed may be seen as 'counter-therapeutic' in terms of current treatment programmes, where the aim is to help the offender to appreciate that the behaviour is within their control.

We conclude that the basic concepts, particularly the emphasis on biological processes, inherent in this model are insufficient to fully explain the role of psychological and social factors in the development and maintenance of sexually abusive behaviours.

The co-occurrence of other addictive behaviours has been examined, with the conclusion that this is not a major feature of sexual offending. Although alcohol can be an important antecedent for sexual offending, there is little evidence that this is dependent on an addictive process.

We have argued that the cognitive behavioural model of addiction is the more useful framework for understanding the 'addictive' aspects of sexual offending such as those highlighted by Salter (1989). She identified some core similarities between substance addiction and sexual offending behaviours, namely: (i) the immediate attainment of short-term positive consequences; (ii) delayed negative consequences; (iii) associated personal and social costs; (iv) difficulty in identifying specific, effective treatments; (v) the lack of unitary aetiological theories which have been satisfactorily validated; (vi) positive short-term treatment effects; and (vii) the difficulty in maintaining change on a long-term basis.

The most significant difference between the disease model and the cognitive-behavioural model is the emphasis placed on environmental, social and psychological influences by the latter. The cognitive-behavioural model is therefore more congruent with current knowledge about sexual offending (Laws & Marshall, 1990, Marshall & Barbaree, 1990) in terms of the role of learning processes, developmental issues, cognitive mediators of behaviour and broader influences on sexual behaviour. Such issues are of particular relevance to the majority of treatment programmes, based on cognitive-behavioural approaches, which have been supported by studies of effective treatment outcome. However, the inclusion of an increasingly wide range of influences into the sexual offending treatment field again demonstrates the limitations of early, learning-theory-based formulations of addictions as applied to sexual abuse.

We have also reviewed other influential models of sexual offending, primarily Finkelhor's four preconditions model. This would appear to have a specific role in providing a framework for treatment approaches and their evaluation, despite its arguably limited impact in academic and training circles (Howells, 1994). The differences between the models in their ability to describe and explain aspects of offending have been discussed and it is clear that the Finkelhor model is more closely related to the cognitive-behavioural addiction model. However, the Finkelhor model does appear to offer a fuller explanation of the whole *process* of offending and it is the only one in which the interaction between the offender and the victim is examined. Neither of the addiction models reviewed appears to define an equivalent social process.

While it is clear that concepts from the addictions field continue to have a major impact on our understanding and management of the problem of sexual offenders, the prevailing tendency appears to be to view sexual offending within an addictions framework without a clear definition of the limits and consequences of such a model. There are inherent problems in assuming a unitary cause or common 'disease' process for a range of ostensibly different sexual offences and offenders. It is clear that certain aspects of such an association have had positive consequences for treatment approaches, particularly in the development of behavioural modification techniques and relapse-prevention components and in the focus on a therapeutic rather than a simply punitive management strategy. However, it is also clear that some concepts conjured up by the notion of 'addiction' as used in the public arena may have a significant negative impact both in terms of the messages conveyed to offenders and in terms of limited empirical rigour. We conclude that it is important to offer clear definitions and to outline clearly conceptual limitations when considering the relationships of specific addiction models to aspects of sexual offending and perpetrators.

REFERENCES

Abel, G. G., Becker, J. V., Murphy, W. D. & Flanagan, B. (1981). Identifying dangerous child molesters. In R.B. Stuart (Ed.), *Violent Behaviour: Social Learning Approaches to Prediction, Management And Treatment*. New York: Brunner/Mazel.

Abel, G. G., Becker, J. V., Mittelman, M., Cunningham-Rathner, J., Rouleau, J. L. & Murphy, W. D. (1987). Self-reported sex crimes of non-incarcerated paraphiliacs. *Journal of Interpersonal Violence*, **2**, 3–25.

Abel, G. G., Becker, J. V., Murphy, W. D. & Flanagan, B. (1981). Identifying dangerous child molesters. In R.B. Stuart (Ed.), *Violent Behaviour: Social Learning Approaches to Prediction, Management And Treatment*. New York: Brunner/Mazel.

Abel, G. G., Becker, J. V. & Skinner, L. (1983). Behavioural approaches to treatment of the violent sex offender. In L. Roth (Ed.), *Clinical Treatment of the Violent Person*. Washington, DC: NIMH Monograph series.

Abel, G. G. & Blanchard, E. B. (1974) The role of fantasy in the treatment of sexual deviation. *Archives of General Psychiatry*, **30**, 467–475.

Bandura, A. (1977). *Social Learning Theory*. Englewood Cliffs, NJ: Prentice-Hall.

Beckett, R., Beech, A., Fisher, D. & Fordham, A.S. (1994) *Community-based treatment for sex offenders: An evaluation of seven treatment programmes*. A report for the Home Office by the STEP Team. London: Home Office Publications Unit.

Beech, H. R., Watts, F. & Poole, A. P. (1971) Classical conditioning of a sexual deviation: A preliminary note. *Behaviour Therapy*, **2**, 400–402.

Bell, C. M. & Khantzian, E. J. (1991). Contemporary psychodynamic perspectives and the disease concept of addiction: Complementary or competing models? *Psychiatric Annals*, **21**, 5.

Bownes, I. T. (1993). Sexual and relationship dysfunction in sexual offenders. *Sexual and Marital Therapy*, **8**, 157–165.

Cook, M. & Howells, K. (1981). *Adult Sexual Interest in Children*. London: Academic Press.

Davey, G. (1981) *Animal Learning and Conditioning*. London: Macmillan.

Davies, J. B. (1992). *The Myth of Addiction: An Application of the Psychological Theory of Attribution to Illicit Drug Use*. Reading, MA: Harwood Academic.

Davis, J. R. and Tunks, E. (1991). Environments and addiction: A proposed taxonomy. *International Journal of the Addictions*, **25**, 805–826.

Ellis, L. (1989). *Theories of Rape: Inquiries into the Causes of Sexual Aggression*. New York: Hemisphere Publishing.

Faller, K. C. (1991). *Polyincestuous families: An exploratory study. Journal of Interpersonal Violence*, **6**, 3, 310–322.

Finkelhor, D. (1984). *Child Sexual Abuse: New Theory and Research*. New York: Free Press.

Fisher, D. & Howells, K. (1993). Social relationships in sexual offenders. *Sexual and Marital Therapy*, **8**, 123–136.

Fisher, D. & Thornton, D. (1993). Assessing risk of re-offending in sexual offenders. *Journal of Mental Health*, **2**, 105–117.

George, W. H. & Marlatt, G. A. (1989). Introduction. In D.R. Laws *Relapse Prevention with Sex Offenders*. New York: Guilford Press.

Groth, A. N. (1978). Patterns of sexual assault against children and adolescents. In A. W. Burgess, A. N. Groth, L. L. Holmstrom & S. M. Sgroi (Eds), *Sexual Assault of Children and Adolescents*. Toronto: Lexington Books.

Hardy, K. (1964). An appetitional theory of sexual motivation. *Psychological Review*, **71**, 1–18.

Harris, M. B., Sutton, M., Kaufman, E. M. & Williamson-Carmichael, C. (1980). Correlates of success and retention in a multi-faceted, long-term behaviour modification program for obese adolescent girls. In W. R. Miller (Ed.), *Advances in Addictions Research, Addictive Behaviours*, **5**, 25–34.

Howells, K. (1979). Some meanings of children for paedophiles. In M. Cook & G. Wilson (Eds), *Love and Attraction*. Oxford: Pergamon.

Howells, K. (1981). Adult sexual interest in children: Considerations relevant to theories of aetiology. In M. Cook & K. Howells (Eds), *Adult Sexual interest in Children*. London: Academic Press.

Howells, K. (1994). Child sexual abuse: Finkelhor's precondition model revisited. *Psychology, Crime, and Law*, **1**, 201–214.

Knopp, F. H. (1984) *Retraining Adult Sex Offenders: Methods and Models*. New York: Safer Society Press.

Lane, S. & Zamora, P. (1984). A method for treating the adolescent sex offender. In R. Mathias, P. Demuro & R. Allinson (Eds), *Violent Juvenile Offenders*. San Francisco, CA: National Council on Crime and Delinquency.

Lanyon, R. I. (1991). Theories of sex offending. In C. R. Hollin & K. Howells (Eds), *Clinical Approaches To Sex Offenders And Their Victims*. Chichester: Wiley.

Laws, D. R. (1984) The assessment of dangerous sexual behavior in males. *Medicine and Law*, **3**, 127–140.

Laws, D. R. (Ed.) (1989). *Relapse Prevention with Sex Offenders*. New York: Guilford Press.

Laws, D. R. (1994). How dangerous are rapists to children? *Journal of Sexual Aggression*, **1**, 1–14.

Laws, D. R. & Marshall, W. L. (1990) A conditioning theory of the etiology and maintenance of deviant sexual preference. In W. L. Marshall, D. R. Laws & H. E. Barbaree (Eds), *Handbook of Sexual Assault: Issues, Theories and Treatment of the Offender*. New York: Plenum Press.

Laws, D. R. & Marshall, W. L. (1991). Masturbatory reconditioning with sexual deviates: An evaluative review. *Advances in Behavioral Research and Therapy*, **13**, 13–25.

Levine, M. P. & Troiden, R. R. (1988). The myth of sexual compulsivity. *Journal of Sex Research*, **25**, 347–363.

Longo, R. E. & Groth, A. N. (1983). Juvenile sex offences in the histories of adult rapists and child molesters. *International Journal of Offender Therapy and Comparative Criminology*, **27**, 150–155.

Maletzky, B. M. (1991). *Treating the Sexual Offender*. Beverly Hills, CA: Sage.

Marlatt, G. (1982). Relapse prevention: A self-control program for the treatment of addictive behaviours. In R. B. Stuart (Ed.), *Adherence, Compliance and Generalization in Behavioural Medicine*. New York: Brunel/Mazel.

Marques, J. K. & Nelson, C. (1989). Elements of high—risk situations for sex offenders. In D. R. Laws (Ed.), *Relapse Prevention with Sex Offenders*. New York: Guilford Press.

Marshall, W. L. & Barbaree, H. E. (1990). An integrated theory of the etiology of sexual offending. In W. L. Marshall, D. R. Laws & H. E. Barbaree, *Handbook of Sexual Assault: Issues, Theories and Treatment of the Offender*. New York: Plenum Press.

Marshall, W. L., Barbaree, H. E. & Butt, J. (1988). Sexual offenders against male children: Sexual preferences. *Behaviour Research and Therapy*, **26**, 499–511.

Marshall, W. L., Barbaree, H. E. & Christophe, D. (1986). Sexual offenders against female children: Sexual preferences for age of victims and type of behaviour. *Canadian Journal of Behavioral Science*, **18**, 424–439.

Marshall, W. L., Barbaree, H. E. & Eccles, A. (1991a). Early onset and deviant sexuality in child molesters. *Journal of Interpersonal Violence*, **6**, 323–336.

Marshall, W. L. & Eccles, A. (1991a). Issues in clinical practice with sex offenders. *Journal of Interpersonal Violence*, **6**, 68–93.

Marshall, W. L., Hudson, S. M. & Ward, T. (1991b). Sexual deviance. In D. H. Wilson (Ed.), *Principles and Practise of Relapse Prevention*. New York: Guilford Press.

Marshall, W. L., Jones, R., Ward, T., Johnston, P. & Barbaree, H. E. (1991c). Treatment outcome with sex offenders. *Clinical Psychology Review*, **11**, 465–485.

Marshall, W. L., Laws, D. R. & Barbaree, H. E. (1990). *Handbook of Sexual Assault: Issues, Theories and Treatment of the Offender*. New York: Plenum Press.

Marshall, W. L. & Pithers, W. D. (1994). A reconsideration of treatment outcomes with sex offenders. *Criminal Justice and Behavior*, **21**, 10–27.

McGuire, R. J., Carlisle, J. M. & Young, B. G. (1965). Sexual deviations as conditioned behaviour: A hypothesis. *Behaviour Research and Therapy*, **2**, 185–190.

Meichenbaum, D (1977). Cognitive-Behavior Modification. New York: Plenum Press

Nelson, C. & Jackson, P. (1989). High risk recognition: The cognitive-behavioural chain. In R. Laws (Ed.), *Relapse Prevention with Sex Offenders*. New York: Guilford Press.

Novaco, R. W. (1975). *Anger Control: The Development and Evaluation of an Experimental Treatment*. Lexington, MA: D.C. Heath.

Orford, J. (1985). *Excessive Appetites. A Psychological View of Addictions*. Chichester: Wiley.

Perkins, D. (1991). Clinical work with sex offenders in secure settings. In C. R. Hollin & K. Howells (Eds), *Clinical Approaches to Sex Offenders and their Victims*. Chichester: Wiley.

Pithers, W. D. (1990). Relapse Prevention with sexual aggressors: A method for maintaining therapeutic gain and enhancing external supervision. In W.L. Marshall, D. R. Laws & H. E. Barbaree (Eds), *Handbook of Sexual Assault: Issues, Theories and Treatment of the Offender*. New York: Plenum Press.

Pithers, W. D., Beal, L. S., Armstrong, J. & Petty, J. (1989). Identification of risk factors through clinical interviews and analysis of records. In R. Laws (Ed.), *Relapse Prevention with Sex Offenders*. New York: Guilford Press.

Pithers, W. D., Kashima, K. M., Cumming, G. F. & Beal, L. S. (1988). Relapse prevention: A method of enhancing maintenance of change in sex offenders. In A. Salter (Ed.), *Treating Child Sex Offenders and Victims: A Practical Guide*. Thousand Oaks, CA: Sage.

Pithers, W. D., Marques, J. K., Gibat, C. C. & Marlatt, G. A. (1983). Relapse prevention with sexual aggressives: A self-control model of treatment and the maintenance of change. In J. G. Greer & I. R. Stuart (Eds), *The Sexual Aggressor: Current Perspectives on Treatment*. New York: Van Nostrand Reinhold.

Quinsey, V. L. & Earls, C. M. (1990). The modification of sexual preferences. In W. L. Marshall, D. R. Laws & Barbaree, H. E. (Eds), *Handbook of Sexual Assault: Issues, Theories and Treatment of the Offender*. New York: Plenum Press.

Quinsey, V. L., Harris, G. T., Rice, M. E. & Lalumiere, M. L. (1993). Assessing treatment efficacy in outcome studies of sexual offenders. *Journal of Interpersonal Violence*, **8**, 512–523.

Rada, R. T. (1978). *Clinical Aspects of the Rapist*. New York: Grune & Stratton.

Ryan, G. D. (1987). Juvenile sex offenders: Development and correction. *Child Abuse and Neglect*, **11**, 385–395.

Sacks M. H. & Sachs, M. H. (1981). *Psychology of Running*. Champaign, IL; Human Kinetics.

Salter A. (1988). *Treating Child Sex Offenders and Victims*. Thousand Oaks, CA: Sage.

Schneider, J. P. & Schneider, B. H. (1990). Marital satisfaction during recovery from self-identified sexual addiction among bisexual men and their wives. *Journal of Sexual and Marital Therapy*, **16**, 230–250.

Segal, Z. V. & Marshall, W. L. (1985). Heterosexual social skills in a population of rapists and child molesters. *Journal of Consulting and Clinical Psychology*, **53**, 55–63.

Seligman, M. E. P. (1970) On the generality of the laws of learning. *Psychological Review*, **77**, 406–418.

Stermac, L. E., Segal, Z. & Gillis, R. (1990). Social and cultural factors in sexual assault. In W. L. Marshall, D. R. Laws & Barbaree, H. E. (Eds), *Handbook of Sexual Assault: Issues, Theories and Treatment of the Offender*. New York: Plenum Press.

Weinrott, M. R. & Saylor, M. (1991). Self-report of crimes committed by sex offenders. *Journal of Interpersonal Violence*, **6**, 286–300.

Wilson, G. T. (1991). The addiction model of eating disorders: A critical analysis. *Advances in Behavioral Research and Therapy*, **13**, 27–72.

Wolf, S. (1984). A multi-factorial model of Deviant Sexuality. Paper presented at the 3rd International Conference on Victimology, Lisbon, Portugal.

Yates. E., Barbaree, H. E. & Marshall, W. L. (1984). Anger and deviant sexual arousal. *Behaviour Therapy*, **15**, 287–294.

CHAPTER 5

Addictions and Multiple Murder: A Behavioural Perspective

David M. Gresswell

Lincoln District Healthcare NHS Trust & Rampton Hospital

and

Clive R. Hollin

University of Leicester & Rampton Hospital

Traditionally, multiple murderers have been said to have an obsession with killing in the sense of having a persistent preoccupation with murder and sadistic fantasy. In a similar vein, they have been said to have a compulsion to kill having an inner drive that causes them to kill repetitively, usually against their will (Danto, 1982; Revitch, 1965). However, the implications of using labels such as obsession or compulsion in terms of psychological processes or psychiatric diagnoses have not been fully explored. The position is very similar when the use of the term 'addiction' is considered in association with multiple murder: the idea of an addiction is generally not developed further than using the term as a shorthand expression for an excessive attachment to violence and violent fantasy. However, as Gresswell (1991) has noted, addiction-based models of behaviour, such as Brown's (1987, 1988) psychologically

Addicted to Crime? Edited by J.E. Hodge, M. McMurran and C.R. Hollin.
© 1997 John Wiley & Sons Ltd.

centred model developed from work with gambling addicts, can usefully be applied to the experiences of some multiple homicide perpetrators. In this chapter the core features of a psychological model of addiction will be described in relation to multiple murder, and then discussed and illustrated with examples from the literature and our own current research into multiple murder. Two case studies also drawn from our current research are presented to illustrate the process by which a killer can be shown to develop the behavioural features of addiction. These case studies illustrate how the principles derived from a psychologically centred model of addictions can be usefully applied to increase our understanding of the aetiology of some multiple murderers.

It could be argued that the adoption of a psychologically centred model of addiction is doing no more than describing a cluster of behavioural patterns, maintaining factors, and associated emotional experiences that can equally well be explained by conventional learning-based models. However, the addiction model would seem to apply to a minority of cases we have studied and there is considerable room to speculate that we are describing a specific phenomenon and one that certainly merits further investigation. The implications of a psychologically centred model of addictions for the identification, treatment, and management of this type of offender are discussed.

MULTIPLE MURDER PERPETRATORS

Multiple murderers are commonly classified under three headings: these are *mass-*, *spree-*, and *serial-murder*. *Mass-murder* involves the taking of several lives (usually three or more) in the same place at the same time. In *spree-murder*, several victims are killed over a longer time period in different locations. With both mass- and spree-murder the killer appears to act impulsively, kills in a frenzy, and makes little attempt to evade detection. By contrast the central feature of *serial-murder* is its planned repetition, often over a long period of time.

We will suggest that concepts from addiction models can be usefully applied to develop accounts of all three forms of multiple homicide. However, before taking this step it is worth briefly considering the existing literature on multiple murder.

Despite a large literature on homicide there have been comparatively few articles on the subject of multiple murder. Indeed, until the 1980s there were few systematic studies of multiple homicide perpetrators and even the more ambitious modern studies

(Holmes & De Burger, 1988; Levin & Fox, 1985; Leyton, 1987) have tended to rely on secondary sources of information such as trial transcripts, newspaper articles, and criminal records. The only large-scale published systematic study involving interviews with perpetrators was carried out by the FBI Behavioural Science Unit. This study was conducted with 36 sexually motivated killers of whom 29 had more than one victim (Ressler et al., 1988). A smaller study by Lunde and Siegal (1990) considers 30 perpetrators, but only 10 through the use of direct interview.

Bearing in mind the limitations of the data, a survey of the literature on multiple murderers reveals a high prevalence of case histories characterised by childhood traumas such as sexual abuse, brutal beatings and abandonment, and problems such as a failure of empathic bonding with parents, bedwetting, firesetting and torturing animals (Ansevics & Doweiko, 1991; Burgess et al., 1986; Levin & Fox, 1985; Norris, 1990). In later life, multiple murderers show a tendency to depersonalise other people (particularly victims), a pervasive sense of isolation and alienation, a lack of acquired inhibitions against violence, and a belief that violence against others is legitimate (Burgess et al., 1986; Ressler et al., 1986). However, as we have previously observed (Gresswell & Hollin, 1994), none of these factors are unique to multiple homicide perpetrators.

When considering sadistic offenders, those who take pleasure in the inflicting of pain and humiliation on victims but who do not necessarily kill, several accounts have stressed the role of fantasy both as a precursor to offending, and as a means by which sadistic offenders cope with life's pressures (Brittain, 1967; MacCulloch et al., 1983; Prentky et al., 1989; Ressler et al., 1988). Brittain (1967) suggested that many sadists have a rich fantasy life that involves imagining their own and other's sadistic acts. More recently, MacCulloch et al. (1983) examined 16 patients detained with a diagnosis of psychopathic disorder in a maximum security mental hospital. They found that the sadistic behaviour of 13 of these patients was explicable only in terms of 'internal circumstances'. This group of patients had a history of habitual use of sadistic sexual fantasies, often used during masturbation; several had acted out elements or sequences of these fantasies prior to committing their sadistic offences. Prentky et al. (1989) also found an association between fantasy and serial sexual murder. They compared 25 serial sexual murderers with 17 single sexual murderers: 86% of the multiple killers disclosed a history of violent fantasy compared to 23% of the single murderers. The use of fantasy and acting out parts of fantasies ('try-outs') can provide the potential perpetrator with intense changes in subjective excitement, physiological arousal and affective reactions. Fantasy provides both pleasurable sensation and relief from aversive emotional states. It can be argued that such physiological and psychological changes may serve the function of maintaining fantasy and try-out behaviours in the absence of other more obvious reinforcers such as sexual activity.

MODELS OF ADDICTION AND MULTIPLE MURDER

At face value, some multiple murderers appear to have features in common with some addicts, notably gambling addicts, and there may be a case for considering the experiences of this group of offenders in terms of a habit or addiction disorder. In considering the application of an addiction model to multiple murder we have drawn upon the work of Brown (1986, 1987, Chapter 1 this volume) who has offered a psychological model for non-substance-based addiction; the model of behaviour developed by Skinner (1974); and on our own research involving a study of nearly 64% ($n = 37$) of all cases of multiple homicide recorded in England and Wales between 1982 and 1991.

Non-Substance-Based Addiction

There is evidence that changes in 'excitement', as measured by subjective ratings and changes in physiological arousal indicated by increases in heart rate, are associated with some forms of gambling. Anderson and Brown (1984) have put forward the hypothesis that such psychological processes may contribute as significantly as instrumental forces to the development of gambling addictions. They suggest that 'arousal and excitement are major mediators of reinforcement and internal cues for gambling behaviour, especially for regular gamblers. Pathological gamblers may become addicted to their own arousal and its physical and psychological effects' (p. 406).

For Brown (1988) the key feature of addiction is activity that has 'strong and immediate effects on hedonic tone, often through altering arousal' (p. 4). Addictive behaviours are thus seen as attempts both to experience pleasure and to escape from the aversive realities of everyday life. Engagement in homicidal fantasy, trial runs and murder may have a similar function for many perpetrators: that is they are activities rewarded by sexual pleasure and a positive feeling of power and control while simultaneously shifting attention from aversive experience. In behavioural terms they are both positively and negatively reinforced.

Brown (1987) has also observed that: 'Many gamblers are trying to repeat a never forgotten "peak experience", perhaps of a big win after a long series of losses or quite often of the special feelings which accompanied their first big win' (p. 117). This description sounds very similar to the experiences of some sadistic offenders and multiple murderers who engage in 'trial runs' in an attempt to make real experience match fantasy. Prentky et al. (1989) have observed that sadistic offenders often aim to make reality match an idealised fantasy murder but, since the match can never be quite perfect, the reality is never quite as satisfying as the fantasies promise. The reinforcing effects of engagement in fantasy enactments and offending are therefore likely to be intense but short-term and, in behavioural terms, give rise to variable-ratio, or intermittent, schedules of reinforcement. According to Skinner (1974) intermittent schedules of reinforcement are those 'in which reinforcement occurs after a given average number of responses but in which the next response to be reinforced cannot be predicted' (p. 60) and that 'it is a characteristic of intermittent reinforcement that behaviour may be sustained over long periods with very little return' (p. 61). These intermittent schedules are likely to make behaviour resistant to extinction and susceptible to reinstatement and are the basis of all gambling systems.

When considering covert behavioural patterns such as repetitive engagement in escapist fantasy it could be anticipated that the consequences of such activities, since they do not lie within the real world, will be subjectively different from the internal/private experiences of a person 'addicted' to an overt activity or substance. With a substance addiction, for example, an addict could in principle manipulate effects of drugs to help cope with any situation up to the point of unconsciousness or lack of awareness. (Although after a time it is possible that due to tolerance effects extreme highs may not be possible or affordable and drugs may be used for maintenance.) With a covert behavioural or private fantasy addiction it would be predicted that there will come a point where such a degree of tolerance is reached that further incorporation of fantasy material no longer enhances arousal or produces the desired changes in attention, arousal, or environment. If this point occurs then the behaviour will fail to achieve the degree of reinforcement required and the individual will, in effect, be on an 'extinction schedule'. Such schedules are generally not advised in clinical practice with potentially dangerous behaviours such as parasuicide or aggressive behaviours because of the risk of a 'post-extinction burst'. A post-extinction burst is a well-documented behavioural phenomenon where individuals increase the frequency or intensity of their behaviour in an effort to obtain the withdrawn reinforcement.

When considering this aspect of behavioural theory and applying it to someone with a dependency on fantasy, it would be expected that any environmental changes that restrict access to reinforcement contingent on the addictive behaviour would in effect place that individual on an extinction schedule. Similarly, when the individual has reached the peak of the utility of their fantasy then this too would have the effect of an extinction schedule with a consequent risk of 'burst' phenomena. The effect of such a schedule could thus be expected to include both a weakening of inhibitions against overt aggression and a decrease in the strength of the triggers necessary to overcome existing inhibitions. In the case of a person with murderous escapist fantasies but with strong inhibitions against overt aggression then presumably any 'post-extinction bursts' would be contained and not result in overt aggressive behaviour. The fantasising or try-outs will become extinct and be dropped from the person's behavioural repertoire, perhaps with a subjective experience of loss of power, disappointment, or deep depression. However, in the case of a person with weakened inhibitions against aggressing the 'burst' would almost certainly involve acting out part or all of the fantasy, in other words progression to murder.

Given the comparisons above, we suggest that there are parallels worth exploring between the experiences of gamblers and of multiple homicide perpetrators. A psychological model of addictions may be particularly useful in explaining the mechanism by which fantasies and try-outs are maintained in the absence of sexual reinforcement, and ultimately facilitate predictions of when overt fantasy enactments are most probable. Thus if some multiple murderers are addicted to aggression it is as likely that they are addicted to fantasy and try-outs and the associated levels of arousal as to murderous acts themselves.

Describing Addiction Variables within a Population of Multiple Murderers

For Brown (1988), addictions are activities intended to produce changes in affect and physiological arousal. As outlined in Table 5.1 they have the core psychological components of salience, conflict, tolerance, withdrawal effects, relief, and relapses.

When the literature on multiple homicide perpetrators is examined all of the features of addiction described by Brown can be found.

Table 5.1. Checklist of the common components of addictions (Brown, 1988)

Salience:
  The addictive activity becomes the most important thing in the person's
  life and dominates thinking (preoccupations and cognitive distortions),
  feeling (craving) and behaviour (deterioration of socialised behaviour)

Conflict:
  Disputes over the extent of the excessive behaviour arise both between the
  addicted person and others around him and within the addicted person
  themselves. Continual choosing of short–term pleasure and relief leads to
  disregard of adverse consequences and long–term damage which in turn
  increases the apparent need for the addictive activity as a coping strategy

Tolerance:
  Increasing amounts of the addictive activity are required to achieve the
  former effects

Withdrawals:
  Unpleasant feelings and/or physical effects when the addictive activity is
  discontinued or suddenly reduced

Relief:
  The effects of the addictive activity are so powerful that there is a rebound
  effect when it ceases (withdrawals) and when it is over the only way to
  avoid feeling more miserable than before (to find relief) is to do it again at
  the earliest opportunity

Relapse and Reinstatement:
  Tendency for repeated reversions to earlier patterns of addictive behaviour
  to reoccur and for even the most extreme patterns typical of the height of
  the addiction to be quickly restored even after many years of abstinence

These components are discussed below with respect to multiple
homicide perpetrators. It will be noted that we include as addictive
activities not only the murderous behaviour itself, but also engagement in fantasy and acting out sequences of established fantasies. It
is likely that if some multiple murderers do have an addiction it will
be to the activities that support killing as much as to the act of
murder itself.

Salience

For many multiple homicide perpetrators the behaviours surrounding
their offences have become salient in the sense that many hours are
spent in fantasy, 'try-outs', acquiring weapons, selecting victims and
locations, 'environmental grooming', i.e. preparing the environment
for an offence, offending, and following their cases in the media.
Great risks are taken to act out elements of the fantasies which are

often developed at the expense of more prosocial activities. Jeffrey Dahmer, an American serial killer (quoted by Masters, 1993, p. 148), offers a good description of this phenomenon:

> Nothing else gave me pleasure towards the end, nothing, not the normal things, especially near the end when things just started piling up, person after person, during the last six months. I could not get pleasure from going out to eat, I just felt very empty, frustrated, and driven to continue doing it. None of these are excuses for what I did, but those are the feelings I had in those last months, really intensive. For some reason I just kept doing it. I knew my job was in jeopardy around February. All I would have had to do was just stop for several months at a time and space it out, but it didn't happen that way. I was just driven to do it more frequently and more frequently until it was just too much—complete overload. I couldn't control it any more.

Conflict

Some offenders do appear to feel conflict and some describe feelings of revulsion and guilt after they have killed. Ressler et al. (1988, p.57) quote one murderer from their sample who said:

> It blew my mind killing those people. I wasn't ready for that. The fantasies were there, but I couldn't handle the death trip and the dead bodies. I freaked out and gave myself up.

Gary Long and Henry Lee Lucas, two American multiple murderers, both with victim totals in double figures, are also documented as having experienced 'conflict'. While serving sentences for other offences both asked not to be paroled and complained to prison and medical authorities that they they felt themselves to be dangerous and likely to kill again if released (Norris, 1990).

Tolerance

There appears to be evidence of increasing tolerance in this population, for example MacCulloch et al. (1983) found clear evidence of a progression in the fantasies of 9 of the 16 sadistic offenders they studied. Several of these offenders stated that their fantasies were continuously changed in order to maintain their efficiency as a source of arousal and pleasure. This increase in the power of fantasies was accomplished by increasing the sadistic content and including new material based on overt enactments and rehearsals of the main fantasy sequence.

Withdrawal

Although withdrawal experiences have not been looked for in this group, Revitch (1965, p. 642) cites Krafft-Ebbing (1934) who reported the case of a man who stabbed women in the genitals:

> For a while he succeeded in mastering his morbid cravings, but this produced feelings of anxiety and perspiration would break out on his entire body.

This description is reminiscent of the withdrawal effects described by some substance addicts.

Relief

It appears that for some multiple murderers killing and associated behaviours may be negatively reinforced by the termination of unpleasant feelings of intense frustrating sexual arousal subsequent to killing. For others, however, killing and associated activities may be their primary strategy for relieving such negative affective states as the experience of powerlessness, anger, or frustration. Norris (1990, p. 143) cites the case of multiple rapist and murderer Gary Long, who provides an illustration of both relief and tolerance phenomenon:

> And after each crime he felt more depressed because he could not recover the feelings of sexual passion that had driven him to commit the crime.

Relapses

Repetition is clearly a feature of this type of offending; however, there are accounts in the literature of individuals who have tried to stop killing but failed.

> With each subsequent victim, picked up in exactly the same way in one of the singles bars, he became more and more depressed. He knew he was sick and needed help, yet he could not stop himself. When he tried to prevent himself from going out, he became so aroused that when he surrendered to the urgings he was more violent than he had been previously. (Norris 1990, p. 143)

In total, the picture that emerges is of an individual who may have failed to achieve normal socialisation, and who is likely to have a well-rehearsed set of violent and/or sadistic fantasies. These fantasies are used both to escape the aversive realities of everyday life (often at the expense of the development of other prosocial coping mechanisms) and to enhance sexual pleasure. He may have a history of acting out sequences of his fantasies. In addition he has a developing and self-maintaining set of beliefs that legitimise and normalise his violence and sadism. The same processes that support these beliefs may also be eroding any acquired constraints against killing.

These processes may be viewed in terms of a psychological addiction with six key features, i.e. salience, conflict, tolerance, withdrawals, relief and relapse/reinstatement. We suggest that individuals with these characteristics have a substantially increased potential for committing murder. Within a behavioural model, however, it would be hypothesised that this potential will be triggered into overt action by a combination of either an extinction experience, the appropriate environmental triggers, or a combination of the two.

In drawing together the ideas described above and considering a population of killers and potential killers the following eight features could be expected in someone who could reasonably be described as having an addiction to multiple murder:

1. Fantasy, try-outs or acts of aggression have become *salient* and dominate the person's life.
2. The person should experience *conflict* about their behaviour.
3. There should be evidence of *tolerance* phenomena, such as use of increasingly sadistic fantasy.
4. *If* the person has attempted to stop the addictive behaviour there should be some evidence of *withdrawal* effects.
5. There may be evidence of *relapse* phenomenon.
6. The addictive activity should provide *relief* from negative mood states.
7. Specific *triggers* for the first homicidal sequence should be evident.
8. Triggers would be most likely to elicit overt aggression in the context of the addictive activity being on an *extinction schedule*.

In the course of our current research into multiple murder we have identified two men who have all these features. We present their cases below.

TWO ILLUSTRATIVE CASE STUDIES OF MURDERERS WITH ADDICTIVE PATTERNS

In our current research we have attempted a psychological examination and description of every case of multiple homicide recorded in England between 1982 and 1991. The research involves examination of official case material on 64% ($n = 37$) of cases involving three or more killings, including interviews with 20 imprisoned perpetrators.

In addition data were collected on a further three serial killers (two by direct interview), and two further cases of men who have features in common with multiple killers. In drawing on our research we will first illustrate the types of processes of interest with two case studies. The first case is that of a man convicted of 6 murders and 2 attempted murders, although he has admitted to a total of 15 murders and 4 attempts. The second case, which is examined in more detail, is that of a man who is convicted of one murder but who claims to have enjoyed the experience so much that he spends all his time fantasising about killing again. In describing these cases we shall use the functional analysis methodology on which our research is based (Gresswell & Hollin, 1992) to show the progression to a possible addicted state. This methodology involves breaking down complex case material into meaningful 'chunks' that are further broken down into antecedent events, 'A', that are triggers for the behaviour. The behaviour, 'B', is further divided into covert behaviours, such as thinking and feeling, and directly observable overt behaviours. Finally the environmental consequences, 'C', which follow the behaviour complete the sequence.

Case 1

Dennis Nilsen

During the course of participating in the current research Nilsen, an intelligent and insightful man, spontaneously described himself as having a compulsion to kill and as being addicted to the behaviours surrounding the murders. His opinions therefore shed a useful light on the phenomenon in question. When questioned on what he might be addicted to Nilsen's view was: 'the whole passion of the ritual; a synthetic courtship ritual'. The major components of the ritual reported by Nilsen were heavy drinking, smoking, food, emotive music, and either a search for sexual partners or, if he did not go out, an elaborate fantasy involving sexual activity with a passive (dead) and anonymous male. This ritual activity allowed him to become 'very focused for the evening with the excitement'. When engaged in this intensely arousing activity he was distracted from everyday problems: 'when Brando did "Superman" he wasn't thinking of "The Godfather": all extraneous detail was blocked out'. The information included is based primarily on over 8 hours of interviews with Nilsen (by DMG), examination of official documentation, and discussion of his case with other informed professionals including his biographer Brian Masters. All quotations included in this chapter are drawn from those interviews. It should be noted that the version of events that Nilsen currently offers is somewhat 'rosier' than that offered to Masters and is probably due to the period of time he has had to consider his position, having been imprisoned for nearly 10 years at the time of the current series of interviews.

Nilsen describes his mother as cold and secretive, and claims to be unable to recall her ever offering him physical comfort. He never met his father, and is certain that he does not share the same father as his older brother and sister. When his mother remarried it was to a man employed as a council roadman, to whom Nilsen never felt close and quickly came to look down on. The strongest male influence in Nilsen's life was his maternal grandfather who died when Nilsen was only 5 years old and whom Nilsen saw laid out in his coffin. The image of his dead grandfather was a powerful one that stuck in Nilsen's mind.

In describing his early life Nilsen stresses feelings of being different from others, and while denying that he was as isolated as other accounts of his life would indicate, he admits to having been aloof and introverted. He had developed an ability to withdraw into fantasy from an early age and claims a phenomenal ability to create wholly absorbing mental images. This ability was nurtured by access to the cinema and has led to a lifelong interest in film and photography. As he progressed into adolescence Nilsen became increasingly aware of homosexual feelings which increased his sense of being different. During his adolescence his sexual experience was reportedly, however, largely restricted to fondling the genitals of his passive sleeping brother with whom he shared a bed. Possibly as a result of this limited experience, perhaps combined with the powerful image of his dead grandfather laid out in his coffin, Nilsen reports that his favoured sexual fantasy came to revolve around thoughts of a passive, unresponsive, perhaps dead, partner. Nilsen reported that he would imagine himself both in the passive and in the active roles: for example, imagining himself to be both a man who finds a perfect dead body and has sex with it and himself as the body itself.

At the age of 15 years he joined the army and thus completed the first stage that we have described in Table 5.2.

Although Nilsen had some homosexual partners while in the army, especially while serving abroad and towards the end of his career, he had difficulty in forming close emotional relationships. His favoured fantasy of the passive dead man became further elaborated and he began to enhance its effectiveness by using his own body suitably made up to simulate a corpse as a 'prop' and often masturbated while observing his reflection in a mirror. While in the army he also

Table 5.2. Stage 1: Childhood experiences: Age 0–15 years

A: Cold, secretive, dominant mother, absent father, weak step–father
   Death of grandfather at 5 years old.

B/Covert: Dependence on fantasy for relief of negative mood states
   Feelings of being intellectually superior to peers, having more drive and
   flair
   Developing homosexual feelings makes him feel different from family and
   peers
   Developed fantasy of passive/dead sexual partner

B/Overt: Homosexual contact with brother
   Development of lifelong interest in cinema and fantasy images
   Becomes increasingly aloof
   Joins army as a boy soldier to escape restrictions of home village

C: Becomes increasingly at odds and isolated from community
   Army life provides relief and distraction

Key learning: (1) He is different
           (2) He can use fantasy as an effective escape strategy from
                aversive situations
           (3) Sexual fantasy of passive, dead partner is most arousing

developed a pattern of heavy drinking which he claims few of his colleagues could match. Over time the pressures of living in the army as a covert homosexual became too great and Nilsen left, subsequently joining the police, which he found to be equally 'homophobic' at that time. After a year he left the police and was unemployed for some time before he found work as a civil servant in the Department of Employment, thus completing stage 2 described in Table 5.3.

In the Civil Service Nilsen also found himself not fully accepted, with no close friends and often at odds with the system. He developed a role for himself as a trade union shop steward but became increasingly frustrated by the apathy of the bulk of the membership. Perhaps as a result of his manner, sexuality, or union activities he felt himself passed over for promotion and became increasingly frustrated at work.

By that time Nilsen had established a pattern of 'cruising' gay pubs, drinking heavily and picking up strangers for sexual contacts. On one of these nights he met the man with whom he would live for nearly two years. 'Twinkle', also a homosexual, was the passive recipient of Nilsen's sexual advances and over the duration of this relationship Nilsen claims that he rarely if ever used the 'passive' fantasy. After two years Nilsen and 'Twinkle' drifted apart and he found himself increasingly lonely and isolated. The relationships he

Table 5.3. Early adult experiences: Age 16–30 years

A: Sequences as in stage 1
  Failure of relationship with other men
  Disciplinary charge as a result of sexual activity
  'Homophobia' in the police

B/Covert: Dependence on fantasy for relief of negative mood states
  Further development of fantasy based on passive/dead sexual partner

B/Overt: Homosexual contacts
  Begins acting out elements of fantasy using own body as a prop
  Begins pattern of heavy drinking
  Leaves army and joins police, leaves police and joins civil service

C: Disciplined for 'entertaining civilian personnel'
  Increasingly a loner in the army and isolated, introverted in the police
  Arrested for indecent assault

Key learning: (1) Has problems forming equal relationships with others
              (2) Strengthening of tendency to use fantasy as an effective
                  escape strategy from aversive situations
              (3) Sexual fantasy of passive, dead partner is most arousing

formed with the men he met at pubs and brought home were always short lived, unsuccessful emotionally and sometimes no sex occurred. On several occasions Nilsen woke to find that he had been robbed by one of his pick-ups. This phase of Nilsen's life left him with increasing feelings of depression which he increasingly relieved by use of drink, cruising and the passive sexual fantasy. It would appear that by this stage, described in Table 5.4, Nilsen was becoming increasingly dependent on one means of short-term relief from negative mood states; he was possibly in the early stages of an addiction.

With a behavioural model, a specific trigger or set of triggers would be seen as antecedent to the homicidal behaviour. These triggers began to occur around late December 1978, as outlined in Table 5.5.

The winter of 1978/79 has been described as 'the winter of discontent' and certainly Nilsen, became increasingly depressed and pessimistic about the British political scene. On a more personal level, the office, his major source of personal contact and support, was closed and he had been lonely and depressed over Christmas. His fantasies and rituals had only provided him with limited relief and the prospect of a lonely New Year's Eve was looming. In order to relieve his feelings Nilsen, as had become his habit, went out cruising and drinking and met a young man who was willing to come home with him. After more heavy drinking it came to Nilsen that this partner would leave him as the others had. In the circumstances this

Table 5.4. Before the murders: Age 31–32 years

A: Sequences as in stage 2
   Not accepted by peers in civil service
   Meets long–standing partner

B/Covert: Protective arrogant belief system maintained
   Increasingly frustrated by inability to motivate union colleagues
   Less use of passive partner fantasy while in relationship
   Increasing feelings of depression, isolation and alienation

B/Overt: Heavy drinking continues
   Establishes pattern of cruising gay bars picking up men for casual sex
   Develops job as union representative

C: Others relate to him in friendly but superficial way
   Passed over for promotion
   Long–standing partner leaves
   Is robbed by several sexual partners

Key learning: (1) Increasing sense of pessimism about forming meaningful
                  relationships
              (2) Increasingly reliant on highly arousing ritual involving
                  alcohol and passive fantasy to distract from negative mood
                  states

Table 5.5. The first murder sequence: Age 33 years

A: Sequences as in stage 3
   'Winter of discontent'
   Office closed for Christmas break
   New Year's Eve looming
   Meets victim who agrees to come home with him

B/Covert: Intense feelings of loneliness and depression
   Fantasy ritual provides only partial relief
   Dread of being abandoned again over the New Year

B/Overt: Goes to bed without sex
   Strangles victim
   Acts out fantasy with body with only limited satisfaction

C: Murder undiscovered and unnoticed
   Body starts to deteriorate

Key learning: (1) He has killed without being discovered
              (2) Acting out fantasy with real body not totally satisfactory

was more than he could bear and he killed the young man. The next
day on waking to the horror of what he had done he initially
panicked, but with his crime undiscovered, and despite his vow that
nothing like this should happen again, he could not resist the

temptation to act out part of his fantasy with the corpse. This was only partly satisfying to him as the real body was not warm and pleasant as it was in fantasy but cold and decaying.

Eventually he hid the body under his floor and promised himself that the episode would not be repeated.

Within the year Nilsen had killed again and he admitted to committing a further seven (in the original police interviews he said ten) murders of young men before he left his flat in late 1981. These further killings took place with much greater rapidity, occurring in a period of a little over 18 months. The victims were young men he met in bars, mainly young down-and-outs, some homosexual, some that Nilsen felt attracted to and others that he did not. At least one appears to have been killed because he was an annoyance rather than as a part of the ritual. It is not necessary for the purposes of this chapter to describe those events in detail (for a fuller account see Masters, 1985). We will therefore pick up the story from the time Nilsen moved to his new flat in October 1981. These events are described in, Table 5.6. By the time Nilsen moved to his new flat he had killed at least nine men. He had decided on at least three occasions to stop killing: once after the first murder; once after he disposed of a collection of bodies towards the middle of the killing sequence; and finally when he disposed of the last few bodies in a

Table 5.6. The last three murders: Age 36–37 years.

A: Sequences as in stage 4
    Further 11 murders
    Disposal of bodies
    Pressured to leave old flat
    Given promotion

B/Covert: Decision to stop killing and start afresh
    When at work constantly wanting to get back to fantasy life, ritual still established
    Ritual provides intense excitement and stimulation
    Increasing feelings of boredom and depression

B/Overt: Gives up union business
    Moves to new flat
    Kills three more times
    Difficulties in disposing of bodies

C: Drains become blocked with remains of victims
    Murders discovered and Nilsen arrested

Key learning: (1) Unable to cope without ritual
          (2) Acceptance of self as compulsive killer

bonfire and moved out to his new place, hoping for a fresh start. He had at last been promoted at work but had given up his union activities, unable to resolve the conflict between the the morality of that area of his life and the immorality of his killings.

Despite his good intentions he continued to feel depressed and isolated, and at work found himself constantly wanting to get back home to the escapist world of his fantasies and rituals. Perhaps inevitably given his state of mind he had, within 5 months, killed again, and went on to kill two more men and to attempt to kill a further two before being arrested after blocking drains with pieces of his victims' bodies that he had attempted to flush down the toilet.

In considering how Nilsen talked about these events in the interviews, the experiences he describes appear to fulfil all of Brown's core features of addiction. In addition, the first murder can be seen to have specific triggers (failure at work, isolation from colleagues over the Christmas break and New Year looming), and to be in the context of his fantasy ritual being on an extinction schedule: by Christmas 1978 the ritual was no longer powerful enough to distract from the overwhelming negative mood states he was experiencing at the time. We have therefore revisited Brown's core features of addiction in the light of Nilsen's interviews.

Salience. During the course of interviews with DMG Nilsen said that he only indulged in his ritual perhaps once or twice a month: it was not 'every Friday night but was episodic'. Nilsen also said he retained other interests such as his love of movies, talking to people in pubs, listening to Brian Hayes on LBC, and his trade union activities. Prior to the first murder and during the early stages of his homicidal career the ritual does not therefore appear to meet the criterion for salience. Nevertheless, Nilsen does appear to have used the ritual as a major means of manipulating his mood. Towards the end of his homicidal career, however, the other activities began to drop away, he spent less time with colleagues and gave up his union activities, unable to reconcile them with his killing. In the months before his arrest Nilsen said that he was 'so wedded to the fantasy that reality felt like fantasy. It distorted perception; the fantasy was constantly available and always in mind'.

Conflict. In describing his own reactions to the murders Nilsen made a number of comments that indicated he was experiencing conflict: 'I had destroyed myself as a good and moral person'; 'after the first one I knew I was a "murderer" and that was more important than whether others knew'.

He also had 'to give up the union business because it made [him] feel like a moral hypocrite'. He could not 'claim the moral high ground' when he had 'the bodies [of his victims] at home'. He only recaptured that feeling of morality again when he made a full confession.

Nilsen knew he would get caught when neighbours called for a plumber to clean out drains blocked with human flesh cut from his victims. He realised he could 'either run, fight or do nothing' and made a half-hearted attempt to cover it up but then went out and got drunk. He did 'not regret being caught—it would have gone on and on'.

Tolerance. Nilsen has described how he had to use his own body suitably made up to look like a corpse because of his need to 'accentuate the fantasy'. He stated more explicitly that: 'Focusing on fantasy, murder, was a way of coping with depression: like a drug I needed more and more of.'

Withdrawals. It is less clear whether Nilsen experienced withdrawal, for example, when he was arrested and stopped from killing. Certainly he appears to have engaged in a good deal of substitute behaviour, writing furiously and filling many exercise books for his biographer, Brian Masters. Nilsen has also had notoriety and attention since his capture, if not the approval of inmates, and much attention in the press which he finds hard to resist. He receives 'fan-mail' so it is possible that the needs that drove his fantasy are being met elsewhere.

Nilsen says that he has never used the fantasy of the dead young man while in prison. Firstly because suddenly 'everyone knew about them: having written them down they cease to be another world. It's like being in a house in the pitch black, the imagination runs wild, every sound takes on significance. Flick the switch—the lights come on: four walls. In writing down what happened to me what I was doing was switching the light on. Everything was suddenly then exposed and ceased'.

Relief. Nilsen says that he made 'heavy use of fantasy even when a child'. The development of the fantasy: 'Met my escape needs—displacement into fantasy: if I couldn't meet my needs in the relationship I could in fantasy.'

Nilsen again offers some insight into the feelings from which relief is sought and the sort of ways in which relief is achieved. In particular relief from feelings of: 'Weakness, the need to be potent.'

In a period of happiness between 1975 and 1978, when living with his partner nicknamed 'Twinkle', he never needed the fantasies.

However, from 1978 to 1981 'I only saw the woman next door three times', and he felt isolated and lonely. In 1978 during 'the winter of discontent' his partner had left, he was lonely with no flatmate, and he had a desolate Christmas, seeing no one as the office was closed. He spent most of the holiday drinking and watching movies. It was during this period that he committed the first murder.

There were other areas of his life that Nilsen reported to be unsatisfactory. He wanted recognition and attention, 'I have a desperate need for people to say "that's good"'. He would get a 'buzz' out of the recognition and appreciation that he got for his cooking in the army: after leaving he never bothered to cook for himself. He felt the other members of the union were not really interested in what he was trying to do for them and that they were content for him to do everything. He did not feel valued by them. He felt he was passed over for promotion because of his sexuality and became increasingly bitter. He needed the ritual particularly at the weekend to help him face 'the Friday night prospect of the long weekend'.

However, all these problems seemed insignificant in comparison with the 'problem' of committing the murders: 'I'm not suicidal, I'm homicidal.' After the first murder he felt isolated and 'totally insecure', while matters were compounded by fear of the 'embarrassment' of someone finding the bodies: 'what are they going to think of me?'.

Relapse and Reinstatement. Nilsen made at least three unsuccessful attempts to stop killing. The first after killing his first victim, the second after disposing of some of the bodies, and the third after moving to a new flat. Nilsen reported that he had attempted to stop after the horror of the first murder but could not resist the temptation to use the body as a prop for his masturbatory fantasy. He also made an attempt to make a new start after he burned the bodies he had stored up and then later, after he moved to a new flat, but on each occasion there were further murders.

Nilsen thus constitutes a case of a convicted multiple murderer who has not only described himself as being addicted but can be shown to have all the features that we have argued should be present.

Case 2

This is the case of a young man who killed one person and claims to have enjoyed the experience so much that he would like to repeat it. He is similar to Nilsen in that both enjoy their notoriety, but is different in other respects. Nilsen does not relish talking about his killings in the way that 'Paul' does. Paul also has a far more overtly disturbed background than Nilsen and was witness to many acts of violence. He perpetrated many violent acts before killing his first victim which, he says was a deliberate and planned act. This case is therefore used here as a contrast to the case of Dennis Nilsen (and also illustrates a person at a much earlier stage of an offending career). Paul was interviewed while still experiencing the processes we were investigating rather than looking back on them as Nilsen was.

The information in this analysis was obtained from an interview lasting approximately three hours, from study of his case file, and discussion with those involved with managing his case. At the time of interview this man was thought to be so dangerous that he was contained on the segregation unit of a maximum security prison and the first author was only permitted to interview him under conditions of the highest security.

Early Experiences

Paul describes a highly charged emotional atmosphere at home. He describes his real father as an entertainer who always left the family short of money and who was subject to mood swings, womanising, violent tempers, street fighting, and religious fervours. In their first house his father would catch mice and burn them alive over the fire. After Paul's parents separated his mother remarried. However, Paul's step-father had a serious drink problem and would frequently beat up his mother, always locking the children out of the house before he began. When his step-father also eventually left, his real father returned to the home briefly but then moved out again, leaving Paul hurt, angry, and wanting revenge for the perceived betrayal.

At school Paul was a small boy; quiet, timid and often bullied by his peers he frequently suffered the humiliation of running away from fights. Throughout his childhood he felt an increasing sense of anger and hostility to those around him which he took out on animals. He described how, from at the age of 11 years, he enjoyed watching worms wriggling when he put them through his grandmother's mangle; at age 13 years he stoned to death a pet rabbit to watch it die, and crushed toads with bricks. Paul reported in the interview that he had 'seen violence as a kid [at home, in the street] and I've grown up feeling that violence is a natural thing. I've got a right.'

Adolescence

At the age of 15 years, after his father had left for the second time, he acted out his revengeful fantasies for the first time: he waited outside a pub where his father, a club entertainer, was doing his act, intending to kill him with a baseball bat. His mother found him and persuaded him that it was not worth it. At around the same age he joined a gang of skinheads and, egged on by his friends, attacked an older bigger boy who had been teasing him, for the first time won a fight, and had the satisfaction of seeing his victim knocked to the ground. These events form the sequences outlined in Table 5.7 and hence the first antecedent event described in Table 5.8.

Winning this fight altered Paul's life. Although it was several months before his next fight, he felt a sense of empowerment he had never previously experienced. The second fight was not, he says, started by him but again involved two gangs; yet again Paul came out on top and 'things accelerated again'. From then on he would join in fights whenever possible and would start them deliberately. He would enjoy fighting even if he lost or came off badly. For him fighting 'was like taking drugs [he] got a buzz out of it [and] felt excited and good'. Paul also said that it 'would make me feel good to see someone on the floor with his nose bleeding thinking that I did that. It put me on a high and I would feel good about myself.'

Table 5.7. Childhood experiences: Age 0–15 years.

A: Father's changes of mood and sadistic acts
   Step–father's violence towards mother
   Bullied by peers while at school
   Father returns to live at home then leaves

B/Covert: Belief that violence is natural
   Feelings of being vulnerable and weak
   Broods on revengeful fantasies after being bullied and victimised
   Fantasises about killing father

B/Overt: Quiet and timid at school
   Sadistic acts towards animals
   Waits for father outside pub with baseball bat
   Has to walk away from fights
   Joins 'skinhead' gang

C: Gang cheer him on to fight with older, bigger youth

Key learning: (1) Violence is natural
           (2) Use of sadistic revengeful fantasies helps overcome feelings of being victimised

Table 5.8. Adolescent experiences: Age 15–20 years.

A: Sequences as in stage 1

B/covert: Sense of empowerment at having won fights
  Feelings of intense satisfaction if he can knock someone to floor
  Depression if goes out and cannot engineer a fight
  Develops exciting fantasy life as gangster

B/Overt: Engages in fights
  Beats up wife if unable to have pub fight
  Supports fantasy with clothes, books, weapons and associated violence
  Commits armed robbery

C: Increased status amongst friends
  Compared to Ronnie Kray by some friends
  Arrested and imprisoned for armed robbery
  Dramatic loss of status (in prison)

At the beginning he was also able to go out for a drink without fighting. He had always wanted a wife and baby, and was pleased when he got a girlfriend whom he married and had a child. However, although he was first able to show and give them affection he found that he lost interest. Instead he was going out more and more looking for fights and found himself feeling annoyed if he got home without having had one, a situation that would put him in a bad mood. His relationship with his wife deteriorated, not least because if he had not had a fight in a pub he would come and start on her or smash up the house. Paul says that his friends stuck with him but they found themselves having many evenings ruined by his aggression and violence.

At home he spent increasing amounts of time reading and watching videos about violent men and criminal gangs. He was particularly fascinated by the Kray brothers and read all he could about them: he bought clothes so he could dress like them, collected knives and airguns, and carried a cut-throat razor. As he spent more and more time fantasising about these men so he increasingly liked the idea of leaving his mundane job in a laundry and becoming a 'proper criminal'. He persuaded a friend to join in an armed robbery of the fish and chip shop where his friend's girlfriend worked and used one of his air pistols to intimidate the staff.

The robbery was not a success as his friend's girlfriend recognised their voices and they were soon arrested. Paul was sentenced to prison, not as a supercriminal but as just another prisoner amongst a group which contained the far more serious and competent villains whom he fantasised joining. The incompetence of his first crime did little to increase the esteem in which he was held by the other prisoners or prison staff: the major and unexpected loss of status he experienced forms the final component in the sequences described in Table 5.8.

The events and processes experienced by Paul thus far have several of the features of an addiction. The violence and fantasies of being a criminal, supported by collections of clothing, reading materials, videos and weapons which helped him to imitate his heroes the Krays, had become *salient* and were indulged in at the expense of almost all other means of gaining satisfaction. His extreme behaviour was leading him into *conflict* with the law, with his friends, and with his family. There is also evidence of *tolerance* phenomena with him needing more and more violence to maintain his excitement and image. *Withdrawal* effects are also apparent in the anger and annoyance he felt if he returned home without having had a fight. Similarly it can be seen that his violence and fantasies were providing him with *relief* from the negative mood states and low self-esteem arising from his early childhood. *Relapse and reinstatement* phenomena are not relevant here as Paul has made no attempt to give up his activities. In addition, his fantasising and pretending to be a supercriminal and violent man was no longer being rewarded in prison, and he was in effect on an extinction schedule. We describe below the triggers that led to the murder.

Imprisonment and Murder

On the night before Paul killed his victim he had decided to kill another prisoner—a man he felt had been staring at him. However, on reflection he thought that if he killed another prisoner then the other men might gang up on him and exclude him: having been out of the group before this was something he could not tolerate occurring again. The idea of killing someone was nevertheless present and appealed to him as a means of increasing his status and making himself more like the Krays, who had both killed. Since he was frightened of the repercussions of killing a fellow prisoner, he decided to kill a member of staff, and focused on a civilian worker who led the work party that he was attached to. Paul had previously tried to impress the worker by describing his violent behaviour prior to his imprisonment. However, according to Paul, the man had been unimpressed and told him he was a 'nutter' who 'should be in Broadmoor hospital': Paul found this response unsatisfactory and insulting. That night Paul says that he could hardly sleep with the excitement of his plan: the next day when the opportunity presented itself he took a hammer and beat his victim to death. Afterwards, while waiting for other officers to arrive, he remembers feeling 'strong like a giant'. He was subsequently convicted of murder and sentenced to life imprisonment. These events form the sequences in Table 5.9.

Table 5.9. Stage 3: Imprisonment and murder: Age 21 years

A: Sequences as in stage 2
  Treated as ordinary prisoner
  Murder victim says he should be in Broadmoor
  Victim leaves toolbox open

B/Covert: Experiences loss of status
  Plans methods to increase status, decides to kill
  Plans to kill fellow inmate then decides on victim

B/Overt: Attacks and kills prison worker
  Talks about enjoying killing and wanting to kill again

C: Convicted of murder
  Given category 'A' status; treated as highly dangerous

When interviewed, Paul said that he now spends most of his time in his cell fantasising about murder. Such fantasies provide him with high states of arousal and in the year since he killed his victim he has found that he will occasionally get an erection when immersed in such fantasy. He said he would prefer to kill his next victim by torturing them to death with a blowtorch but recognises that this would be impractical in prison, he would be content therefore just to kill someone quickly. His ambition is to become a serial killer and the Krays have to some extent been dropped from his fantasies in favour of the fictional character 'Hannibal Lecter', the homicidal psychiatrist featured in the novels *Red Dragon* and *Silence of the Lambs*. He does not expect to be released from gaol but has heard there are two 'cages' in British prisons and would enjoy the status of being incarcerated in one of those. At the time of interview he was receiving little by way of therapy as he has identified psychologists as 'soft targets' and as his likely next victims.

CONCLUSIONS

All the core features predicted from a psychologically centred model of addictions can be found in the literature on multiple murder. Furthermore, examination of a sample of 22 English murderers interviewed for the purposes of our own research into multiple murder revealed two men who fit this model. Examination of these cases can be shown to confirm our predictions that the addiction in such cases is likely to be to fantasy or overt enactments of fantasy. These elements of fantasy are associated with major changes in arousal and affect and provide both pleasure and relief from negative aversive mood states.

It can thus be seen that there are examples that illustrate the key features of addiction that Brown has described. These illustrations also indicate the type of experiences that should be looked for in an individual who may be 'addicted'. While the role of addiction in multiple homicide offending is necessarily speculative at present, there appear to be sufficient parallels to make further investigation worthwhile.

Clearly a model that may account for only a small number of individuals within a very small population, has limited utility as an aid to prediction. Nevertheless, application of the addiction model draws attention to such processes as tolerance phenomena and the possible role of extinction schedules in the timing of overt offending. These processes have to date not yet been thoroughly explored in psychological approaches to offending. Applying an addiction model to serious repetitive offending behaviours therefore has the potential to be more than just an interesting exercise. Analyses of the type reported here could have repercussions for understanding, prediction, early intervention, and treatment of other less serious forms of violent behaviour.

REFERENCES

Anderson, G. & Brown, R. I. F. (1984). Real and laboratory gambling, sensation-seeking and arousal. *British Journal of Psychology*, **75**, 402–410.

Ansevics, N. L. & Doweiko, H. E. (1991). Serial murderers: Early proposed developmental model and typology. *Psychotherapy in Private Practice*, **9**, 107–122.

Brittain, R. P. (1967). The sadistic murderer. *Medicine, Science and the Law*, **10**, 198–207.

Brown, R. I. F. (1986). Arousal and sensation seeking in the general explanation of gambling and gambling addictions. *International Journal of Addictions*, **41**, 1001–1016.

Brown, R. I. F. (1987). Classical and operant paradigms in the management of gambling addictions. *Behavioural Psychotherapy*, **15**, 111–122.

Brown, R. I. F. (1988). Gambling addictions: Commonalities and peculiarities. Implications for a value-free and psychologically centred concept of addiction. Paper presented to the Scottish Branch of The British Psychological Society, University of Strathclyde, Glasgow.

Burgess, A. W., Hartman, C. R., Ressler, R. K., Douglas, J. E. & McCormack, A. (1986). Sexual homicide: A motivational model. *Journal of Interpersonal Violence*, **1**, 251–272.

Danto, B. L. (1982). A psychiatric view of those who kill. In B. L. Danto, J. Bruhns & A. H. Kutscher (Eds), *The Human Side of Homicide* (pp. 3–20). New York: Columbia University Press.

Gresswell, D. M. (1991). Psychological models of addiction and the origins and maintenance of multiple murder. In M. McMurran & C. McDougall (Eds), *Proceedings of the First DCLP Annual Conference*, Vol. 2. Leicester: The British Psychological Society.

Gresswell, D. M. & Hollin, C. R. (1992). Towards a new methodology for making sense of case material: An illustrative case involving attempted multiple murder. *Criminal Behaviour and Mental Health*, **2**, 329–341.

Gresswell, D. M. & Hollin, C. R. (1994). Multiple murder: A review. *British Journal of Criminology*, **34**, 1–14.

Holmes, R. M. & De Burger, J. (1988). *Serial Murder*. Newbury Park, CA: Sage.

Krafft-Ebbing, R. von (1934). *Psychopathia Sexualis*, trs. F. J. Rebman. New York: Physicians' and Surgeons' Book Co.

Levin, J. & Fox, J. A. (1985). *Mass Murder: America's Growing Menace*. New York: Plenum Press.

Leyton, E. (1987). *Hunting Humans: The Rise of the Modern Multiple Murderer*. Harmondsworth: Penguin Books.

Lunde, D. T. & Siegal, H. (1990). Multiple victim killers. In R. Bluglass & P. Bowden (Eds), *Principles and Practice of Forensic Psychiatry* (pp. 625–30). Edinburgh: Churchill Livingstone.

MacCulloch, M. J., Snowden, P. R., Wood, P. J. W. & Mills, H. E. (1983). Sadistic fantasy, sadistic behaviour and offending. *British Journal of Psychiatry*, **4**, 20–29.

Masters, B. (1985). *Killing for Company: The Case of Dennis Nilsen*. London: Jonathan Cape.

Masters, B. (1993). *The Shrine of Jeffrey Dahmer*. London: Hodder & Stoughton.

Norris, J. (1990). *Serial Killers*. London: Arrow.

Prentky, R. A., Burgess, A. W., Rokous, F., Lee, A., Hartman, C., Ressler, R. & Douglas, J. (1989). The presumptive role of fantasy in serial sexual homicide. *American Journal of Psychiatry*, **146**, 887–891.

Ressler, R. K., Burgess, A. W. & Douglas, J. E. (1988). *Sexual Homicide: Patterns and Motives*. Lexington, MA: Lexington Books.

Ressler, R. K., Burgess, A. W., Douglas, J. E., Hartman, C. R. & D'Agostino, R. B. (1986). Sexual killers and their victims: Identifying patterns through crime scene analysis. *Journal of Interpersonal Violence*, **1**, 288–308.

Revitch, E. (1965). Sex murder and the potential sex murderer. *Diseases of the Nervous System*, **26**, 640–646.

Skinner, B. F. (1974). *About Behaviourism*. London: Jonathan Cape.

CHAPTER 6

Joy-Riding: An Addictive Behaviour

Rosemary Kilpatrick
Queen's University of Belfast

Given the extent of motor-related crime in contemporary Britain and the serious consequences of the offence the sociological and psychological literature on the topic is surprisingly limited. There has been little significant work on the subject and much of the recently published material on joy-riding is through investigative journalism and the media. The available research that there is has been conducted primarily by the Home Office Research Unit (e.g. Houghton, 1991; Light et al., 1993), crime prevention organisations (most notably EXTERN in Northern Ireland), and Probation Boards in England, Wales and Northern Ireland. There is also a smattering of unpublished postgraduate theses examining various aspects of car theft.

Legally the crime of car theft covers two broad categories of offences:

1. theft of a motor vehicle where the intention is to permanently deprive the rightful owner (e.g. where the thief plans to resell the vehicle for profit); and
2. theft of a motor vehicle where the car is stolen for temporary use and is usually recovered within 30 days after being stolen.

This latter offence is referred to in England and Wales as 'Taking Without the Owner's Consent' (TWOC) and in Northern Ireland as

Addicted to Crime? Edited by J.E. Hodge, M. McMurran and C.R. Hollin.
© 1997 John Wiley & Sons Ltd.

'Taking and Driving Away' (TADA). While the legislation and courts do distinguish between the two offences, with TWOC (TADA) being considered the less serious, official statistics do not.

As with the crime of car theft the car thieves themselves can be divided into two groups, though these are not mutually exclusive. Firstly, those who steal with a view to reselling the car for permanent use, sometimes referred to as the 'professional' car thieves, and those who steal for temporary use, commonly known as joy-riders. It is this latter group that is the focus of this chapter.

CAR CRIME IN NORTHERN IRELAND

Overall Northern Ireland has a much lower crime rate than Great Britain and car theft in England and Wales is twice as high as in Northern Ireland, though levels of car crime continue to rise throughout the United Kingdom.

Out of a total of 2983 cars stolen in Northern Ireland in one year over half (56.9%) were stolen in the city of Belfast, and particularly South Belfast, an affluent area which encompasses a university campus, a business and commercial sector, a residential sector and an entertainment sector. At all times of the day and night high-performance cars, which are most popular models with the car thief (Houghton, 1991), are parked in this area which makes it a Mecca for the joy-rider.

Recovery rate for stolen cars is high and nearly all vehicles (85%) are recovered within one or two days of being stolen. Two-thirds of these cars are found in West Belfast and the surrounding area and in one week over 60 stolen cars can be recovered in this part of the city. Furthermore, in almost one-third of these crimes the thief was apprehended and in more than 90% of the crimes which were 'cleared up' the offender was living in West Belfast. The pattern which emerges from this information would suggest that many of the car thieves in Belfast steal vehicles from outside their own home area and then bring them back to that area, abandoning them close to where they live.

It is important here to draw the reader's attention to the fact that the studies on which the above information is based were published in 1990 (McCullough et al.) and 1992 (Sandby-Thomas) with the actual research being conducted prior to publication. While the pattern remains the same there will, naturally, be some variation in the actual figures quoted and it has been suggested that the advent of the cease-fire in the sectarian strife in the province resulted in a reduction in car theft.

COURT DISPOSALS

The courts in England and Wales and in Northern Ireland have a variety of disposals available to them when convicting individuals found guilty of a criminal act, including car-related offences. These disposals range from conditional discharges through to fines, probation orders and custodial sentences. A further disposal available in Northern Ireland when convicting juveniles is that of the Training School Order (TSO). Training schools provide residential accommodation for young people between the ages of 10 to 16 years placed there by means of a Court Order for either care or justice reasons, each group being accommodated separately. Training School Orders for Justice provide for a maximum period of two years detention. The young person may be released by the Training School after six months on licence or before that with the approval of the Secretary of State. In 1991 in Northern Ireland TSOs were the most frequently used disposal for the 14–16 year old convicted of car-related offences (Marks & Cross, 1992).

CAR THIEVES

The studies of car thieves that have been conducted tend to concentrate on young offenders who have usually been apprehended for offences of car crime, an easier sample to locate than those who have not been caught. They mostly focus on the where, why and how of car crime and many have come up with similar findings. Five of the studies most relevant to the current paper have been carried out in Sunderland (Spencer, 1992), Greater Manchester (Smyth, 1990), Northumbria (Briggs, 1991; Gulliver, 1991) and Belfast (McCullough et al., 1990). There has also been a comprehensive study by Light et al. (1993), in which car thieves from five geographical areas in England and Wales were interviewed.

While these studies were spread throughout the United Kingdom there was a certain degree of consistency in the reported findings and a profile of the car thief can therefore be drawn together. Invariably the car thief is male and generally comes from a socially deprived inner city area, where the population is overwhelmingly working class and both poverty and unemployment are high. Generally speaking he will be within the 12 to 21 age range though he may be as young as 11 and as old as 35; the average age will be 15–16 years. When actually stealing cars it is unusual for a car thief to work on his own, and there is some suggestion of gaining status and identity through the group. These teenagers have commonly severed their ties with any form of formal education; very rarely will they have any formal qualifications and few will have any experience of employment outside of Government Training Schemes. For most their aspirations for the future will be very conventional and when asked about this, car thieves usually see themselves as getting a job, being married, settling down and having children.

Reasons for car theft consistently have an excitement component as well as being a means of gaining status and identity. These psychological motivators were frequently combined with financial gain. These were very strong influences that resisted not only the danger of accidents and of being apprehended by the police, but also the threat of paramilitary punishment in Northern Ireland.

Of particular interest in the Belfast study (McCullough et al., 1990) was the joy-riders' sense of their own identity. They see themselves as 'joy-riders' and are often proud of that fact. Although involved in regular criminal activity many would strongly resent being classified as 'hoods', i.e. young men who are involved in a wide range of illegal activities such as house-breaking, and this sense of identity is strongly reinforced by their treatment. They are isolated within their own community and are frequently the subject of paramilitary punishments, which range from warnings to 'placarding' (where the joy-rider is forced to stand outside the local shops with a placard saying 'joy-rider' around his neck), to severe gunshot wounds, including knee-capping (now the most frequent punishment for persistent offenders), to being ordered out of the country (to remain means death). Such punishments often provoke an angry reaction from the joy-riders and may lead to greater cohesion in the group.

CAR THIEF'S CAREER

The studies on which the above profile is based outline the activities of an extremely wide age range of young people; while there is a degree of consistency in the findings it is also important to note that even within each study there was some variation and car thieves could not be described as a homogeneous group. This was true particularly when the motivation for car crime was considered. Here, while some of the respondents appeared to be involved in car theft purely for profit and could be described as 'professional car thieves', others indicated that they were solely involved in car theft for the excitement and thrill of it.

This difference in motivation was clearly identified by two quotes from a study by McAuley (1989):

> Hell of a lot excitement driving down the road at 100 mph; definitely exciting. (Joy-rider, 17 years)
>
> Stealing's our work—we'll only stop if we get jobs. (Joy-rider, 18 years)

McCorry and Morrissey (1989), in their description of car theft in West Belfast, argue that there is a continuum of joy-riding during which those involved are liable to move from psychological satisfactions (e.g. thrills, adventure) to seeking economic gain—a move from what they describe as 'expressive' to 'instrumental' delinquency. Discussion with these authors led Kilpatrick (1988) to describe this continuum as follows:

> In West Belfast experience of stolen cars begins at an early age. Children playing in the street will be aware of the excitement in the area as a stolen car is raced about. Eventually the cars are dumped and stripped or burnt out, becoming temporary playgrounds for children. However, often stolen cars which have been abandoned in an estate will be taken by youngsters and driven around. This is probably how most young people, perhaps at the age of ten or eleven, get their first taste of being driven in, and eventually of driving a stolen car. The next step, once the skills of driving have been acquired by trial and error, is to steal a car for yourself. Here a new set of skills are learned, breaking into and starting the engine of a car. Young people, once they have acquired these skills, may continue stealing and racing cars to a lesser or greater extent. Accompanying the stealing of cars will be the selling of parts. Some of these young people will become serious and extremely persistent joy-riders while others may simply be on the periphery of the activity. Most of the serious joy-riders will reach a turning point in their careers in their early twenties. While a proportion of them graduate to a criminal career the majority of them are absorbed back into the community through relationships and marriage or employment.

This description is very similar to that outlined more recently by Light et al. (1993) who refer to 'an apprenticeship' in car theft.

These studies indicate that as car crime careers progress the opportunity for financial gain begins to feature more prominently in motivation for offending, though excitement is clearly still a factor. Thus it would appear that many of the older 'professional' car thieves began their delinquent career as joy-riders who stole cars with no intention of permanently depriving their owner, but then progressed on to 'instrumental delinquency'.

JOY-RIDING AND ADDICTION

The suggestion of a career in car crime may help to explain the progressive nature of joy-riding but it does not provide any enlightenment into the question as to why some adolescents try the activity and then stop, why some continue in the activity on a casual basis, and why some appear to be extremely attracted to the experience and become persistent joy-riders. Light et al. (1993), while indicating that it is important to proceed with caution, suggest that the combination of what is perceived as unlimited opportunity and personal gratification seems to lead to a degree of offending that may be described as more compulsive in nature than is the case with other acquisitive crimes. Of their sample, 41% felt that being 'hooked' on cars was a possibility, and over a third said that nothing felt as good as stealing cars, with a further quarter saying that only the effect of drugs was comparable.

This notion of joy-riding as an extremely compulsive or addictive behaviour goes beyond the traditional idea of addiction being a physiological dependency on substances which have addictive properties, such as alcohol or heroin. Recent psychological work on non-substance addictions, for example gambling, sexual behaviour and overeating, led Orford (1985) to argue against the definition of addiction as a disease, and to suggest that it is rather an excessive, appetitive behaviour that is oriented towards a psychologically based rather than a physiologically based model.

Drawing on the problem behaviour theory of Jessor and Jessor (1977), Orford suggests that the degree of a person's involvement in an addictive activity has multiple interacting determinants within both the personal and social domains. These include features of personality but some of the strongest determinants will be social or ecological, including the availability of opportunities for the activity and the normative influence of friends. Orford stresses that this does not imply an additive model but that personal factors interact with the social context in which the behaviour occurs, and there are thus different pathways to addiction. Engaging in the appetitive behaviour can serve numerous personal functions for different individuals, and even within the same person. These include forms of mood modification, which links into the work of Brown (see Chapter 1, this volume), as well as the enabling of many different forms of self-expression and the enhancing of many different kinds of self-identity (Peele, 1985). Orford further suggests that a longitudinal perspective is vital for understanding appetitive behaviour since changes in behaviour are the rule rather than the exception, and frequently occur as part of a developmentally normal change in a whole constellation of attitudes, experiences, values and activities.

Within the field of psychiatry and clinical psychology there is general agreement that there are common characteristics of addiction to psychoactive substances on which diagnosis by one of the several systems of classification can be based. Hodge (1991) expands this notion and argues that these characteristics would also be found in psychological addictions. These common characteristics are as follows:

1. Tolerance—the need for more to produce the same effect
2. Salience—increasing importance of addiction in lifestyle
3. Conflict—increasing awareness of negative consequences
4. Withdrawal—distress after a period of non-engagement
5. Craving—distress associated with desire to re-engage
6. Relapse—reinstatement after decision to stop or reduce.

There is some recent evidence that some of the above characteristics may be present in joy-riders. Reeves (1993) considered the prevalence of car crime amongst incarcerated young offenders between the ages of 15 and 21 years. She examined her data for evidence to indicate that car crime should be regarded as a compulsion or addiction in its own right and found some support for this argument. There was some indication that there was a group of emotional motivations (i.e. buzz, excitement) for car crime, some of which were significantly related to higher rates of car offences. The results, however, did not indicate a clear-cut addicted group though this study was a quantitative one with closed questions and was not specifically designed to examine addiction to car crime.

McCorry (1992) conducted an exploratory study to consider whether persistent joy-riders displayed the six characteristics of addiction outlined above and concluded that joy-riding can become an addiction. However, this study, like that of Reeves, used highly structured questionnaires which failed truly to assess any of the addictive characteristics. Having said this it was a useful base for the present in-depth study.

THE STUDY

The above theories move addiction from the traditional clinical or disease model, which has tended to focus more narrowly upon aspects of individual personality which were thought to promote addictions, into a clearly identifiable form of social learning theory which allows social and ecological variables to have a role. The study described in this chapter examined persistent joy-riders to consider their behaviour within this framework. It addressed the following questions:

1. What are the personal functions served by joy-riding?
2. What is the social context in which joy-riding occurs?
3. Is there are evidence of the six characteristics of addiction (given above) in joy-riders?

The sample consisted of 15 juvenile offenders who had been placed in St Patrick's Training School, Belfast, for one or more car-related offences during the period of the research (January–May 1994). The range of offences included: taking and driving away; allowing self to be carried in a stolen car, theft of goods from a car, careless driving; reckless driving; driving without licence; driving without insurance; going equipped when related to car offences (e.g. carrying a screwdriver or other means of breaking into a vehicle). In each case the young person had committed several of these offences and the fact that he had been given a custodial sentence indicated that he had a fairly extensive criminal record. The criminal record for each individual was also checked to ensure that the young person had been primarily involved in car-related crime and could be described as a persistent joy-rider.

All the individuals who were placed in St Patrick's Training School during the research period and who met the criteria were invited to take part in the study, with no refusals. A semi-structured interview schedule designed to collect a range of information relating to the above questions was administered and responses were tape-recorded. Prior to the interview the purpose of the research (i.e. to find out more about joy-riding) was explained to the respondents and the confidentiality of the material assured. All of the young men spoke openly and freely in the interview situation, and though some accounts of certain incidents were most probably embellished and inflated, they did provide a good insight into the individual processes of becoming involved in car-related crime.

Several reasons determined the selection of a qualitative approach to this research, there being three major ones. Firstly, the topic under investigation was the processes involved in joy-riding, not the measurement of numbers of young people engaged in the activity or how many offences they had committed; it therefore required a technique where the researcher could explore and probe an individual's responses in depth. Secondly, previous researchers in this area (e.g. Reeves, 1993; McCorry, 1992) had both pointed to the limitations of structured questionnaires when investigating this topic and had suggested that more qualitative research is required to help interpret and further illuminate the whole question of joy-riding and addiction. Finally, the research population was not only extremely small, but also somewhat difficult to locate and this, as Walker (1985) suggests, lessens concern about representativeness and inference and tips the balance away from quantification.

PROFILE OF THE SAMPLE

Of the group, seven came from intact families where both parents were living together, and four came from homes where their parents had separated and they were living with one parent. The remaining four had all been living with extended family before being admitted to training school. This placement with extended family had been due to a variety of reasons including abuse by the parents and problem drinking. Of those who came from intact families, eight had at least one parent who was working (six fathers were working and two mothers worked where the father was unemployed). All of the sample came from families where they had two or more siblings and were variously placed in the family. Four had brothers who had been involved in joy-riding and four others had siblings who had been involved in some other form of criminal activity. Two of the boys were 17 years (having been placed in Training School before their seventeenth birthday), six were 16 years, four were 15 years and the remaining three 14 years of age.

PERSONAL FUNCTIONS SERVED BY JOY-RIDING

There was a considerable degree of consistency when the responses to questions assessing the personal functions served by joy-riding were considered. The most frequently used words to describe the good things about joy-riding were 'the buzz' and 'the excitement'. The vast majority of respondents also mentioned feeling scared when they first stole cars or raced them and several indicated how they still felt scared when being chased. Many described the mixture of nerves and excitement which they experienced, especially when racing or being chased. However, it was interesting to note that going looking for chases with the police was not as common as might have been anticipated and typical responses here were as follows:

> Sometimes we would go looking for a chase but the peelers don't always chase you anyway—it really depends on who you're with but definitely not unless you're with a good driver and in a fast car so you know you'll get away.

> Sometimes we would go looking for a chase, but not always—no
> way—anything can go wrong in a chase—it's stupid going and looking
> for them; but it's exciting when they happen.

Thus it would appear that it is not the excitement of the chase that is
the priority but rather the thrill of racing and flying around with
one's peers. This general sense of excitement appears to be increased
by the crowds standing on the roadside watching. This feeling, or
heightened sense of arousal, can also be generated by just cruising
around:

> Cruising around—that feels really good cruising's better than
> racing—just cruising around all day—the freedom of it—it's just really
> good.

The other very consistent response to these questions was the
status associated with joy-riding and the sense of 'showing off', which
was a frequently used phrase in this context:

> It's exciting racing with your mates and flying round—it makes you
> feel good but the best thing is showing off.

> Showing off—that makes me feel good—it's great when someone says 'I
> saw you in that Cosworth you had—it was a cracker'.

There was clear evidence that for this group of young men joy-riding
provided them with an intense emotional experience which also could
be used to manipulate emotional arousal. The intensity of the
experience was also very apparent in the accompanying facial
expressions and other non-verbal communication throughout the
interviews.

While all of the sample mentioned such personal functions it is
important to note that they also referred to financial rewards to be
gained as a result of stealing cars, though these appeared to be
secondary in importance. These findings are remarkably consistent
with those reported in other offender studies (e.g. Spencer, 1992;
Light et al., 1993).

Peele (1985) argues that these intense emotional experiences are
associated with an enhanced sense of control, power and self-
esteem, all of which were evident: the control over the car, the sense
of power when driving the car and the enhanced status, were all
frequently mentioned as the positive consequences of joy-riding.
Brown's theory that addiction is to a behaviour which can be used to
manipulate emotional arousal is less readily assessed by verbal
responses. However, here again it could be argued that the continued use of words which refer to such arousal must be supportive
of the theory.

THE SOCIAL CONTEXT IN WHICH JOY-RIDING OCCURS

Peer influence clearly played an important part in joy-riding activities, and this did not come solely from other joy-riders. Many of the sample talked about the image and status that they gained from joy-riding and how this came from the on-lookers and bystanders.

Everyone sees you in a stolen car especially the girls—being able to show off—it makes you feel superior.

There was, of course, peer influence from other joy-riders as well:

It's like a big game—who can get the biggest and the fastest—as you get better the crack gets better and it gets more and more competitive—you've got to keep up your image.

For those who wanted to give up joy-riding the pressure from other joy-riders and the wider group was particularly difficult to handle:

Seeing the others doing it [joy-riding], and they're always on at me—sometimes I think I'll just give in and go back to it.

Every respondent indicated that they rarely, if ever, stole alone. Sometimes they would be driving alone but this usually happened only if they were bringing a stolen car back into the neighbourhood. This situation would occur when a group of two or three had gone to steal a car, and perhaps had decided to take two, resulting in one person returning by themselves. Part of the 'crack' was being in the group. Most of the sample also indicated that solvents and drink were closely associated with stealing cars, and as one respondent indicated:

When you've been sniffing or drinking it's easier because you don't worry about being caught or anything.

The daily pattern seemed to vary depending on time of year (they would steal more in the summer time) and time of day. Some stealing seemed to be very opportunistic, for example:

I was just walking down the streets with my mates—we were bored—and someone said 'come on let's get a car' so we went to the shopping centre.

Some thefts however, appeared to be planned:

We took a black taxi out to Carryduff—it's good for cars—and took a couple there and then just cruised around.

For most respondents stealing cars was an everyday occurrence:

It's an everyday thing—after lunch I'd call into Belfast and get a car ... most probably keep it for the evening if it was good. The days we don't take cars we're catching up on the sleep we lost cruising around.

Two of the respondents reported that their parents or family did not seem to be particularly concerned about their joy-riding activities. However, for the remainder of those who lived with their family, all referred to the high degree of concern and worry that their activities brought to the home. Parents were usually reported to be worried while siblings, if not involved in car crime themselves, tended to be described as angry and/or embarrassed. Sometimes the worst thing about joy-riding was: 'getting caught by my parents', 'the hassle from my parents'; as well as: 'the worry I cause my family', 'when my Mum cracks up—that makes me feel bad'.

All of the sample also indicated the ease with which they could steal most cars: 'no car's impossible to steal—some are just more difficult than others'. Opportunities to steal were numerous. One respondent, when asked if he ever stole alone said:

> Yes, but not often—but sometimes it's just too tempting like when I was walking along the Lisburn Road and there was this car sitting there with its keys in it.

While most of the respondents indicated that alarms were a deterrent, everyone claimed that they could break into any car. Indeed, for some a new model of a car was almost a challenge, and a high degree of status accompanied being the first in an area to bring that new model into the neighbourhood. Throughout the interviews there was a strong sense of the importance of the social context within which joy-riding took place, and both immediate peers and the wider group had a major role to play here. The positive attitudes and benefits accrued as a result of this seemed to outweigh the negative consequences and attitudes of families, a finding supported by other studies (e.g. Briggs, 1991).

In examining the effect the social context has on drug consumption it has been argued that the taking of drugs can be described as constituting, on occasions, a 'group entry' requirement (Stone et al., 1984). Further, the socialisation process of the group can shape and direct a wide variety of behaviour, and as the influence of parents wanes that of the peer group increases (Raistrick & Davidson, 1985). These authors continue by stating that redefinition will almost invariably run contrary to the establishment view and such a change will be optimised if the individual views his peers as a credible and acceptable reference group. Such a group can direct, at least in part, the individual's orientation and view of the world. While this description of the process of group identification applies to becoming involved in drug consumption, the evidence from the present study suggests it could just as readily apply to how young men become involved in joy-riding.

Another aspect of the social context which is referred to frequently in relation to drug addiction is that of initial availability of the substance ingested (Raistrick & Davidson, 1985). All of the young men interviewed indicated how easy it was to steal a car. Furthermore, the beginning of a career in joy-riding has been identified as being closely related to the opportunity to travel in, and drive, cars stolen by others and brought into the neighbourhood (Kilpatrick, 1988).

Problem-behaviour theorists (e.g. Jessor & Jessor, 1977) suggest a cluster of antisocial behaviours including delinquency, problem drinking and illicit drug use in adolescents. The young men in this study engaged in all these behaviours, (solvent abuse being equated with illicit drug use), and Reeves (1993) similarly reports 'clusters' of problem behaviours in young men committed to a Young Offenders Centre in England. Social learning through the group as described above could account for such clustering of antisocial activity although there may be other possible pathways (Hodge, 1991). This entire area would need further and much more detailed investigation before any definitive comments could be made here.

It would seem that in the same way as models and theories of dependence on psychoactive substances take into account the social context in the development of that behaviour, so must models of psychological addiction. The present study has focused on the immediate and wider peer group since their influence was particularly apparent in the interviews, though opportunity and availability have also been commented on. It is obviously important that other aspects of the social context as outlined by Orford, (1985) and Jessor and Jessor (1977) be considered in future work examining psychological addiction.

SIX COMMON CHARACTERISTICS OF ADDICTION

Tolerance: the Need for More to Produce the Same Effect

There was clear evidence that the group of joy-riders interviewed went for more and more cars as they became more expert at stealing them. When they first started they were only taking one or two a week but this quickly increased to several a day. None of the respondents could remember exactly how many cars they had stolen and estimates ranged from a modest 50 to 'Oh hundreds'. There was also clear evidence of respondents stealing better and faster cars as well as cars that were more difficult to break into. Several described the first car they stole as being a small car (e.g. a Fiesta, Metro, etc.), which was 'just sitting there so I thought I'd try it', or one that was easy to get into: 'the first car I took was an Astra "cause they're dead easy", but as they moved up in the joy-riding world they needed to be seen in more prestigious cars. Which cars brought more standing was not clear; some respondents felt that the car just needed to look good, others stated that it had to be powerful, while still others said they had to be good to drive. While such points were frequently mentioned it should also be noted that the joy-riders invariably also talked about stealing on demand or when they needed the money.

Salience: Increasing Importance of Addiction in Lifestyle

All subjects reported joy-riding to be a highly important aspect of their lives and this had increased since they first became involved in cars. There did not appear to be a clear pattern of stealing every day; the pattern rather seemed to be to steal several for two or three days and then go home and sleep it off—or as one respondent put it: 'Well I'd sometimes rather go and get a good night's sleep if I'm knackered from the night before.' Stealing cars was generally more important than having a meal, getting a night's sleep, going out with a girl, drinking or using drugs of any sort. However, several of the young men were quick to point out that it was not quite as simple as preferring to go joy-riding. Usually they stated they would be drinking or, particularly with the younger ones, sniffing solvents, and then they would go on to steal a few cars. One or two of the respondents also felt that cars could be useful when trying to pick up girls. Other respondents, particularly the older ones, said they had got a steady girlfriend and she was their main interest now. All of them described stealing cars as a way of life — part and parcel of everyday living.

The increasing importance of cars and joy-riding was also demonstrated when the respondents were asked about other hobbies and interests. Several of the sample indicated that they used to be interested in boxing, snooker, playing video games, swimming and weight training, but were seldom involved in these activities nowadays.

Conflict: Increasing Awareness of Negative Consequences

All of the young men spoken to were aware of the negative consequences of joy-riding though whether this was an increasing awareness was difficult to assess. One respondent did state:

> When I think what I put my Dad through—I used to think 'old faithful
> will sort it out'—I didn't realise at the time—I do now.

Another respondent made it vividly clear how difficult it was to
remain in a training school set in the heart of West Belfast, from
where he could hear and see the stolen cars being raced around, yet
he was very aware of the negative consequences both for himself and
his family should he abscond and go and join his mates in their
activities. Many other respondents also referred to the consequences
for their families:

> My family are really cracking up: they say I bring trouble to the door
> and I do—both the provies [provisional IRA] and the cops.

All of the sample except two had experienced some form of paramilitary threats or punishment and several were currently under
exclusion orders (where the paramilitaries order an individual out
the country). Responses to these punishments were varied, with two
of the respondents reporting that it was the worst thing that had
happened as a result of joy-riding, but the remainder reported
feelings of anger towards the paramilitaries.

For those nine respondents who said they were trying to stop,
awareness of the negative consequences seemed to be a determining
factor. For example one joy-rider who had currently stopped for
approximately two months said that he had begun to see how stupid
it was. Another respondent clearly identified the conflict within him
when he stated that he himself had been beaten up by the provies
and his brother had been in a serious crash but added:

> I don't know why this doesn't stop me—it just doesn't—nothing else
> can make me feel like I do when I'm in a car so I don't care what
> happens after.

Withdrawal: Distress after a Period of Non-engagement; and Craving: Distress Associated with Desire to Re-engage

These two characteristics are dealt with together because firstly, they
are difficult to distinguish, and secondly, they were assessed by the
same interview questions. Within the sample there appeared to be
two distinct groups here: those who said they were trying to stop
($N = 9$) and those who were not concerned about stopping ($N = 6$).
Those who were in the latter group tended to have been involved in
joy-riding for a shorter period of time (usually 2 years and under),
and responses here were typified by comments such as: 'it feels "cat"

[local slang meaning terrible or awful] when you're not out cruising'
and 'I'd rather joy-ride than anything else'. When these boys felt like
stealing a car they reported that they simply absconded from the
training school (which is an open setting and not intended as a 'lock-
up' facility). Previous research has also indicated that joy-riders are
more likely to abscond from custody than any other type of offender
(Laycock, 1977; Curran, 1992) and it could be argued that this
absconding is related to withdrawal and craving symptoms.

All of the group who stated that they were trying to stop indicated
that it was not easy and they felt very tempted for a variety of
reasons. Among these were the fact that they missed both the buzz
and the money. Other negative consequences were being bored and
peer group pressure. Three of this group said they had tried to stop in
the past and had succeeded for short periods of time but all for less
than one month. Now they felt that they had almost outgrown the
activity:

> I just ran out of the buzz and got fed up with it—kind of bored with it
> and couldn't be bothered with the hassle anymore.

> I really just want to spend more time with my girlfriend now and
> anyway she doesn't like me being in cars.

Other indicators of withdrawal and craving are day-dreams or
fantasies (Hodge, 1991). When asked about these two aspects
respondents again gave a mixed response with five of the sample
saying 'No', they did not day-dream about stealing cars or joy-riding;
three respondents reported that they talked about their past
escapades with their mates and also relived these experiences in their
thoughts; seven gave a clear indication of real day-dreams, for
example:

> I'm lying on my bed and I imagine I'm driving this big flashy
> Cosworth—it's metallic blue—and I'm flying up round the estate—no-
> one's watching—just a couple of wee girls—I can make that car do
> anything I want.

> I go to this quiet car park, there's no-one about, and steal this Manta ...
> then I'm racing up and down with my mates—showing off—racing
> with other stolen cars—but always beating them.

Relapse: Reinstatement after Decision to Stop or Reduce

This could only be gauged from the responses of the nine respondents
who indicated they were trying to stop joy-riding. There was some
evidence of great difficulty here and this was not solely because they
missed the financial rewards, though this did play a part. Several of

the responses suggested the hardest time was when first placed in training school. Most of this group referred to being 'pissed off' for the first couple of weeks when they were unable to joy-ride and five subjects indicated that they had absconded at this time in order to go and 'get a car and cruise'.

Three of this group indicated they had tried to stop in the past but had not been successful for a variety of reasons including:

> I missed being in amongst the big guys—everyone watching you—the showing off—nothing else makes you feel like that.

> I missed the money—so I just went back to stealing—I don't think I really missed the buzz.

Various strategies had been used by these three in their attempts to stop joy-riding, including cutting down, stopping completely and staying away from your mates. One respondent stated:

> Well, I just decided I was going to stop but it wasn't easy I had to be really disciplined and keep myself busy—anyway I went back—that's why I'm in here isn't it? but next time I'll do it.

Six Common Characteristics: Overview

This section will consider the presence or absence of each of the outlined characteristics within individuals. This was achieved by a close examination of the responses to the open-ended questions identified as being indicators of each characteristic. The assessment was done in consultation with a second psychologist experienced in working with people who have been diagnosed as dependent on substances.

All 15 subjects were assessed as displaying the characteristics of Tolerance, Salience and Conflict though the strength of Conflict felt by three of the respondents did not appear to be as highly developed as for the remaining twelve. Nine of the subjects could definitely be described as having four of the common characteristics, the above three plus Relapse, while at least seven displayed five of the characteristics. It is important to note here that it was the difficulty in distinguishing between Withdrawal and Craving that made it impossible to state that all six characteristics were present in these cases.

Addictions to chemical substances are traditionally diagnosed by means of a standard classification system such as the *Diagnostic and Statistical Manual* (DSM-III-R), which is widely used in the United States, and the *International Classification of Disease* (ICD-10), which is generally seen to be the European equivalent to DSM-III-R.

Both of these diagnostic systems state that at least three of the six common characteristics of addiction must be present to make a diagnosis of dependence on a psychoactive substance. The current study is concerned with psychological dependence which is not, as yet, recognised by either of these classification systems; however, it would seem reasonable to apply the same criteria in order to diagnose psychological dependence. On the basis of such criteria at least 12 of the sample could be diagnosed as psychologically dependent on joy-riding, with there being some indication that the remaining three were very close to such dependence.

There was some evidence of stepwise transition or progression through the various characteristics of addiction. Tolerance and Salience seemed to be the first two to be developed, followed by Conflict. Only when there was some indication of Conflict was there a suggestion of the remaining three characteristics, Craving, Withdrawal (with the attendant difficulties of separation previously outlined) and Relapse, which usually appeared last in the sequence, unless the cycle had started over again. This hypothesised developmental progression through the various characteristics of addiction would obviously need to be examined in greater detail. If it did stand up to closer scrutiny it would serve to give a clearer understanding of the development and nature of persistent joy-riding.

Several of the sample referred to the idea of 'growing out' of joy-riding and this parallels the concept of 'spontaneous remission' in the addictions field. This phenomenon refers to the fact that many people successfully give up their addictions with no recourse to formal intervention (McMurran & Hodge, 1993), and this question in relation to joy-riding could also benefit from a closer examination. This would give greater insight into factors involved in behavioural change, which could, in turn, contribute to the development of effective interventions.

IMPLICATIONS OF THE PRESENT STUDY

Among many professionals who work with joy-riders there is a strong resistance to the use of the concept of addiction in relation to this behaviour. This resistance is partly because these professionals believe that the concept bolsters the joy-riders' glamorous image of themselves, and it excuses them from the responsibility of thinking about their behaviour (Chapman, 1993).

However, the other side of this argument is that if joy-riding, as has been argued in this chapter, can be an addiction for some, then methods used to facilitate change and enable people to overcome their addictions could be an extremely effective means of working with these individuals. It would thus seem sensible to examine the most successful methods of working with addictions and consider adapting these for work with joy-riders who present with similar difficulties.

STAGE MODEL OF FACILITATING CHANGE IN ADDICTIONS

The most recent and perhaps most influential model of change in addiction is what is known as the Integrative Model first proposed by Prochaska and DiClemente in 1983, and further developed by the same authors in 1984. This model suggests that people who are addicted to a behaviour or psychoactive substance are at various stages in their willingness to change. These stages are:

1. Pre-contemplation—in which individuals are not aware of their difficulty and therefore are not thinking of change.
2. Contemplation—the individual is admitting something is wrong and is seriously thinking about change. This can last for months, even years and indeed some people never get beyond contemplation.
3. Action—where the individual is actively attempting change. This stage is much shorter yet is where most progress is made.
4. Maintenance stage—in which new habits are strengthened. This continues until the individual feels in control of the addiction.

Prochaska and DiClemente (1984) go on to point out that it is in the maintenance stage that the individual struggles to avoid a relapse. If he should relapse he will either exit back to the pre-contemplation stage and give up trying or alternatively re-enter the change process. Stall and Biernacki (1986) suggest a three-stage model of spontaneous remission (where people give up their addictions of their own volition), from problematic use of substances:

1. Motivation to change as a result of negative consequences.
2. Redefinition of economic, emotional, and social relationships that are influenced by or predicated upon the problematic use of a substance.
3. Development of a new lifestyle to avoid problematic substance use.

These stage models have clear similarities and are at present attracting much interest in the addictions field, where the focus is on identifying stages of change and designing appropriate interventions to match those stages (Davidson et al., 1991). Others working in the field of criminology, particularly McMurran and Hodge (1993), have suggested that this area of research has much relevance for the treatment of offenders, and argue that stages of offending could be identified and matched with intervention programmes for clients. In the present study there were examples of joy-riders at each of Prochaska and DiClemente's (1983, 1984) stages and the hypothesised progression through the various characteristics of addictions appeared to be linked to these stages, thus it would seem to be an approach that could be useful when working with this group of young people.

EFFECTIVE ADDICTION TREATMENTS

Methods of working in the field of addiction treatments are wide and varied. Correspondingly, there is a vast array of literature in this area which it would be impossible to do justice to in the confines of this chapter. The reader is therefore referred to Davidson et al. (1991) for an exceptionally useful 'cook-book' of effective methods of working with clients at different stages in the Integrative Model proposed by Prochaska and DiClemente; what follows simply highlights some useful suggestions from this text and other sources.

The interventions which appear most useful are those based on cognitive-behavioural principles. Non-directive counselling, 'casework' and scare tactics have been shown not to be effective when working with addictions (McMurran & Hodge, 1993).

Motivational interviewing techniques (Miller, 1983), which are based on cognitive-behavioural principles, can be used to encourage clients to recognise their problems and accept the need for change. This approach has been shown to be particularly beneficial with problem drinkers who are at the pre-contemplation stage (Tober, 1991) and with offenders in special hospitals (St Ledger, 1991), and could well be a productive means of working with the joy-rider who still does not see the negative consequences of the activity and who gains much of his self-esteem and status through his position in the group hierarchy.

Other treatment approaches based on cognitive-behavioural principles include self-control training, skills training and problem-solving training, all of which have been used with some success with offenders (McGuire & Priestley, 1985), as well as clients with addictions (Davidson et al., 1991). Such interventions would seem to be particularly appropriate at the action and maintenance stages in the Integrative Model, where the individual is actively trying to change and maintain new behaviours. Other techniques such as creative visualisation (which combines relaxation with guided imagery) have also been used by the present author with joy-riders who are trying to change their behaviour (none of whom were in the sample for the described study), and have been reported as useful by the individuals themselves. Pithers (1990) used fantasy to prevent relapse and distress associated with craving and withdrawal in sex offenders, and given the stated use of day-dreaming amongst the young people interviewed this technique could also be of benefit with addicted joy-riders.

There is also some value in examining programmes aimed at preventing relapse in clients who are overcoming their addictions—for example Marlatt (1985) has designed a programme aimed at preventing relapse by teaching clients how to recognise and cope with high-risk situations. Given some of the comments identified regarding the social context of joy-riding, such an approach is unquestionably worth exploring when working with joy-riders.

Innovative techniques such as drama groups are becoming more and more important in general therapeutic terms and have been used in addiction treatment in Northern Ireland, as well as with juvenile delinquents. Similar techniques have also been used by Turas (meaning *journey* in Irish), a project run by the Probation Board for Northern Ireland for persistent joy-riders. This project combined such techniques with a range of personal development interventions and activity-based programmes and an evaluation of it indicated that a number of individual participants had made progress. Additionally, there had been a reduction in car theft in the three estates targeted by the project, during the first six months of 1992, compared to the same period in 1991.

Another innovative development in interventions with offenders is the use of cognitive-behavioural techniques based on personal construct theory, in the form of Identity Structure Analysis (Weinreich, 1980). This technique has been used in personal development work aimed at helping joy-riders develop a more positive self-image (Tunney, 1992).

On a more general note, it is important to realise that whatever the type and style of treatment, both therapist and client bring personal characteristics to the therapeutic dialogue which can significantly influence outcome (Davidson, 1991). Clearly therapists differ in terms of personality, training, orientation and experience. Indeed, in the treatment of general psychological disorder, Murphy et al. (1984)

found that most clients tended to attribute the effectiveness of treatment to empathy and understanding on the part of the therapist while most therapists attributed success to their particular technique. Similarly, client characteristics may influence treatment (Davidson, 1991), and in this respect the provision of multiple approaches, which are varied according to the specific needs of the client, are likely to be the most effective.

ASSESSMENT TECHNIQUES

The above brief overview of methods of facilitating change in the treatment of addictions, and in offending behaviour, presents some suggestions to be considered when designing a programme of work for persistent joy-riders who appear to be addicted to the behaviour. However, this does raise the problem as to how to assess that addiction. Self-report screening questionnaires are frequently used to identify drug and alcohol dependence. However, Davidson (1987) points to problems when using this method, particularly the difficulty in obtaining reliable information and ensuring accurate memory recall. Given the sense of status that joy-riding provides for the car thief, and the associated propensity to exaggeration, it would seem that self-report questionnaires would not be an appropriate method of assessing addiction in joy-riders. It may be that the most appropriate means of assessment is an abbreviated version of the semi-structured interview used in the present study, though this obviously would make greater demands on the therapist's time.

PREVENTING JOY-RIDING

Overall there is substantial evidence, both from the present study and other research (e.g. McCullough et al., 1990) that neither the traditional justice system, nor the more brutal punishment of the paramilitaries effects a long-term solution to the problem of joy-riding. In a continued search for appropriate ways of addressing the issue there have been many initiatives aimed at reducing car crime, including:

1. Target hardening—aimed at making cars more difficult to steal by improving security devices.
2. Situational crime prevention approaches—aimed at identifying locations where cars are most at risk of being stolen so that specific measures may be taken to improve security in that area.

3. Raising public awareness through a variety of means such as advertising campaigns, community groups and work in schools.
4. Diversionary projects which aim at diverting the joy-rider from car theft.

The limited success of the first three types of approaches has been highlighted by Clarke and Harris (1992) and Sandby-Thomas (1992). The comments of the joy-riders in the present study would certainly suggest that target hardening and situational crime prevention might have some limited effect as deterrents, but that they would not have a major impact.

Diversionary projects have also been demonstrated to have limited success (Burns, 1993). These projects do not usually have any clear selection criteria and thus, in some ways, fail to acknowledge that their clients are a heterogeneous group. For some, joy-riding may be an addiction; for others it may be a means of financial gain; and for yet others it may be a bit of fun which they can take or leave. On the basis of the present study it would seem that diversionary projects should be more targeted at different levels and types of joy-riders and be flexible enough to meet individual needs.

Orford's theory, drawing as it does on the social context and personal functions served by appetitive behaviour, would suggest that to really impact on car theft and joy-riding a co-ordinated approach combining a wide range of preventive strategies would be required. Simultaneously with individualised programmes targeted at various types of joy-riders there also needs to be increased surveillance and target hardening, combined with public awareness campaigns in the local communities. The results from the present study would suggest that only if the joy-rider is 'hit from all angles' is there a realistic hope of making a major impact on car crime.

CONCLUSIONS

The chapter has drawn on identified commonalities in the theory and practice of addiction and crime and has shown how these can be linked within the field of joy-riding. Based on these findings it was concluded that intervention programmes for joy-riders could usefully build on treatment programmes in the field of addictions.

However, preventive measures should remember that all joy-riders are not addicted to the behaviour, and accurate assessment and targeted interventions are essential. Furthermore, diversionary projects directed at working with joy-riders are only one means of addressing the problem—a co-ordinated and multi-disciplinary approach is required if any real inroads are to be made in reducing car-related crime.

Note: With the implementation of The Children Order (NI) on 4 November 1996 training schools no longer provide residential accomodation for care cases.

ACKNOWLEDGEMENTS

This research was conducted when the author was employed as a forensic psychologist with the Adolescent Psychology and Research Unit. It would not have been possible without the support of colleagues in the Unit but a special word of thanks must go to Mr Roger Bailey for his help in the categorisation of responses.

REFERENCES

Briggs, J. (1991). A profile of the juvenile joyrider and a consideration of the efficacy of motor vehicle projects as a diversionary strategy. Unpublished MSc dissertation, University of Durham.

Burns, M. (1993). Joyriding—what drives them to it? Unpublished dissertation submitted for MA in Administrative and Legal Studies, University of Ulster at Jordanstown.

Chapman, T. (1993). The search for an effective community based strategy for preventing the theft of cars: The west Belfast experience. *Social Action*, 1, 4, 19–23.

Clarke, R. V. & Harris, P. M. (1992). Auto theft and its prevention. In M. Tonry (Ed.), *Crime and Justice. A Review of Research*, Vol. 16. Chicago, IL: University of Chicago Press.

Curran, J. D. (1992). *Absconding Behaviours in the Rathgael Centre for Children and Young People*. APRU, Whitefield House, Belfast.

Davidson, R. (1987). Assessment of the alcohol-dependence syndrome: A review of self-report screening questionnaires. *British Journal of Clinical Psychology*, **26**, 243–255.

Davidson, R. (1991). Facilitating change in problem drinkers. In R. Davidson, S. Rollnick & I. MacEwan (Eds), *Counselling Problem Drinkers*. London: Tavistock/Routledge.

Davidson, R., Rollnick, S. & MacEwan, I. (Eds) (1991). *Counselling Problem Drinkers*. London: Tavistock/Routledge.

Gulliver, N. (1991). Unpublished questionnaire survey. Northumbria Probation Service.

Hodge, J. E. (1991). Addiction to crime. In M. McMurran & C. McDougall (Eds), *Proceedings of the First DCLP Conference. Issues in Criminological and Legal Psychology*, Vol. 17, No. 2. Leicester: British Psychological Society.

Houghton, G. (1991). *Car Theft in England and Wales: The Home Office Car Theft Index*. Home Office Police Research Group, Crime Prevention Unit Series Paper 33. London: HMSO.

Jessor, R. & Jessor, S. (1977). *Problem Behaviour and Psycho-Social Development. A Longitudinal Study of Youth*. New York: Academic Press.

Kilpatrick, R. (1988). The archetypal car thief. Paper presented to the Let's Crack Car Crime Conference in Newcastle-on-Tyne, Northumbria Police, November 1988.

Laycock, G. K. (1977). *Absconding from Borstals*. Home Office Research Unit, Study 41. London: HMSO.

Light, R., Nee, C. & Ingham, H. (1993). *Car Theft: The Offender's Perspective*. Home Office Research and Planning Unit. London: HMSO.

McAuley, M. (1989). *Patterns of Car Crime in Belfast: A Review of Strategies for Intervention*. Belfast: Policy Planning and Research Unit.

McCorry, H. (1992). Joyriding and its addictive aspects. Unpublished dissertation submitted for MSc in Developmental and Educational Psychology, Queen's University of Belfast.

McCorry, J. & Morrissey, M. (1989). Community, crime and punishment in West Belfast. *Howard Journal of Criminal Justice*, **28**, 282–90.

McCullough, D., Schmidt, T. & Lockhart, B. (1990). *Car Theft in Northern Ireland*. CIRAC Paper No. 2. Belfast: Extern Organisation.

McGuire, J. & Priestley, P. (1985). *Offending Behaviour: Skills and Stratagems for Going Straight*. London: Batsford.

McMurran, M. & Hodge, J. E. (1993). Current issues in the treatment of addictions and crime. Unpublished paper, Rampton Hospital, Notts.

Marks, J. & Cross, G. (1992). *An Evaluation of the Turas Project*. CIRAC. Belfast: Extern Organisation.

Marlatt, G. A. (1985). Cognitive assessment and intervention procedures for relapse prevention. In G. A. Marlatt & J.R. Gordon (Eds), *Relapse Prevention*. New York: Guilford Press.

Miller, W. (1983). Motivational interviewing with problem drinkers. *Behavioural Psychotherapy*, **11**, 147–172.

Murphy, P. M., Cramer, D. & Lillie, F. J. (1984). The relationship between curative factors perceived by patients in their psychotherapy and treatment outcome: An exploratory study. *British Journal of Medical Psychology*, **57**, 187–192.

Orford, J. (1985). *Excessive Appetites: A Psychological View of Addictions*. Chichester: Wiley.

Peele, S. (1985). *The Meaning of Addition: Compulsive Experience and Its Interpretation*. Lexington, MA: Lexington Books.

Pithers, W. D. (1990). Relapse prevention with sexual aggressors. In W. L. Marshall, D. R. Laws & H. E. Barbaree (Eds), *Handbook of Sexual Assault*. New York: Plenum Press.

Prochaska, J. O. & DiClemente, C. C. (1983). Stages and processes of self-change of smoking: Towards an integrated model of change. *Journal of Consulting Clinical Psychology*, **51**, 390–395.

Prochaska, J. O. & DiClemente, C. C. (1984). *The Transtheoretical Approach: Crossing Traditional Boundaries of Therapy*. New York: Daw–Jones Irwin.

Raistrick, D. & Davidson, R. (1985). *Alcoholism and Drug Addiction*. Edinburgh: Churchill Livingstone.

Reeves, S. (1993). The addicted joyrider: Fact, fiction or fad? Unpublished dissertation submitted for MSc in Applied Criminological Psychology. Birkbeck College, University of London.

Sandby-Thomas, M. (1992). *Preventive Strategies to Reduce Car Theft in Northern Ireland*. Extern Report No 2. Belfast: Extern Organisation.

Smyth, G. (1990). Greater Manchester Probation/Police Car Crime Campaign. Results of Probation Offenders Questionnaire, Greater Manchester Probation Service (unpublished).

Spencer, E. (1992). *Car Crime and Young People on a Sunderland Housing Estate*. Home Office Research Unit, Crime Prevention Unit Paper. London: HMSO.

Stall, R. & Biernacki, P. (1986). Spontaneous remission from the problematic use of substances: An inductive model derived from a comparative analysis of the alcohol, opiate, tobacco and food/obesity literature. *International Journal of the Addictions*, **21**, 1–23.

St Ledger, R. J. (1991). Motivational Interviewing with Special Hospital Patients. Paper presented at The British Psychological Society, Division of Criminal and Legal Psychology Annual Conference, University of Kent.

Stone, N., Fromme, M. & Kagan, D. (1984). *Cocaine: Seduction and Solution*. New York: Potter.

Tober, G. (1991). Helping the pre-contemplator. In R. Davidson, S. Rollnick & I. McEwan (Eds), *Counselling Problem Drinkers*. London: Tavistock/ Routledge.

Tunney, P. (1992). Joy-riders: Their self-concept compared to non-offenders. Unpublished dissertation submitted in partial fulfilment of the degree of BS, Psychology Dept., Queen's University of Belfast.

Walker, R. (1985). *Applied Qualitative Research*. London: Gower.

Weinreich, P. (1980). *Manual for Identity Exploration Using Personal Constructs*. Research Papers in Ethnic Relations, No. 1. Centre for Research in Ethnic Relations, University of Warwick, Coventry.

CHAPTER 7

The Development of a Brief Intervention for Car Theft

Mary McMurran

East Midlands Centre for Forensic Mental Health & University of Leicester

and

Jessica Whitman

Formerly HMYOC Glen Parva

Car theft is one type of offence for which intervention programmes are few and far between in British prisons, perhaps because a relatively small percentage of offenders is imprisoned for stealing motor vehicles. The prison statistics available when the survey reported in this chapter was conducted (Home Office, 1987) showed that 1.94% of all male prisoners and 0.33% of all female prisoners were imprisoned for theft of a motor vehicle or taking and driving away. The highest proportion of imprisonments for vehicle theft was evident in young male offenders between the ages of 14 and 20 years, with 5.74% of this group being imprisoned for these two motor vehicle offences. The figure for imprisoned young female offenders was 0.64%.

Vehicle theft may be recognised as a criminologically significant problem for some young male offenders; it is an offence behaviour which requires attention to reduce recidivism. In order to help design an appropriate intervention, a survey was conducted of a sample of motor vehicle offenders in HM Young Offender Centre, Glen Parva. The information gathered was examined with reference to models of

Addicted to Crime? Edited by J.E. Hodge, M. McMurran and C.R. Hollin.
© 1997 John Wiley & Sons Ltd.

addictive behaviours and an intervention derived from the addictions field was designed. The results of this survey, a conceptual basis for intervention, and the intervention designed for car thieves are described in this chapter.

THE SURVEY

This research was conducted in an English male young offender institution between 1988 and 1989. Four of the eight living units were randomly selected as sources of participants. All inmates housed in these four units who reported any occurrence of taking a car without owner's consent, or stealing a car, were selected as participants. From a total 240 inmates, 110 (45.83%) were identified as having a history of one or more of these offences. Participants were all convicted young offenders between the ages of 15 and 21 years (the mean age was 19.5 years). Each young offender was given a structured interview to gather information about factors related to his motor vehicle offending.

On average, participants began to take cars at 15.2 years of age (SD = 1.91) and had an offending career of 38.74 months duration (SD = 28.65). The average number of cars stolen was 3.28 cars per month (SD = 7.53). Most offenders (64.5%) operated in groups, with an average of 2.45 (SD = 1.88) co-offenders of the same average age as themselves. Those who offended alone showed a higher car theft rate (4.14 cars per month; SD = 10.37) than those who offended in groups (2.81 cars per month; SD = 5.33).

Most offenders (57.3%) said that their reason for starting to steal cars was that their friends were already involved in this activity; other reasons were to learn to drive (19.1%) and to have the opportunity to drive (15.5%). Some offenders (13.6%) could give no specific reason for starting to steal cars ('It just happened'). By contrast, a large number of specific reasons was given for continuing to take cars: fun of driving (84.4%); going fast (63.3%); convenience (60.6%); freedom (54.1%); excitement (37.6%); feeling of power (34.9%); boredom (26.6%); trying different models (24.8%); challenge (21.1%); status (17.4%); and to sell the vehicle (16.5%).

It emerged that 20% of offences were planned in advance and 47.7% were committed at the suggestion of the respondent himself. The use of alcohol (30.3%), drugs (29.4%), or solvents (8.3%) prior to taking cars was not uncommon. Those who took cars for the feeling of power or speed were more likely to have used alcohol; those who desired freedom or wished to sell the car were more likely to have planned the crime; and those who wished to try different models were more likely to have suggested committing the offence. The average time spent driving a stolen car was 3.01 hours (SD = 2.86). Reasons given for stopping driving were apprehension by the police, mechanical failure, tiredness, and boredom.

In this sample, 41.4% claimed to have stopped taking cars. The major reasons given for this change were: taking up other activities (33.6%); finding other methods of transport (23.6%); wishing to avoid the adverse consequences of offending (22.7%); deciding to obey the law (17.3%); no longer feeling tempted (13.6%); and a change of friends (12.7%). Although many offenders (62.2%) reported having been involved in an accident, the majority of these (72.1%) had not subsequently stopped taking cars. Therefore, being involved in an accident is not likely to precipitate change.

The majority of offenders (59.6%) lived with family members. Most (72.5%) had a girlfriend at the time. Most had criminal friends (91.8%) and many had family members who had committed offences (51.4%). Over half were unemployed (55%). Most (72.2%) spent their leisure time mainly with male friends, and this group stole on average 2.87 cars per month (SD = 5.35). Offenders who spent their leisure time mainly in female company stole an average of 8.87 cars per month (SD = 19.90).

CAR THIEF TYPOLOGIES

A profile of the 'typical' young male car thief is one who starts stealing cars at around age 15 years. He lives with his family and he is unemployed. He is a sociable person who associates with a group of male friends and also has a girlfriend. His friends introduce him to stealing cars and it is with a group of friends that he operates. He continues to steal cars at a rate of around three per month because he finds the activity fun. He is likely to have an accident at some point when driving a stolen car, but this does not deter him. In fact, as Briggs (1991) discovered in his interviews with 30 young offenders in a Newcastle assessment centre, accidents may actually add to the excitement, enhance an offender's self-image and improve his status within the group; accidents are viewed as conferring prestige. The car thief eventually grows out of stealing cars when he takes up other activities, finds a legitimate method of transport, or decides against participating in crime.

This description of the 'typical' car thief accords with that of Kilpatrick (1988), who formulated a career path from interviews with car thieves in Belfast. Youngsters, mostly boys and usually under the age of 12 years, begin by watching older youths racing around in stolen cars which they have brought into the area. These youngsters will ask for or accept offers of a ride in a stolen car, and by the age of 15 or 16 years, they will have progressed to stealing cars for themselves. Their reasons for stealing cars are excitement, risk, fun, relief from boredom, escapism, status, and feelings of power and importance. Most car thieves will stop committing offences in their twenties as they settle down to relationships and jobs, or simply 'wise up'.

The appellation given to the type of car thief described above is generally 'joy-rider', and the joy-rider's hedonistic motives appear to be the most common in young offenders. Some researchers have suggested other typologies. Briggs (1991) suggests five categories of car thieves: (i) joy-riders, who are motivated by having a good time, striving for status and recognition, and proving masculinity; (ii) profit-makers, who resell cars; (iii) utilitarians, who steal for transport; (iv) those who take cars for long-term personal use; and (v) those who steal cars for use in other crimes because they offer anonymity and mobility. There is tentative support for the first three of these typologies in the data presented in this chapter.

Further research is clearly required to add detail to these typologies, establish their validity, and to examine whether there is any value in separating out these types in terms of differential interventions. Some hypotheses regarding intervention may, however, be based on the results of this survey.

THEORETICAL APPROACH

One feature of successful interventions with offenders is that they are based on a conceptual model (Izzo & Ross, 1990). The theme of this book is to investigate crime in relation to models of addiction, which raises the fundamental question 'What is addiction?'

Orford (1985) suggests that 'there are a number of apparently dissimilar activities which have in common the capacity to create what, in familiar parlance, we call an "addiction" (p.109). The examples Orford chooses are drinking, gambling, drug use, eating, and sex, although he suggests that other behaviours could be included, for instance firesetting, work, and electronic game playing. The attribute 'addictive' is clearly not reserved only for behaviours which involve substance use and if we accept 'behavioural addictions' then the potential exists to admit a wide variety of behaviours, including stealing cars. At first sight, these so-called addictive behaviours share no apparent unifying feature. Involvement in them is, up to a point, quite normal and in some cases even essential (eating), yet there appears to be a point beyond which a need or an indulgence is labelled an addiction.

Orford (1985) views involvement in an addictive behaviour as determined by a balance of incentives and disincentives. These are based in a number of domains—cultural, social, familial, psychological, and physical—and they are personal; that is, each person will have a unique pattern of incentives and disincentives. The personal balance varies across time in relation to fast-changing variables such as time of the day, day of the week, location, and mood, as well as to slow-changing variables such as peers, work status, and family commitments. The functions served by the behaviour during the phase of initiation are not necessarily those that apply in later stages of that behaviour.

Whilst most people remain abstinent or moderate in their involvement, a minority of people develop an increasing attachment to addictive behaviours. Strong attachment, or addiction, may develop as follows (McMurran, 1994). The behaviour provides rewards to the individual, including social validation, mood enhancement, and relief of unpleasant feelings. Mood management is one of the major explanatory factors which appears in the addictions literature; the addictive behaviour may serve to give access to positive experiences or highs, or to avoid negative mood states such as tension, boredom, or depression. The rewards often accrue immediately, whereas any adverse consequences usually appear only after a delay. These adverse consequences are often accompanied by low mood, which can, paradoxically, lead to further engagement in the behaviour to help the individual cope with the situation.

Change towards moderation or abstinence may occur at any stage and such change is best construed as a personal decision. The balance-of-incentives model suggests that ambivalence is likely to characterise the behaviour at all levels of involvement and increased levels of attachment will result in a more obvious conflict of motives. The stronger the attachment, the more fragile will be the decision to change, and the greater the likelihood of relapse.

The person who decides to cease or moderate the behaviour is likely to experience control problems. Subtle emotional and environmental triggers for the behaviour may have developed outwith the individual's awareness and these can be difficult to access for rational problem solving. Attempts at cessation or moderation highlight the functions that the behaviour served in the first place, and because the behaviour has been routinely used as a source of reward or a coping strategy, alternative ways of coping with life have not had a chance to develop. Failure to cope without recourse to the addictive behaviour leads to low self-efficacy expectations (e.g. 'I can't give up'), and meanwhile positive outcome expectancies relating to the addictive behaviour are maintained (e.g. 'It helps me cope'). At this stage, the person may rationalise his or her position by developing beliefs that the addictive behaviour is not a problem after all, expression of these beliefs commonly being labelled 'minimisation' or 'denial' by the outsider.

Before going on to look at car theft within this framework, it is instructive to examine the literature on risk factors for substance use and crime.

DEVELOPMENTAL RISK FACTORS

Developmental models of both substance use and crime suggest that there are a number of risk factors throughout the lifespan which increase the likelihood of initiation to and escalation of these behaviours, and that the two classes of behaviour share many of those risk factors. Indeed, it is apparent that problem behaviours frequently appear in a cluster in the same individuals. In a longitudinal study of young people over a 12-year period from age 13–15 years through to age 25–27 years, Jessor (1987) found a pattern of interrelationships among problem drinking, illicit drug use, cigarette smoking, precocious sexual activity, and delinquency, that was systematic enough to suggest a 'syndrome' of adolescent problem behaviours.

The shared risk factors for the development of substance use and crime include hyperactivity in childhood, poor family management practices, modelling and acceptance of problem behaviours within families, low bonding to the family, poor school performance, school truancy, and the influence of antisocial peers (Graham & Bowling, 1995; Hawkins et al., 1992; Loeber, 1988, 1990). In tracing a developmental pathway, these factors may be seen as interactive and also set within a context which may exacerbate or protect against the development of problem behaviours. For example, a child who is hyperactive is likely to be difficult to manage and parents may have trouble being consistent in their control and discipline; the child may consequently fail to learn self-control and will be unable to settle in the classroom, resulting in poor school performance; this in turn may lead to truancy and mixing with peers who engage in a variety of problem behaviours. The likelihood of following this pathway may be exacerbated or attenuated by external circumstances, such as school atmosphere and resources, and opportunities for leisure and work activities.

Most young people grow out of problem behaviours in their mid-twenties as they settle down to work and family life, although these days 'maturing out' appears to be less common than it used to be amongst young men (Graham & Bowling, 1995; Loeber, 1988; Temple & Ladouceur, 1986). Where crime is concerned, males are more likely to desist if they have had strong bonding with their parents during adolescence, feel they did well at school, break away from delinquent peers, do not drink heavily, and do not use controlled drugs (Graham & Bowling, 1995). Some do not desist from crime, and a lifestyle of substance use and crime may become entrenched. Amongst this group, some may be classified as addicted to antisocial behaviours.

ADDICTED TO CAR THEFT?

It is evident that this cluster of problem behaviours identified by Jessor (1987) contains those which have long been labelled addictive—drinking, drug use, and smoking—and a recent recruit to the addictions—sex. What, then, is the position of delinquency as an addictive behaviour? It may be that the connection between the disparate behaviours currently gathered under this umbrella term is that they are *functionally similar*; they bring similar rewards.

Initial engagement in an addictive behaviour is often culturally normal; indeed, almost half the offenders approached to participate in this study had stolen a car at some stage. It appears that social rewards draw youngsters into the behaviour in the first place and thereafter the experiences of fun, excitement and power of driving are added to the list of incentives. Most of the offenders interviewed appeared to engage in car theft within the 'normal' limits of this specific group, and many desisted in time. Some offenders, however, seem to 'overindulge' in stealing cars; solitary offenders and those who socialise with girls seem to fit this category. It is possible that over the developmental span, hyperactivity, self-control deficits, poor problem-solving skills, and failure to access rewards through prosocial means lead to a greater degree of reliance upon 'joy-riding', amongst other problem behaviours, in order to satisfy various needs.

The survey reported here was not, however, designed to examine an addiction model of car theft, and further research into excessive involvement in stealing cars and the difficulties some offenders have in controlling their behaviour is warranted.

Whilst we are awaiting theoretical developments in this area, there exists an urgent need to develop effective interventions for people who steal cars. If the functions of delinquency are similar to those of other addictive behaviours, then the solutions may also be similar. Therefore, it seems reasonable to look to the field of addictions for interventions which may be applied to stealing cars. Other practitioners have successfully adopted interventions developed in the addictions field for use with 'joy-riders'. Chapman (1995) described a community-based intervention aimed at lifestyle modification, which successfully stopped offending in 43% of participants.

It is interesting to note that delinquency precedes other behaviours in the problem cluster (Elliott et al., 1985; Temple & Ladouceur, 1986). If, as Jessor (1987) suggests, involvement in one problem behaviour is a risk factor for involvement in other problem behaviours, then to address delinquency becomes important not only for reducing crime itself but for reducing the risk of involvement in other problem behaviours in the cluster.

INTERVENTIONS

Two interventions which show promise in the addictions field are behavioural self-control training and relapse prevention. The broad principles behind such interventions are:

1. To teach people to become aware of their behaviour, its antecedents and its consequences through systematic analysis, so that they may 'scientifically' identify ways of bringing it under control.
2. To increase self-efficacy by acknowledgement and early identification of circumstances which present a risk of relapse, developing skills for coping with risk of relapse, and encouraging beliefs about the change process which do not militate against success.

These interventions are described in greater length by McMurran (1994) and McMurran and Hollin (1993). A self-help manual based on behavioural self-control training and relapse prevention was designed for application to stealing cars. The script of this manual is presented in the Appendix to this chapter, although a printed version with graphics was prepared for actual use.

Behavioural self-control training is essentially the process of teaching people the skills and strategies they require to control a specifically targeted behaviour. The techniques are self-monitoring, goal setting, altering the antecedents to the behaviour, changing the form of the behaviour, and generating incentives for maintaining change. Behavioural self-control training has been shown to be effective with problem drinkers (Miller, 1978; Miller et al., 1981b; Miller & Taylor, 1980). The procedure has also been effectively translated into self-help manuals for problem drinkers (Heather et al., 1987; Heather et al., 1986; Miller & Baca, 1983; Miller et al., 1981a).

Relapse prevention is 'a self-control programme designed to teach individuals who are trying to change their behavior how to anticipate and cope with the problems of relapse' (Marlatt & George, 1984, p.261). Marlatt (1985) has identified eight common determinants of relapse common to a range of addictive behaviours: *intrapersonal* determinants are unpleasant emotions, physical discomfort, pleasant emotions, testing personal control, and urges or temptations; *interpersonal* determinants are conflict, social pressure, and pleasant times.

Relapse-prevention techniques include education about the coping versus cure rationale; coping with temptation through positive self-statements, decision review, and distraction; coping with lapses by treating them as learning experiences and avoiding the 'goal violation effect'. Relapse prevention has been successfully applied with smokers (Shiffman et al., 1985), dieters (Sternberg, 1985), illicit drug users (Stallard & Heather, 1989), and sex offenders (Laws, 1989; McMurran, 1991; Pithers et al., 1983). Although relapse prevention has not been translated into a self-help manual, some components may be suitable for this form of presentation.

Self-help manuals present a number of potential advantages in work with prisoners and other groups of clients:

1. A greater number of people may benefit from intervention since less, or even no, therapist time is required and manuals may be made available to prisoners where no therapist is available.
2. Problems may be tackled earlier than might be possible via protracted and, for some clients, off-putting referral systems.
3. Prisoners who are reluctant to be seen taking advice from staff may accept a self-help manual.
4. Where the targeted behaviour is not evident in prison, a self-help manual allows the intervention to be taken away and used in the community when required.
5. Maintenance of change may be enhanced through increased self-attribution for change.
6. Self-help manuals are cheap relative to therapist time and cheaper by far than the legal and penal costs incurred by offending.

However, as Heather (1986) points out, 'the use of self-help manuals must always be accompanied by critical evaluative research' (p.334) and optimism, face validity, and cheapness should not lead to a failure to do so. It is important to gather empirically based information about who benefits from self-help manuals, how people use them, and what components are effective (Barrera et al., 1981). The manual presented here is based on psychological principles but it comes with no guarantee; rather, it is presented as one possible intervention for car theft which requires careful evaluation.

REFERENCES

Barrera, M., Rosen, G. M. & Glasgow, R. E. (1981). Rights, risks, and responsibilities in the use of self-help psychotherapy. In G. T. Hannah, W. P. Christian & H. P. Clark (Eds), *Preservation of Client Rights*. New York: Free Press.

Briggs, J. (1991). A profile of the juvenile joy-rider and a consideration of the efficacy of motor vehicle projects as a diversionary strategy. Unpublished MA thesis, University of Durham.

Chapman, T. (1995). Creating a culture of change: A case study of a car crime project in Belfast. In J. McGuire (Ed.), *What Works: Reducing Reoffending*. Chichester: Wiley.

Elliott, D. S., Huizinga, D. & Ageton, S. S. (1985). *Explaining Delinquency and Drug Use*. Newbury Park, CA: Sage.

Graham, J. & Bowling, B. (1995). *Young People and Crime*. Home Office Research Study No. 145. London: Home Office.

Hawkins, J. D., Catalano, R. F. & Miller, J. Y. (1992). Risk and protective factors for alcohol and other drug problems in adolescence and early adulthood: Implications for substance abuse prevention. *Psychological Bulletin*, **112**, 64–105.

Heather, N. (1986). Change without therapists: The use of self-help manuals by problem drinkers. In W. R. Miller & N. Heather (Eds), *Treating Addictive Behaviors*. New York: Plenum Press.

Heather, N., Robertson, I., MacPherson, B., Allsop, S. & Fulton, A. (1987). Effectiveness of a controlled drinking self-help manual: One year follow-up results. *British Journal of Clinical Psychology*, **26**, 279–287.

Heather, N., Whitton, B. & Robertson, I. (1986). Evaluation of a self-help manual for media-recruited problem drinkers: Six month follow-up results. *British Journal of Clinical Psychology*, **25**, 19–34.

Home Office (1987). *Prison Statistics, England and Wales, 1986*. London: HMSO.

Izzo, R. L. & Ross, R. R. (1990). Meta-analysis of rehabilitation programmes for juvenile delinquents: A brief report. *Criminal Justice and Behavior*, **17**, 134–142.

Jessor, R. (1987). Problem-behaviour theory, psychosocial development, and adolescent problem drinking. *British Journal of Addiction*, **82**, 331–342.

Kilpatrick, R. (1988). The archetypal car thief. Paper presented to the Let's Crack Car Crime Conference, Northumbria Police, Newcastle.

Laws, D. R. (Ed.) (1989). *Relapse Prevention with Sex Offenders.* New York: Guilford Press.

Loeber, R. (1988). Natural histories of conduct problems, delinquency, and associated substance use: Evidence for developmental progressions. In B. B. Lahey & A. E. Kazdin (Eds), *Advances in Child Clinical Psychology,* Vol. 11. New York: Plenum Press.

Loeber, R. (1990). Development and risk factors of juvenile antisocial behaviors and delinquency. *Clinical Psychology Review,* **10**, 1–41.

Marlatt, G. A. (1985). Situational determinants of relapse and skill training interventions. In G. A. Marlatt & J. R. Gordon (Eds), *Relapse Prevention.* New York: Guilford Press.

Marlatt, G. A. & George, W. H. (1984). Relapse prevention: Introduction and overview of the model. *British Journal of Addiction,* **79**, 261–273.

McMurran, M. (1991). A cognitive-behavioural intervention with a sex offender. *Delinquencia,* **2**, 311–330.

McMurran, M. (1994). *The Psychology of Addiction.* London: Taylor and Francis.

McMurran, M. & Hollin, C. R. (1993). *Young Offenders and Alcohol-Related Crime: A Practitioner's Guidebook.* Chichester: Wiley.

Miller, W. R. (1978). Behavioral treatment of problem drinkers: A comparative outcome study of three controlled drinking therapies. *Journal of Consulting and Clinical Psychology,* **46**, 74–86.

Miller, W. R. & Baca, L. M. (1983). Two year follow-up of bibliotherapy and therapist directed controlled drinking training for problem drinkers. *Behavior Therapy,* **14**, 441–448.

Miller, W. R., Gribskov, C. J. & Mortell, R. L. (1981a). Effectiveness of a self-control manual for problem drinkers with and without therapist contact. *International Journal of the Addictions,* **16**, 1247–1254.

Miller, W. R., Pechachek, T. F. & Hamburg, S. (1981b). Group behavior therapy for problem drinkers. *International Journal of the Addictions,* **16**, 829–839.

Miller, W. R. & Taylor, C. A. (1980). Relative effectiveness of bibliotherapy, individual, and group self-control training in the treatment of problem drinkers. *Addictive Behaviours,* **5**, 13–24.

Orford, J. (1985). *Excessive Appetites: A Psychological View of Addictions.* Chichester: Wiley.

Pithers, W. D., Marques, J. K., Gibat, C. C. & Marlatt, G. A. (1983). Relapse prevention with sexual aggressives: A self-control model of treatment and maintenance of change. In J. G. Greer & I. R. Stuart (Eds), *The Sexual Aggressor: Current Perspectives on Treatment.* New York: Van Nostrand.

Shiffman, S., Read, L., Maltese, J., Rapkin, D. & Jarvik, M. E. (1985). Preventing relapse in ex-smokers: A self-management approach. In G. A. Marlatt & J. R. Gordon (Eds), *Relapse Prevention.* New York: Guilford Press.

Stallard, A. & Heather, N. (1989). Relapse prevention and AIDS among intravenous drug users. In M. Gossop (Ed.), *Relapse and Addictive Behaviour.* London: Tavistock/Routledge.

Sternberg, B. (1985). Relapse in weight control: Definitions, processes, and prevention. In G. A. Marlatt and J. R. Gordon (Eds), *Relapse Prevention.* New York: Guilford Press.

Temple, M. & Ladouceur, P. (1986). The alcohol–crime relationship as an age-specific phenomenon: A longitudinal study. *Contemporary Drug Problems,* **13**, 89–115.

The Behavioural Self-Help Manual

DRIVEN TO CRIME?

1. What Will You Get out of this Book?

This booklet is for people who want to stop taking cars and who are interested in finding out *how* they can change.

The booklet will help you think about your behaviour and it will give you ideas about how to change. But there is no magic solution. *You* do the work. *You* make the choices.

As you go through the book you will find lists and charts to fill in. The booklet is yours to keep and you may write in it.

2. Controlling the Balance

Most of the things we do have a good side and a bad side. Taking cars is like anything else—you do it for the sake of going along with the gang, having a bit of fun and excitement, or because you like to feel good at something. But afterwards you may wish you hadn't pinched some ordinary bloke's car, driven like a maniac, and broken the law.

There is a balance of good things against bad things.

The balance for stealing cars may look like this:

GOOD	BAD
Fun	Trouble with police
Something to do	Might have an accident
Could steal music system	Might get banned from driving

Addicted to Crime? Edited by J.E. Hodge, M. McMurran and C.R. Hollin.
© 1997 John Wiley & Sons Ltd.

The balance of good and bad is different for everybody. Write down your own balance of the good things about stealing cars and the bad things about stealing cars.

GOOD   BAD

_____   _____

_____   _____

What this book will help you do is to *take control* over the balance and *take control* over your offending. How do you take control?

- you set rules for yourself
- you learn ways to resist temptation
- you learn how to handle problems
- you reward your successes

Now... what do you want to do about stealing cars? If you want to stop, or at least try to, *READ ON...*

3. Rule Setting

Before you set rules for yourself, you need to know what makes taking cars more likely for you. Think back over the last few months and answer these questions:

(a) Are there people who are always around when you decide to take a car? Name them _____

(b) Which of your friends never take cars? Name them _____

(c) Are there places you usually go to find cars? Name the places _____

(d) Do you carry equipment (e.g. keys) to help you get into cars? Name the equipment _____

(e) What are you usually doing before you offend? (e.g. drinking, sniffing glue, hanging about getting bored) _____

Now, make some decisions about who you are going to hang about with, where you are going to go, and what you are going to do.

I WILL STOP HANGING AROUND WITH THE FOLLOWING PEOPLE:
_____
_____

I WILL GO AROUND MORE WITH THE FOLLOWING PEOPLE:

I WILL STOP GOING TO THE FOLLOWING PLACES:

I WILL NOT TAKE THE FOLLOWING EQUIPMENT WITH ME WHEN I GO OUT:

I WILL TAKE UP THE FOLLOWING ACTIVITIES:

Taking up new activities will stop you getting bored, and help you meet new friends who do not steal cars. Here are some suggestions of things you could do: football, swimming, martial arts, cycling, running, weight training, snooker, pool, fishing, cinema, discos, concerts, odd-jobbing, gardening, decorating.

You will find it easier to stay out of trouble if you plan your spare time. Don't hang about with nothing to do. Try making a timetable of activities for yourself each day.

Example: SATURDAY

Morning	Afternoon	Evening
Get some money by doing odd-jobs	Go to the cinema	Visit brother

4. Resisting Temptation

There are going to be times when you feel tempted to steal a car. You should watch out for especially risky situations such as when you're bored, or when you're having a good time with your mates and they suggest nicking a car. When you feel tempted, *activate your defences*! There are three stages to go through, as follows:

(a) Talk yourself out of it.
Just because you feel tempted to steal a car, doesn't mean you've got to do it. Say to yourself things like:
    'I expected to feel tempted and I'll just live with it.'
    'I won't let temptation beat me.'
    'I don't have to do everything my mates do.'

(b) Review your decision to stop.
You wanted to stop stealing cars because of all the bad things about it. You know there are good things too, but the bad side needs thinking about. List

all the reasons you had for wanting to stop: getting in trouble with the police, disappointing your parents, being banned from driving, and so on. A bit of fun for an hour or so could cost quite a lot in the long term.

(c) Do something else.
Don't argue with yourself for too long—just get off and do something else. Be careful though! Don't do anything that will make you *more* likely to steal a car. *Don't* visit a friend that you used to get into trouble with. *Don't* go for a walk round the back streets where you used to find your cars.

Write down a few ideas of things to do so that you'll have them ready for emergency use:

Activities for coping with temptation

_____

_____

_____

5. Coping with Problems

When you stop stealing cars, you may notice some problems appearing. This may be because you are missing the good things that you got out of stealing cars. You have to find other ways of getting what you want out of life. 'Problem solving' is a technique which you can use to help you sort out many kinds of problems.
Problem solving requires you to ask six key questions.

Bad feelings? Bad feelings can mean most anything you don't like—boredom, anger, loneliness, sadness, tension, and so on. You have to learn to pay attention to your bad feelings and not ignore them. They are the cue that problem solving is required.

What's my problem? Ask yourself what is causing your bad feelings. Try to be specific. For example, 'I'm bored' is a bad feeling; the problem might be 'It's Saturday afternoon, I've not heard from my mates, and I can't think of anything to do.'

What do I want? After you've decided what the problem is, decide what you want instead. If you're bored on a Saturday afternoon, you might decide that you 'want something to do between 3 o'clock and teatime'.

What could I do? Now is the time to let your imagination run riot! Think of all the things you *could* do. Forget the practicalities for now—the more ideas you have, the more likely it will be that you come up with one or two good ones.

What's my plan? Now is the time to select your best ideas to make a realistic plan. To continue with the example of being bored, the plan could be to go to the cinema, or go for a swim, or walk to the library to look at the books about hobbies and sports, or to go out and have a coke or a coffee in a café.

How did I do? Afterwards, check out how well your plan worked.

6. Rewards

For every week that you stay out of trouble, reward your success. Decide at the beginning of the week what reward you will aim for. It doesn't have to be anything expensive. How about a Big Mac, a magazine, or a decent haircut?

As time goes on, you can stop rewarding yourself every week and stretch it out to every month instead. You can save up for something special, for example a new tape or disc, or something to wear, or you may treat yourself to some tickets for a rock concert.

Use the chart below for rewarding your successes.

Week	Reward	Success (yes or no)
1		
2		
3		
4		
5		
6		
7		
8		

7. The Future

This booklet has asked you questions which make you look at your behaviour and make decisions. You have been given ideas about how to carry out those decisions. This book isn't the sort of book you pick up, read, and never look at again. You can look through it again and again to remind yourself of your aims. You can even work through it all over again and set different rules, activities, and rewards.

Try to involve friends and family in what you are doing. They'll be able to help and encourage you.

If you need some extra advice or help, contact one of these people: your probation officer or social worker; a school teacher; or your doctor, who will be able to put you in touch with someone who can help.

CHAPTER 8

'Irrational' Shoplifting and Models of Addiction

James McGuire
University of Liverpool

THE OFFENCE OF SHOP THEFT

A chapter on shoplifting in a book called *Addicted to Crime?* To many this may appear an unlikely topic for coverage, but one objective of this book is to pose exploratory questions, and the issue of whether the act of shop theft can have any 'addictive' components is one which will be addressed in the present chapter.

Thefts of one form or another usually account for approximately half of all reported crime. In England and Wales in 1994, a total of 5.26 million offences was recorded by the police. Of these, 2.56 million (48.7%) were of theft. The largest single proportion of them consisted of thefts from, or of, motor vehicles. Shop thefts, the crime commonly known as shoplifting, totalled 269 683. This constituted approximately 10.5% of all thefts, and 5.1% of all crimes recorded in that year (Home Office, 1995).

However, the figures for recorded acts of shop theft, as with most forms of crime, are likely to be a considerable underestimate of the real incidence of this activity. Studies of crime frequency based on victim reports, such as the British Crime Survey (Mayhew et al., 1993; Home Office, 1995) have generally indicated that for the types of 'personal' crimes examined (burglary, criminal damage, vehicle crime, and violence), recorded crime represents only just over a

Addicted to Crime? Edited by J.E. Hodge, M. McMurran and C.R. Hollin.

quarter, on average, of the likely real total. This proportion has probably changed over time, as the rate of reporting of crime is generally thought to have increased. No direct comparison along such lines has been made for shop theft as it is not included in the British Crime Survey. However, there are indications that for this type of offence, official statistics may be even more of an underestimate than they are for other types.

This emerges strongly from research conducted by the British Retail Consortium (Burrows & Speed, 1994), which under its *Retail Crime Initiative* carried out a large-scale survey of over 54 000 retail outlets in the UK. The principal aim was to establish rates of a range of offences including criminal damage, burglary, theft by staff, theft by customers, fraud, arson, violence to staff, and terrorist attack. Extrapolated across the industry as a whole, this work shows that in the financial year 1992–93, over 1.5 million incidents of theft by customers were experienced by retailers; forming the largest single share of the 2.1 million crime incidents reported. The majority of these thefts were discovered through stocktaking. Retail staff apprehended 1 172 477 suspects, of whom 706 840 (63%) were notified to the police. However, as is evident from Home Office statistics, only a small proportion of this group was subsequently prosecuted, many being dealt with instead by informal cautions.

The net loss to retailers in financial terms as a result of theft by customers (the gross amount stolen less the value of goods recovered), was £471.2 million. Thefts by staff accounted for an even higher figure of £549.2 million. Retail crime as a whole formed 57% of the overall amount of *shrinkage*, or audited stock losses, which are defined differently by different retailers but usually include losses from damaged goods, short deliveries, administrative errors, or products which pass their 'sell-by' date. The total for shoplifting is more modest than that reported earlier by Ekblom (1986) who cited the Association for the Prevention of Theft in Shops, which in the mid-1980s took the view that shoplifting accounted for the loss of goods worth a billion pounds per year. In the United States in the early 1980s it was estimated that the annual cost of shoplifted goods was in the region of $16 billion. In the middle of the decade, shop thefts were calculated to occur at the rate of twenty per minute (Glasscock et al., 1988).

INCIDENCE OF SHOPLIFTING

The true incidence of shoplifting is difficult to determine, but it is evidently much higher than officially recorded rates suggest. Home

Office statistics show that the trend of the latter over recent years differs slightly from that for other types of crime. While for 10 out of the 14 years from 1981 to 1994 (the exceptions being 1983, 1988, 1993 and 1994) the total number of recorded crimes, and of all thefts combined, generally increased, the pattern for shop theft was much more stable. Figure 8.1 shows the trends for all offences of theft; for theft from vehicles; and for theft from shops, over that period. The drop in theft from shops in the second half of the 1980s, whilst other thefts continued to rise, is almost certainly more apparent than real. Farrington and Burrows (1993) have questioned whether the observed decrease of 11% in shop theft between 1985 and 1990 represents an actual decline in its frequency, when other thefts rose by 33% over the same period. To explore this further, information was collected by them from the chief security officers of 16 of the best known retail chains (with a total of 7873 outlets) in Britain. They were asked to provide details of numbers of shoplifters apprehended during each of the years 1985–1990. Analysis of these figures suggested that the rate of shoplifting remained roughly constant, as did the rate at which apprehended shoplifters were reported to the police. The decline in the criminal statistics for numbers prosecuted or cautioned was therefore due to a decrease in the use of official action by the police. Most notably, these companies alone,

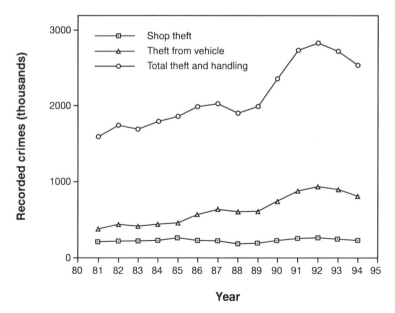

Figure 8.1. Statistics for theft, England and Wales, 1981–1994.

representing only a small proportion of the retail outlets in the UK, apprehended 112 224 shoplifters in 1990; a year when for England and Wales as a whole only 250 301 shop thefts were recorded by the police. The true figure for acts of shop theft is likely therefore to be several times this number.

Given the wide discrepancy between recorded shop theft and known losses of retailers, attempts have been made to assess the frequency of the crime by other methods such as self-report surveys and direct observation. Ray (1987) distributed a thousand questionnaires to randomly selected shoppers in Spokane, Washington. Information was requested concerning whether respondents had ever shoplifted; the questionnaires, which also sought basic demographic data, and information on stress levels and attitudes to shop theft, were to be returned anonymously to the researchers. Of the 382 usable questionnaires recovered, 34 contained an admission of shoplifting during the previous year. Ray thus estimated that the general frequency of shoplifting amongst adults was one in twelve. Given the response rate, this figure of course may be an erroneous estimate, and it is at the top end of the range obtained from other studies. Similar surveys amongst adolescents, however, find self-reported shoplifting rates that are much higher, ranging between 22% and 37% within a single year or less (Cox et al., 1990; Klemke, 1982). Overall, on the basis of these studies it has been suggested that as many as 60% of consumers shoplift at some time (Cox et al., 1990).

Buckle and Farrington (1984) conducted a field study in which shoplifting was examined through direct observation by two researchers working conjointly in a single department store in Peterborough over a period of three weeks. One in every six customers entering the store was followed, kept under scrutiny, and detailed notes recorded of the amount of time he or she spent in the store, and the parts of the store visited. Various other features such as the estimated age and social class of shoppers, and whether or not they were accompanied, were also noted. Of a total of 503 customers followed, nine (1.8%) were observed to shoplift. These figures are concordant with those obtained from an earlier observational study (cited by the authors) conducted by a UK security firm. However, they are lower than rates reported in both Irish and American studies: the corresponding figure for a study in Dublin was 5.5%, and for one New York department store it was 8.4%. The latter figure closely approximates that obtained by Ray's self-report survey, but it is the highest amongst the results of the seven observational studies cited by Buckle and Farrington. A later replication study by Buckle and Farrington (1994) in another department store in a different town yielded a lower observed shoplifting rate of 1.2%. Even at the modest rate of 1.8% however, Buckle and Farrington (1984) calculated that the store which they had used for observation, which had an average of 600 customers entering per hour, experienced over 500 thefts each week. Comparing this with statistics for the police division in which the store was based, they estimated that the actual number of shop thefts in the area was more than ten times that recorded by the police.

Overall therefore, it appears fairly certain that the recorded frequency of shop theft is even more of a distorted estimate of its real occurrence than is the case for other thefts. Offences of shop theft are dissimilar from most other forms of theft in two further respects. First, setting aside a small proportion of thefts in which nothing of value was stolen, in England and Wales in 1991 the average value of goods stolen in all forms of theft combined exceeded £1000 for the first time. By contrast, the average value of goods stolen in shop thefts was much lower at £76. Second, the 'clear-up rate', or number of recorded offences for which someone is charged, summonsed, cautioned, or has admitted guilt, is much higher than for most types of offence: in 1994 it was 77%. Although for some other kinds of theft, such as that by employees, the clear-up rate (1994) was higher still (81%), the average for all thefts combined was only 24%, and for all types of offence only 26%.

ADDICTIONS MODELS

The hypothesis of the present volume is that it may be possible to apply models derived from the study of the 'addictive behaviours' to an understanding of aspects of criminal conduct not previously encompassed within that framework. Before examining relevant studies of shop theft in more detail, it will be helpful first to consider what is meant by the word 'addictive'.

The concept of 'addiction' is most familiar and best established in accounts of the mechanisms underpinning repetitive substance abuse. This typically involves alcohol, tobacco, heroin, tranquillising drugs or other agents, which in certain amounts or consumed over long periods have toxic, even lethal, effects. In recent years the concept has been extended to non-substance-abuse disorders, such as overeating and gambling. More recently still it has been applied to offence behaviours such as sexual assaults.

Major controversies have arisen over the question of the nature of 'addiction', whether there are 'addiction-prone personalities', and what forms of treatment follow from the endorsement of various models of the behaviour. But perhaps the most radical issue currently at stake is that of whether, even in substance abuse, it is the substance *per se* and its immediate physiological effects to which sufferers are addicted. In place of such a view, a number of models of psychological dependence have been formulated, for example by Fingarette (1988) or by Davies (1992).

Probably the most widely researched example of a non-substance 'addiction' is gambling. Moran (1970) described similarities between some individuals' dependence on gambling and the experience of alcohol abuse; noting fluctuations in tension, loss of control, symptoms of craving, and persistence of the behaviour despite heavy personal cost. Wray and Dickerson (1981) conducted a survey of members of Gamblers Anonymous and reported mood disturbances and other symptoms of 'withdrawals' in a similar proportion to that found amongst persons recovering from alcohol abuse. There was also a relationship between experience of these symptoms and the likelihood of return to gambling. Peck (1986) drew close parallels between the learning processes involved in becoming a 'compulsive' gambler and those leading to other forms of addiction.

The possibility that concepts central to the notion of 'addiction' might be applicable to behaviours far removed from substance abuse is not new. De Coverley Veale (1987) collated evidence that some individuals may develop a dependence on physical exercise. For example, a proportion of regular runners, when compelled to stop (e.g. by injury or circumstances), developed irritability, sleep disturbance and other disorders of mood. Results of several studies supported the contention that running 'is best viewed as a coping strategy for the regulation of affect' (De Coverley Veale, 1987, p. 736). While this might occur as a function of the release of opioids in the central nervous system, psychophysiological evidence regarding this is equivocal and the desire for exercise was thought to occur independently of such reinforcement. Glatt and Cook (1987) have described the case of a 24-year-old woman with a six-year history of 'pathological spending'. During this time she accumulated debts totalling £55 000; bought numerous items she did not need and in some cases already possessed; exhibited 'tolerance' in that over time she spent progressively larger sums of money; and continued to spend in the face of mounting complications, including criminal proceedings and acute personal distress.

Brown (1989, 1993, chapter 1 this volume) has elaborated a theoretical model of gambling which is potentially applicable across the entire range of behaviours usually classed as 'addictive'. This perspective is founded on social learning principles but also utilises concepts drawn from reversal theory in an attempt to explain a variety of phenomena observed in addictions.

Addictive behaviours have been described by Brown (1993) as being marked by a number of common components, and these perhaps can be used as a crude form of checklist for deciding whether a pattern of behaviour is genuinely an 'addiction'. They are:

1. *Salience:* the dominance of the addictive activity over the individual's thoughts, feelings and behaviour.
2. *Conflict:* inter- and intrapersonal, and between present and future goals.
3. *Tolerance:* the need for increasing amounts of the activity to achieve desired effects.
4. *Withdrawals:* aversive feeling states when the activity is discontinued.
5. *Relief:* need for the activity and rapid reduction in aversive state when it is recommenced.
6. *Relapse:* repeated return to the behaviour after periods of cessation, and its capacity for complete reinstatement even when these periods have been lengthy.

MOTIVATIONS FOR SHOPLIFTING

Holding this proposed set of features in mind, let us return to studies of shop theft. The clear-up statistics given earlier might suggest that, were systematic studies of those found guilty of shop theft to be undertaken by researchers, it might for once be possible to work with samples which were genuinely representative of those who committed such acts: as opposed to the more usual case in which offender samples are probably not very typical of the populations from which they are drawn. However, given the likely size of the gap between recorded shoplifting and actual shoplifting, those apprehended are in all probability only a small proportion of those who commit the offence, and those officially adjudicated a smaller proportion still.

In any case, the number of such studies undertaken has been comparatively small. This may be because the motivations for shop theft are assumed to be predominantly economic, and by virtue of this are to some extent seen as rational, comprehensible, and therefore requiring little further investigation. On the other hand it may simply reflect the relatively low seriousness of this type of offence (disregarding its substantial cumulative cost). Looking more widely, much more psychological research has been carried out with those who commit personal crimes of a violent or sexual nature than with those who commit property offences of any kind. This may have helped to shape an image of psychology as having 'pathologised' the study of offenders, and contributed to its relative marginalisation by mainstream criminological theories.

Available research on shoplifting suggests that there is a variety of factors which contribute to it and a range of motivations may be involved. Studies do tend to confirm that one principal motivation for it is economic. But this is by no means the whole story. To obtain a perspective on the thesis that a proportion of shop theft may have addictive properties, existing studies of the factors influencing shop theft will be briefly reviewed.

It is worth noting first, however, that there may be separate reasons for shoplifting amongst adolescents and adults respectively. While an economic element may be common to both, there is considerable evidence that other factors such as experiential risk-taking and peer-group influence may be principal motivators for adolescent offending. Cox et al. (1990; Cox et al., 1993) conducted an anonymous questionnaire survey of a large sample of teenagers ($n = 1750$) in the age range 11–16. Factor analysis of their responses showed the single strongest set of motives to be associated with fun, excitement, and 'to see if I could get away with it', and comparison of shoplifters with non-shoplifters suggested the former were more prone towards rule-breaking in multiple respects. Social influence was the second most important factor. A third factor, labelled 'contraband', was associated with stealing items to pass them on to others, because purchase of the items was legally forbidden, or because it was embarrassing to be seen buying them. As the authors point out this represents another, indirect form of social influence. Straightforward economic motives emerged as a fourth factor in this analysis. Lo (1994) has put forward a model of the determinants involved in shop theft by juveniles, and also endorsed the role of amusement, thrill-seeking, and peer pressure in its occurrence. All of these authors additionally emphasise the important part played in teenage shoplifting by opportunity and the easy access to goods permitted by modern retail design. None of these studies investigated personality factors or the possibility of there being addictive components in this behaviour, and it seems unlikely for this age group that such a pattern would be found.

Amongst adults by contrast, Ray (1987) and Ray and Briar (1988) found that there was a strong association between economic hardship and shoplifting. Based on the self-report questionnaire survey described above (Ray, 1987), and on a separate database of 200 court-adjudicated shoplifters, these authors found a significant relationship between lower income level and shoplifting, and a significantly higher rate of unemployment, and of concern about owing money, amongst shoplifters as compared to other shoppers. Whilst a proportion of shoplifters had high incomes, they nevertheless reported experiencing concurrent economic problems at the time prior to the offence. The importance of economic benefit was also underlined by Moore (1984) who found that this was the primary motivational factor in nearly seven out of ten of his sample of 300 shoplifters; and by Yates (1986) who reported a preponderance of economic motives in 64% of her sample ($n = 101$).

Contrasting with this are the findings of Beck and McIntyre (1977). They studied an undergraduate student sample ($n = 170$) using a shoplifting questionnaire and the Minnesota Multiphasic Personality Inventory (MMPI). Those who admitted to having shoplifted many times ('chronic shoplifters') were found to be significantly different from other groups ('one-time' and 'non-shoplifters') on several MMPI scales. The scales which differentiated them were those for Psychopathic Deviancy and Mania; a profile was constructed for the 'chronic' group, who were thought to be typified by poor judgement; shallow, superficial relationships; and general maladjustment. 'One-time' shoplifting amongst women was thought to be caused by depression. Situational or environmental factors were discounted as likely primary causes. Another study using the MMPI was undertaken by Ray et al. (1983). A sample of 94 first-offender shoplifters were found to have elevated but subclinical scores on the Psychopathic Deviancy and Schizophrenia Scales; and there were significant correlations between number of previous shoplifting episodes and the Depression, Masculinity-Femininity and Paranoia Scales. On a test of self-regard, shoplifters scored in a range indicative of 'unsure' and 'confused' self-image.

These two sets of findings on shop theft by adults and accompanying explanations are somewhat at odds with each other. In the first the importance of economic circumstances is highlighted, in the second personal factors are seen as more influential. The position is clarified somewhat by a number of studies which have addressed the question of whether there are distinct, identifiable patterns or subgroups amongst those found guilty of shop theft. This strategy was adopted by Moore (1984) and by McShane and Noonan (1993). Moore (1984) attempted to classify a sample of 300 shoplifters, using a range of assessments including a shoplifting attitudes questionnaire, personality and intellectual tests, an interview conducted by a probation counsellor, and a diagnostic interview by a psychologist.

Five subtypes were distinguished (rounded percentages thought to belong to each are given in brackets): 'Impulse' (15.4%); 'Occasional' (15%); 'Episodic' (1.7%); 'Amateur' (56.4%); and 'Semi-professional' (11.7%). Economic gain was thought to be a prime operative factor in the last two groups (together constituting 68% of the sample). Membership of the Episodic group was associated with the presence of fairly severe psychosocial stress. The pattern closest to any addictive behaviour was amongst the Impulse group, who though not having a prior intent to steal, experienced fluctuations in arousal and loss of self-control whilst in shops. It should also be noted that of those individuals identified in the assessments as having substance-abuse disorders, a sizeable proportion (65.2%) were chronic shoplifters.

The latter finding is paralleled by studies as it were from the opposite direction, where the primary focus of interest has been substance abuse. For example, studies of heroin usage have indicated that shoplifting plays a large part in the financing of this habit. In interviews with a sample of 61 frequent heroin users, Jarvis and Parker (1989) found that acquisitive crime was the principal means of securing funds to buy the drug, admitted by 87% of the sample. Within this shop theft, reported by 41% of the sample, was the commonest type of offence. Other studies cited by these authors also confirm this relationship, though shoplifting sometimes comes second to burglary in the 'frequency table' of crimes committed.

McShane and Noonan (1993) assessed a group of 75 shoplifters soon after arrest and prior to any formal legal processing. Back-ground demographic data were collected and individuals were administered two measures of purposefulness (the Purpose in Life Test and the Seeking of Noetic Goals Test; the latter specially designed for the study) and in addition, a measure of stressful life events, the Social Readjustment Rating Scale. Through the use of cluster analysis, four subgroups emerged: 'Rebels', 'Reactionaries', 'Enigmas' and 'Infirm'. However, the distinctions between these groups were not strong, and none of them conformed to a pattern bearing any similarity to addictive behaviours, at least as defined in terms of the features listed earlier. All of the 'Infirm' group and a majority of the 'Enigma' group had enough money to buy the articles they had stolen; larger proportions of the other two groups had low incomes. The only group distinguished by a high level of prior criminality were the 'Rebels'; the only group apparently free of significant life stress were the 'Enigmas'. In a separate study, the purposefulness tests and other measures were used to compare this whole sample with a non-shoplifting group (McShane et al., 1991).

Shoplifters were found to have less purpose or meaning in their lives; to be less motivated to find meaning; and to have lower levels of social participation, and lower incomes, than the comparison group.

A different focus of investigation is exemplified in a study by Arboleda-Florez et al. (1977). Amongst a sample of referrals ($n = 42$) to a psychiatric clinic in Ottawa, three subgroups were identified: 'snitches', who were recidivistic shoplifters, generally younger and in financial difficulties; 'psychotic', who were diagnosed as suffering from delusions; and 'unusual', who could afford to buy the items they had stolen, and whose behaviour was thought to be influenced by high levels of psychosocial stressors.

There is evidence then that amongst adults, economic factors, life stress and personal attributes probably interact in the causation of shoplifting. Broadly speaking, larger sample studies using apprehended or court-adjudicated individuals yield higher proportions in which economic deprivation is a probable causal factor; while clinic-based, psychiatrically oriented studies detect more evidence of mental illness or behavioural disorder. Where substance-abuse has been present, it has been associated with high rates of shoplifting. However, none of the studies reviewed here has explicitly isolated any form of addiction to shop theft itself, though some features have been present in some subgroups.

Another approach to categorising shoplifting types, which might be more suitable for the present inquiry, is to distinguish 'rational' from other kinds of shoplifting motivations. We have seen that economic factors emerge quite clearly from several studies and the resultant theft can be depicted as rational: the individual needed or wanted the item but did not have the money to buy it. But it has consistently been reported in the research literature that some shop thefts are not committed for material gain. Such theft has variously been called 'irrational' or 'nonsensical' shoplifting (Schlueter et al., 1989; Yates, 1986) and several of the subgroups named in other studies exhibit patterns of this kind. One characteristic which might be thought to be definitive is that the individual has adequate funds to buy the item but despite this steals it. However, possession of the necessary resources is not the key to the 'rational/non-rational' distinction. Schlueter et al. (1989) emphasise a range of motivations all of which involve the notion that the theft was goal-directed in some sense. Goods might be stolen for financial gain; because individuals thought they could get away with it; because it was a challenge; they were in a hurry and had no time to pay; or they felt angry at the store and sought retribution. Thus although the stolen item might not be needed, other goals were being accomplished.

Of 132 middle-class shoplifters interviewed by Schlueter et al., 59% fell into this broadly defined 'rational' category. Another group, comprising 24% of the sample, were classed as 'non-rational' in that they were not motivated by any conscious goal. The remaining 17% were said to have 'mixed' rational and non-rational motives. Comparing the rational and non-rational groups, the latter were older; a higher proportion were married; they had more years of education; were more likely to hold religious beliefs; and had more personal problems prior to the offence (all differences statistically significant). Schlueter et al. saw the non-rational group as a greater threat to shop security, as they seldom considered the possibility of being caught and their attitudes remained unaffected by arrest; in the authors' phrase they seemed to be 'undeterrable'. Another important difference was that the non-rational group reported thinking about their problems immediately before the theft, and claimed to have acted impulsively. By contrast, members of the rational and mixed groups were thinking instrumentally about the theft itself and about avoiding detection. Again however, the possibility that any of the behaviours described may have been 'addictive' is not investigated by these researchers.

Yates (1986) used the more straightforward yardstick of whether individuals were economically disadvantaged and were stealing items they could not afford. Approximately two-thirds of the sample she studied fell into this category, which also contained the highest proportion with a previous criminal history. The remainder were allocated into two 'non-sensical' subgroups. Both could have paid for the items they stole. Members of one subgroup (22% of the sample) claimed they had no intention of stealing, but the items taken made some sense in that they were things they could use. Members of the third subgroup (15% of the sample) stole, apparently at random, items which they did not need or desire and which were in fact useless to them. This group was significantly older, more likely to be married, more often socially isolated, and emotionally depressed, than the other two.

The traditionally held stereotype of the emotionally distressed middle-aged female shoplifter is not supported by many of the foregoing research results. Such a pattern was portrayed in psychiatric studies for example by Gibbens et al. (1971; Gibbens, 1981). However, there is probably a substantial sampling bias in these studies, given the selection processes likely to be at work in channelling women offenders towards the psychiatric region of the network of criminal justice agencies. Some studies (e.g. that of Arboleda-Florez et al., 1977) were based only on psychiatric clinic referrals, so there are serious difficulties in generalising from these samples to shoplifting as a whole. Both in the observational studies (Buckle & Farrington, 1984, 1994) and in the majority of studies of apprehended or self-reported shoplifters, male offenders (Beck & McIntyre, 1977; Cox et al., 1990; Ekblom, 1986; McShane & Noonan, 1993; Moore, 1984; Munday, 1986) or younger female offenders (Ray et al., 1983; Schlueter et al., 1989; Yates, 1986) predominated. The underlying trend across all of these studies is of an interaction between age and gender: the ratio of female to male shoplifters increases with increasing age. Higher proportions of older, emotionally distressed women offenders are likely to be found amongst referrals to mental health services.

It is also plausible that the age and gender distribution of those who shoplift is likely to be associated with the nature of a store and the kinds of merchandise on sale. This suggestion is borne out by Ekblom's (1986) study of the Oxford Street, London, branch of recorded music retailers HMV. On a busy day 20 000 customers entered this store. The majority of those caught shoplifting were young (91% aged 24 or under) and male (91%). Amongst early adolescents, there is evidence that the most frequently stolen goods are relatively low-cost food items (Jackson, 1990). For those aged 17 and over, Munday (1986) found that, whereas clothes were the items most often stolen by females regardless of age, the pattern for males changed, with those under 30 most often stealing clothes but those over 30 being marginally more likely to steal food.

An innovative approach to the analysis of shoplifting was implemented in a study by Carroll and Weaver (1986). These authors used a 'process-tracing' method to examine decisions to steal by two groups of individuals, one (the 'experts') with an extensive history of shop theft (admitting to a median of 100 previous offences), the other (the 'novices') who had not previously engaged in shop theft. All were recruited as volunteers from an advertisement placed in Chicago newspapers. These recruits, accompanied by a graduate student researcher, were asked to go on a 1-hour shopping trip and 'think aloud' as they did so; each had a lapel microphone and a concealed microcassette recorder. Results showed that the 'experts' were much more skilled in their assessment of shoplifting opportunities, and more likely to focus on immediate strategic issues concerning the feasibility of taking an item, than on 'distal' prospects of arrest or court appearances. Carroll and Weaver typified shoplifting decisions as occurring within a form of bounded rationality, using decision-making heuristics that are applicable to the crime situation, but which are not 'rational' in the normative sense implied in economic models of human behaviour. This study also illustrated the crucial distinction between decisions made at crime-opportunity points and those processes involved in entry into crime in general.

Factors other than a *mens rea* to steal may also result in shoplifting. There is evidence that individuals could be behaving in a condition of automatism due to metabolic states such as narcolepsy (Zorick et al., 1979). Use of or withdrawal from anti-depressant medication has also been implicated (Coid, 1984; Williams & Dalby, 1986), though the phenomenon of 'pharmacogenic shoplifting' has been dismissed by Lamontage et al. (1994). Case studies have been described in which shop theft was linked to brain damage or deterioration (Murray, 1992). Alternatively, individuals could simply be acting absent-mindedly (Cunningham, 1975); in one survey, 18% of respondents acknowledged having left stores without paying (Reason & Lucas, 1984). All of these circumstances might be admissible as defences in court for persons accused of shoplifting.

SHOPLIFTING AND MENTAL HEALTH PROBLEMS

From the research reviewed above it is clear that there is a proportion of shop theft which is associated with life stress and with symptoms of mental ill-health. In those studies (e.g. Arboleda-Florez et al., 1977; Gibbens, 1981; Gibbens et al., 1971) in which individuals who have shoplifted are referred for psychiatric examination, a regular pattern of difficulties has been found. The extent to which shoplifting is a symptom of underlying emotional problems or mental disorder has been a matter of debate for some time in the psychiatric literature (Bradford & Balmaceda, 1983; Goldman, 1991; Lamontage et al., 1994; Russell, 1973). It is probably unwise however to place too heavy an emphasis on the possible interconnections. In one survey of 1649 shoplifting convictions in a Montreal court (Lamontage et al., 1994), only 53 individuals (3.2% of the sample) had diagnosed mental illnesses. The importance of separating the profiles of routine court cases from those referred to mental health services has been underlined by a number of writers (Cupchik & Atcheson, 1983; Murray, 1992).

Most studies have reported fairly congruent findings and a similar constellation of difficulties amongst those who have been arrested for shop theft and referred for psychiatric assessments or reports. The most common finding is of depression (Bradford & Balmaceda, 1983; Fishbain, 1987; Gibbens, 1981; Gibbens et al., 1971; Gudjonsson, 1987), though this sometimes comes second in frequency to substance abuse disorders (Lamontage et al., 1994). Many of those who 'non-sensically' shoplift are socially isolated; almost all have poor or doubtful self-esteem (Ray et al., 1983); a proportion have recently suffered some personal loss (Cupchik & Atcheson, 1983); others are frequently under severe stress, for example through having relatives who are ill or have disabilities (e.g. McShane & Noonan, 1993; Moore, 1987; Roy, 1988; Yates, 1986). A small proportion of those seen by Arboleda-Florez et al. (1977) were described as suffering from psychotic delusions. There have been indications of an increased risk of shoplifting amongst individuals suffering from eating disorders (Bridgeman & Slade, 1996; Goldner et al., 1991).

One recurring question within this debate has been the extent to which repeated non-rational shop theft can be subsumed under the clinical diagnosis of *kleptomania*. This concept has a varied history in having been at times excluded and at other times included in the Diagnostic and Statistical Manual of Mental Disorders (DSM). It is included in DSM-IV (Code 312.32) under the category of 'Impulse-Control Disorders Not Elsewhere Classified', alongside apparently similar dysfunctions such as pathological gambling, pyromania and intermittent explosive disorder. The definition incorporates: recurrent failure to resist impulses to steal objects that are not needed for personal use or for their monetary value; increasing tension before, and pleasure, gratification or relief at the time of committing the theft; and which is not explicable in terms of other identifiable motives or disorder (for example to express anger, or in response to a delusion). Earlier Murray (1992), using DSM-III-R criteria, reviewed this area and indicated the paucity of studies of individuals who satisfactorily met the criteria. For example, in the study of psychiatric referrals by Arboleda-Florez et al. (1977) no individual showing this pattern was found. The largest single study was undertaken by McElroy et al. (1991) who describe a series of 20 cases meeting DSM-III-R diagnostic criteria. However, all of these individuals were also diagnosed as suffering from mood disorders, and 17 of them were classifiable in terms of several other disorders in addition. There were evident links, for nearly all of the patients, between fluctuations in their moods and acts of theft. Many of these patients could be described as manifesting features of addiction or dependence, with shoplifting an integral component of their behavioural disorder. Another pertinent study was carried out by Sarasalo et al. (1997, in press). Detailed assessments were conducted with 50 shoplifters caught red-handed and interviewed at the scene of the thefts. While features of kleptomania-like behaviour were discovered amongst several members of this sample, none possessed enough of them to fulfil DSM-IV criteria for the disorder. These authors suggested, and others such as Cupchik (1992) agree, that diagnosable kleptomania is likely to be extremely rare; their results call into question the reliability of studies reporting its presence in several per cent of shoplifters. Overall then, the real applicability of the concept remains to be demonstrated.

In general terms, the uncertain foundation of some of the distinctions contained within DSM has been criticised by Blackburn (1993). Recently Clark et al. (1995) have questioned the entire basis of taxonomic systems such as DSM-IV. Impulse control disorders are diagnosed when a behaviour has no function that is obvious to the perpetrator or observer; in the absence of identifiable motive, the concept of 'mania' is invoked. Ultimately this is a pseudo-scientific fiction. So too is the distinction between rational and non-rational motives described above, which simply attempts to assimilate patterns of behaviour into culturally acceptable norms. As a way out of these contradictions, the behaviour of repeated shop theft might be approached instead in social-learning terms. It may have developed, for example, as a maladaptive solution to problems which the individual cannot solve by other means. In this respect, models drawn from the study of addictive behaviours may offer an alternative formulation with greater validity and utility.

INTERVENTION METHODS

This chapter cannot deal in any depth with approaches to intervention with shoplifters. However, by way of summary it may be useful to outline the scope of the methods which have been adopted. Interventions have for the most part entailed the use of behavioural methods, though a smaller number of studies have been undertaken using cognitive and allied approaches, or counselling. Most structured activities have been in the context of programmes of diversion from prosecution.

The behavioural methods used have included systematic desensitisation (Marzagao, 1972); contingency management (Guidry, 1975); covert sensitisation (Gauthier & Pellegrin, 1982; Glover, 1985); self-management (Aust, 1987); and activity scheduling (Gudjonsson, 1987), to date applied in single-case studies. By contrast Kolman and Wasserman (1991) have described counselling groups designed exclusively for women offenders. Use of a cognitive group therapy based on Rational-Emotive principles has been outlined by Solomon and Ray (1984). A more eclectic format was adopted by Edwards and

Roundtree (1982) using methods drawn from reality therapy, transactional analysis, assertiveness training and behaviour modification. Structured psycho-educational methods were used in a six-session group programme by MacDevitt and Kedzierzawski (1990). Finally, evaluations of diversion programmes for first-time shoplifters have been reported by Casey and Shulman (1979) and by Royse and Buck (1991). The latter programme included community service and a number of group sessions of 'rational behaviour therapy'.

In all of these studies, reductions in shop theft have been obtained. The single-case interventions were uniformly successful. In the group-based studies by Solomon and Ray (1984) and by MacDevitt and Kedzierzawski (1990) long-term reoffence rates were remarkably low: in the former, 1% after one year; in the latter, 5% after seven years. However, neither of these studies included a control group. Kolman and Wasserman (1991) compared offence rates of women offenders in the year before and the year after attending a counselling programme, and found a substantial reduction (23% to 6%). The study by Edwards and Roundtree (1982) employed a no-treatment control. At a 90-day follow-up, both groups had very low reoffence rates. In the study of juvenile shoplifters by Casey and Shulman, one-year recidivism rates of the treatment and control groups were 5% and 11% respectively. Finally, the two-year recidivism rate for the diversion programme evaluated by Royse and Buck (1991) was 4%. This contrasted favourably with three comparison groups each of which had a recidivism rate in the region of 25–26%.

CASE STUDIES OF POTENTIALLY 'ADDICTIVE' SHOP THEFT

Using the tentative checklist for features of an 'addiction' given earlier, in the remainder of this chapter the possibility will be explored that the features listed are present in a small number of individuals ($n = 3$) thought to have developed an addiction to shoplifting. It has first to be recognised, however, that a proportion of those regularly arrested for shop theft do suffer from concomitant substance-abuse disorders. The precise links between the two problems can themselves take several forms. For example, alcohol may be repeatedly stolen for direct consumption; goods may be stolen to obtain money to sustain substance-abuse habits; and so on. However, none of these connections is at the centre of the present hypothesis. The question asked focuses instead on the possibility that shoplifting as an activity may, for some individuals, become established as a form of addictive behaviour in itself, or at the very least, may be rendered more explicable from such a standpoint.

One of the difficulties of identifying any such pattern in the existing literatures has been that the highest frequency rates of previous offending are almost always amongst economically motivated shoplifters. Where subgroups with some features suggestive of addictive behaviour have been delineated, they are usually much less recidivistic than those with so-called 'rational' motivations. In the case studies to be outlined, ingredients of 'non-sensical' shoplifting co-existed alongside high rates of offending behaviour.

These descriptions do not purport in any way to be results of a systematic survey. They were obtained through contacts with staff of offender services, with whom the issue of potential addictiveness in shop theft had been informally discussed. One case was seen by the present author; the other two were obtained, respectively, from a probation officer and a clinical psychologist, each working in different parts of the United Kingdom.

To 'standardise' the kinds of information collected, a short questionnaire was designed and presented to the above workers. This requested information concerning various aspects thought to be relevant to a formulation of 'addictive behaviour', using concepts similar to those itemised above, though information was sought concerning levels of *arousal* in the offence, rather than the existence of conflict. Case reports, suitably anonymised, were also obtained, in each instance with the permission of the client being described.

Case 1. C. D., a woman, 36 years of age. This woman had 22 convictions for theft with 42 offences 'taken into consideration' by the police; in addition to other convictions for assaults on police, forgery, and taking vehicles. C. D. stated that she had begun to shoplift in her teens, in the company of peers, but later was forced to shoplift to support her husband's drug use. Later she was separated from her husband, who had been violent towards her, and also lost custody of her two daughters. Two offences in which she stole baby clothes and subsequently a child's plastic swimming pool were committed within two days of each other. Often depressed, at the time of these offences C. D. was even more so as a result of a miscarriage. However, thoughts of shoplifting were constantly with her; her level of excitement rose greatly at the thought of shopping; and when in stores she would feel a sense of compulsion to take goods she did not need. She described experiencing a 'high' when this occurred; and used thoughts of shop theft to control her mood and raise herself from depression at other times. When not able to steal (e.g. when accompanied by someone who would disapprove), she became irritable and morose. She showed a pattern of modulating her emotional level by stealing small items and also when in shops by manipulating the level of risk of being detected.

Case 2. E. F., a woman aged 56, had a 40-year history of shoplifting, though with a six-year break in her mid-forties. In her earlier years she had shoplifted with friends and later in financial hardship regarded it as an economic necessity. She was divorced from her husband, who was a heavy drinker; it was reportedly as a result of his spending the family income on alcohol that her habit of shoplifting took hold. She was thought to have developed a pattern of 'compulsive' shop theft following a series of five offences. On each occasion she believed she had no option but to steal; and while mostly she took items she believed she needed, in her two last offences she had stolen items she did not need and had no idea why she did so. Her two children and their families were unable to understand her behaviour; she had adequate resources to meet her material needs. In one offence the stolen item was a size-44 man's suit; in the other, make-up accessories which she stated she did not need. She had formed no intention to shoplift, but once inside the stores could not resist the temptation to do so, disregarding the consequences of her behaviour.

Case 3. G. H., male, aged 63, suffered from diabetes. At the time of assessment, this man had a total of 55 convictions for a total of 107 offences, the majority of them of shoplifting; though he had also committed a variety of other crimes including burglary, forgery, deception, indecent exposure, and indecent assault. In interviews, he admitted a very large number of other shoplifting offences for which he had never been caught. His offence behaviour followed a highly repetitive, almost ritualised pattern. His general mood was one of depression, and to alleviate it he would leave home in the late morning, taking a bus to another town. In the shopping centre, he would often (but not always) enter a pub and drink one pint of beer. Later, he would go into shops and once inside would feel a rising sense of excitement. Thoughts of being able to get away with theft, and of getting back at retailers, would rush into his head, and the impulse to steal would become overwhelming. Even describing this situation, G. would show evident signs of absorption and excitement. This behaviour recurred despite its serious personal consequences for G. H., including almost complete alienation from his family, and occasional short prison sentences. There may have been a possible effect of his diabetic condition on his mood state just prior to the offences, especially when alcohol had been consumed, though this was not an essential component of the sequence. G. occasionally stole large quantities of usually small items, despite having sizeable sums (e.g. in the region of £80) in his pocket. At an earlier stage of his life, while in the navy, G. H. stated he had committed no offences for an eight-year period.

There are marked differences between the behaviour of the three persons just described, but for present purposes our focus is upon the structural features they may have in common. The hypothesis under consideration is whether some aspects of their offences can be understood more fully if viewed from the perspective of an 'addictions' model. To facilitate this perspective-taking, some further details are given in Table 8.1 where the three cases are analysed alongside each other in terms of six core components of addiction. On the basis of the table it is contended that there is at least an initial degree of support for the value of addictions concepts in providing a coherent account of the offences of the three people described. All were characterised by a high degree of salience in that the problem, despite their awareness of its severe consequences, had an enormous

Table 8.1. Components of 'addiction' in three cases of shoplifting.

	Case 1	Case 2	Case 3
Salience	Very marked	Very marked	Very marked
Arousal	Depressed mood modulated by thoughts & behaviour	Depressed mood modulated by offence behaviour only	Depressed mood modulated by behaviour; to a lesser extent by thoughts
Tolerance	Strong evidence of development of tolerance	Limited evidence of tolerance development	Strong evidence of development of tolerance
Withdrawals	Marked presence	Generally depressed moods; evidence of withdrawals unclear	Marked presence
Relief	Strong evidence of excitement and relief	Limited evidence of excitement and relief	Strong evidence of excitement and relief
Relapse	Frequent despite attempts to control	Moderately frequent; reinstatement after lengthy absence	Frequent despite attempts to control; reinstatement after lengthy absence

impact on their lives. The behaviour was repeated often and a high level of compulsion was experienced. There was evidence of tolerance in two out of three cases, and of withdrawal phenomena in all three, though in Case 2 the details of it were unclear. Each also showed evidence of marked conflict, arousal and relief. Relapses were frequent despite attempts to reduce the behaviour and in two cases they occurred after long intervals of 'abstinence'. The case is weaker concerning the value of the model in Case 2, nevertheless some components of addiction are present. It is interesting to add that in each of the cases, shop theft first appeared much earlier in life as an economically motivated peer-group activity, but has since evolved into a strikingly different pattern. Finally, these individuals are all, to different extents and for quite different reasons, depressed. In a mode that is unique to each of them, shoplifting may also be a temporary relief from that mood state and anticipation of it may be a basic setting condition for the repetition of the behaviour.

CONCLUSION

Based on the findings of research reviewed above, and on the patterns shown in the three case studies described, it is suggested that shoplifting can have features for which the 'best fit' interpretation is derived from an addictions model of self-damaging behaviours. A proper test of this suggestion would require systematic assessment of a representative sample of shop thefts, bearing in mind the spread of motivational factors mapped out earlier. It is envisaged that 'addictive' shop theft, if this proves a viable supposition, probably constitutes only a small proportion of offences of this type. But where it might be present, it is vital that it be accurately identified. This is important firstly, in that it may affect the contents of reports prepared for courts, and subsequent sentences; the nature of interventions used; and the evaluation of outcomes. Even where not all of the components of addiction or psychological dependence are established, the presence of some of them may have implications for the type of work that is feasible with individuals, and appropriate to offer them.

This proposal is important, secondly, for theory construction in relation to the study both of offending and of addictions. That applies not only to shop theft, but also to the types of offences considered elsewhere in this volume, and to the overall prospect of developing an integrative social-learning framework applicable across the whole spectrum of behaviour.

ACKNOWLEDGEMENTS

I wish to thank Mark Gresswell and Cheree Hall for supplying information concerning two of the case studies described in this chapter.

REFERENCES

Arboleda-Florez, J., Durie, H. & Costello, J. (1977). Shoplifting—an ordinary crime? *International Journal of Offender Therapy and Comparative Criminology*, **21**, 201–207.
Aust, A. (1987). Gaining control of compulsive shop theft. *National Association of Probation Officers Journal*, December, 145–146.
Beck, E. & McIntyre, S. (1977). MMPI patterns of shoplifters within a college population. *Psychological Reports*, **41**, 1035–1040.
Blackburn, R. (1993). *The Psychology of Criminal Conduct: Theory, Research and Practice*. Chichester: Wiley.
Bradford, J. & Balmaceda, R. (1983). Shoplifting: Is there a specific psychiatric syndrome? *Canadian Journal of Psychiatry*, **28**, 248–253.
Bridgeman, J. & Slade, P. D. (1996). Shoplifting and eating disorders: A psychological-medical-legal perspective. *European Eating Disorders Review*, **4**, 133–148.
Brown, R. I. F. (1989). Relapse from a gambling perspective. In M. Gossop (Ed.), *Relapse and Addictive Behaviour*. London: Tavistock/Routledge.
Brown, R. I. F. (1993). Planning deficiencies in addictions from the perspective of reversal theory. In J. H. Kerr, S. Murgatroyd and M. J. Apter (Eds), *Advances in Reversal Theory*. London: Swets and Zeitlinger.
Buckle, A. & Farrington, D. P. (1984). An observational study of shoplifting. *British Journal of Criminology*, **24**, 63–73.
Buckle, A. & Farrington, D. P. (1994) Measuring shoplifting by systematic observation: a replication study. *Psychology, Crime and Law*, **41** 133–141.
Burrows, J. & Speed, M. (1994). *Retail Crime Costs 1992/93 Survey*.London: British Retail Consortium.
Carroll, J. & Weaver, F. (1986). Shoplifters' perceptions of crime opportunities: A process-tracing study. In D. B. Cornish and R. V. G. Clarke (Eds), *The Reasoning Criminal: Rational Choice Perspectives on Offending*. New York: Springer-Verlag.
Casey, L. R. & Shulman, J. L. (1979). Police-probation shoplifting reduction program in San José, California: A synergetic approach. *Crime Prevention Review*, **6**, 1–9.
Clark, L. A., Watson, D. & Reynolds, S. (1995). Diagnosis and classification of psychopathology: Challenges to the current system and future directions. *Annual Review of Psychology*, **46**, 121–153.
Coid, J. (1984). Relief of diazepam-withdrawal syndrome by shoplifting. *British Journal of Psychiatry*, **145**, 553–554.
Cox, A. D., Cox, D., Anderson, R. D. & Moschis, G. P. (1993). Social influences on adolescent shoplifting: Theory, evidence, and implications for the retail industry. *Journal of Retailing*, **69**, 234–246.
Cox, D., Cox, A. D. & Moschis, G. P. (1990). When consumer behavior goes

bad: An investigation of adolescent shoplifting. *Journal of Consumer Research*, **17**, 149–159.

Cunningham, C. (1975). Absent mind versus guilty mind in cases of shoplifting. *Medico-Legal Journal*, **43**, 101–106.

Cupchik, W. (1992). Kleptomania and shoplifting. *American Journal of Psychiatry*, **149**, 1119.

Cupchik, W. & Atcheson, J. D. (1983). Shoplifting: An occasional crime of the moral majority. *Bulletin of the American Academy of Psychiatry and Law*, **11**, 343–354.

Davies, J. B. (1992). *The Myth of Addiction: An Application of the Psychological Theory of Attribution to Illicit Drug Use*. Reading: Harwood Academic Publishers.

De Coverley Veale, D. M. W. (1987). Exercise dependence. *British Journal of Addiction*, **82**, 735–740.

Edwards, D. & Roundtree, G. (1982). Assessment of short-term treatment groups with adjudicated first offender shoplifters. *Journal of Offender Counseling, Services and Rehabilitation*, **6**, 8–102.

Ekblom, P. (1986). *The Prevention of Shop Theft: An Approach Through Crime Analysis*. Home Office Crime Prevention Unit Paper 5. London: HMSO.

Farrington, D. P. & Burrows, J. (1993). Did shoplifting really decrease? *British Journal of Criminology*, **33**, 57–69.

Fingarette, H. (1988). *Heavy Drinking: The Myth of Alcoholism as a Disease*. Berkeley, CA: University of California Press.

Fishbain, D. A. (1987). Kleptomania as risk-taking behavior in response to depression. *American Journal of Psychotherapy*, **41**, 598–603.

Gauthier, J. & Pellerin, D. (1982). Management of compulsive shoplifting through covert sensitization. *Journal of Behavior Therapy and Experimental Psychiatry*, **13**, 73–75.

Gibbens, T. C. N. (1981). Shoplifting. *British Journal of Psychiatry*, **138**, 346–347.

Gibbens, T. C. N., Palmer, C. & Prince, J. (1971). Mental health aspects of shoplifting. *British Medical Journal*, **3**, 612–615.

Glasscock, S., Rapoff, M. & Christopheresen, E. (1988). Behavioral methods to reduce shoplifting. *Journal of Business and Psychology*, **2**, 272–278.

Glatt, M. M. & Cook, C. C. H. (1987). Pathological spending as a form of psychological dependence. *British Journal of Addiction*, **82**, 1257–1258.

Glover, J. H. (1985). A case of kleptomania treated by covert sensitization. *British Journal of Clinical Psychology*, **24**, 213–214.

Goldman, M. J. (1991). Kleptomania: Making sense of the nonsensical. *American Journal of Psychiatry*, **148**, 986–996.

Goldner, E. M., Cockhill, L. A., Bakan, R. & Birmingham, C. L. (1991). Dissociative experiences and eating disorders. *American Journal of Psychiatry*, **148**, 1274–1275.

Gudjonsson, G. H. (1987). The significance of depression in the mechanism of 'compulsive' shoplifting. *Medicine, Science and the Law*, **27**, 171–176.

Guidry, L. S. (1975). Use of a covert punishment contingency in compulsive stealing. *Journal of Behavior Therapy and Experimental Psychiatry*, **6**, 169.

Home Office (1995). *Criminal Statistics England and Wales 1995*. Cmn 3010. London: HMSO.

Jackson, J. (1990). An investigation into theft from shops among juveniles. *Practice*, **4**, 16–42.

Jarvis, G. & Parker, H. (1989). Young heroin users and crime: How do the 'new users' finance their habits? *British Journal of Criminology*, **29**, 175–185.

Klemke, L. W. (1982). Exploring juvenile shoplifting. *Sociology and Social Research*, **67**, 59–75.

Kolman, A. S. & Wasserman, C. (1991). Theft groups for women: A cry for help. *Federal Probation*, **55**, 48–54.

Lamontage, Y., Carpentier, N., Hetu, C. & Lacerte-Lamontage, C. (1994). Shoplifting and mental illness. *Canadian Journal of Psychiatry*, **39**, 300–302.

Lo, L. (1994). Exploring teenage shoplifting behavior: A choice and constraint approach. *Environment and Behavior*, **26**, 613–639.

MacDevitt, J. W. & Kedzierzawski, G. D. (1990). A structured group format for first offense shoplifters. *International Journal of Offender Therapy and Comparative Criminology*, **34**, 155–164.

Marzagao, L. R. (1972). Systematic desensitization treatment of kleptomania. *Journal of Behavior Therapy and Experimental Psychiatry*, **3**, 327–328.

Mayhew, P., Maung, N. A. & Mirrlees-Black, C. (1993). *The 1992 British Crime Survey*. Home Office Research Study No.132. London: HMSO.

McElroy, S. L., Pope, H. G., Hudson, J. I., Keck, P. E. & White, K. L. (1991). Kleptomania: A report of 20 cases. *American Journal of Psychiatry*, **148**, 652–657.

McShane, F. J., Lawless, J. & Noonan, B. A. (1991). Personal meaning in the lives of a shoplifting population. *International Journal of Offender Therapy and Comparative Criminology*, **35**, 190–204.

McShane, F. J. & Noonan, B. A. (1993). Classification of shoplifters by cluster analysis. *International Journal of Offender Therapy and Comparative Criminology*, **37**, 29–40.

Moore, R. H. (1984). Shoplifting in middle America: Patterns and motivational correlates. *International Journal of Offender Therapy and Comparative Criminology*, **28**, 53–64.

Moran, E. (1970). Gambling as a form of dependence. *British Journal of Addiction*, **64**, 419–428.

Munday, R. (1986). Who are the shoplifters? *New Society*, 14 February, 274–276.

Murray, J. B. (1992). Kleptomania: A review of the research. *Journal of Psychology*, **126**, 131–138.

Peck, C. P. (1986). Risk-taking behavior and compulsive gambling. *American Psychologist*, **41**, 461–465.

Ray, J. (1987). Every twelfth shopper: Who shoplifts and why? *Social Casework: Journal of Contemporary Social Work*, **68**, 234–239.

Ray, J. & Briar, K. H. (1988). Economic motivators for shoplifting. *Journal of Sociology and Social Welfare*, **15**, 177–189.

Ray, J. B., Solomon, G. S., Doncaster, M. G. & Mellina, R. (1983). First offender adult shoplifters: A preliminary profile. *Journal of Clinical Psychology*, **39**, 769–770.

Reason, J. & Lucas, D. (1984). Absent-mindedness in shops: Its incidence, correlates and consequences. *British Journal of Clinical Psychology*, **23**, 121–131.

Roy, M. (1988). Shop-lifting as a symptom of stress in families of mentally handicapped persons: A case report. *British Journal of Psychiatry*, **152**, 845–846.

Royse, D. & Buck, S. A. (1991). Evaluating a diversion program for first-offence shoplifters. *Journal of Offender Rehabilitation*, **17**, 147–158.

Russell, D. H. (1973). Emotional aspects of shoplifting. *Psychiatric Annals*, **3**, 77–79.

Sarasalo, E., Bergman, B. & Toth, J. (1997). Kleptomania-like behaviour and psychosocial characteristics among shoplifters. *Legal and Criminological Psychology*, **2**, 1–10.

Schlueter, G. R., O'Neal, F. C., H C., Hickey, J. & Seiler, G. L. (1989). Rational vs nonrational shoplifting types: The implications for loss prevention strategies. *International Journal of Offender Therapy and Comparative Criminology*, **33**, 227–239.

Solomon, G. S. & Ray, J. B. (1984). Irrational beliefs of shoplifters. *Journal of Clinical Psychology*, **40**, 1075–1077.

Williams, R. & Dalby, J. (1986). Benzodiazepines and shoplifting. *International Journal of Offender Therapy and Comparative Criminology*, **30**, 35–39.

Wray, I. & Dickerson, M. G. (1981). Cessation of high frequency gambling and 'withdrawal' symptoms. *British Journal of Addiction*, **76**, 401–405.

Yates, E. (1986). The influence of psycho-social factors on non-sensical shoplifting. *International Journal of Offender Therapy and Comparative Criminology*, **30**, 203–211.

Zorick, F. J., Salis, P. J., Roth, T. & Kramer, M. (1979). Narcolepsy and automatic behavior: A case report. *Journal of Clinical Psychiatry*, **40**, 194–197.

Index

Index compiled by Caroline Sheard

Related titles of interest from Wiley...

Therapeutic Communities for Offenders

Eric Cullen, Lawrence Jones and Roland Woodward

Foreword by John Gunn

Drawing from the authors' extensive experience, this book summarises examples of 'best practice' that therapeutic communities can offer to offenders in the UK, Europe and the US.

0-471-96545-6   300pp 1997 Hardback
0-471-96980-X   300pp 1997 Paperback

Clinical Approaches to Working with Young Offenders

Edited by Clive R. Hollin and Kevin Howells

Examines clinical approaches used with specific groups of offenders, including adolescent sex offenders, firesetters, and alcohol and drug related crime, and reviews successful prevention programmes.

0-471-95348-2 300pp 1996 Hardback

What Works: Reducing Re-Offending

Guidelines from Research and Practice

Edited by James McGuire

Offers a critical review of research and practice with the focus on identifying interventions and models of offender treatment that really do work and are practical, and ways of evaluating treatment and offender services.

0-471-95053-X 264pp 1995 Hardback
0-471-95686-4 264pp 1995 Paperback

Handbook of Psychology in Legal Contexts

Edited by Ray H.C. Bull and David Carson

Highlights and emphasises both the extent to which psychologists are already assisting and informing the legal system and the potential that exists for collaboration between lawyers and psychologists.

0-471-94182-4 694pp 1995 Hardback

Visit the Wiley Home Page at http://www.wiley.co.uk